Frommer's®
Portable
Bahamas

by Darwin Porter & Danforth Prince

WILEY
John Wiley & Sons, Inc.

Published by:
JOHN WILEY & SONS, INC.
111 River St.
Hoboken, NJ 07030-5774

ISBN 978-1-118-02883-4 (paper); ISBN 978-1-118-16469-3 (ebk);
ISBN 978-1-118-16467-9 (ebk); ISBN 978-1-118-16468-6 (ebk)

Editor: Andrea Kahn
Production Editor: Katie Robinson
Cartographer: Guy Ruggiero
Photo Editor: Richard Fox
Production by Wiley Indianapolis Composition Services
Front cover photo: Palmetto Point, Eleuthera, Bahamas. © Purestock /
AGE Fotostock, Inc.

For information on our other products and services or to obtain technical support,
please contact our Customer Care Department within the U.S. at 877/762-2974,
outside the U.S. at 317/572-3993 or fax 317/572-4002.

Wiley also publishes its books in a variety of electronic formats. Some content that
appears in print may not be available in electronic formats.

Manufactured in the United States of America

5   4   3   2   1

CONTENTS

LIST OF MAPS

917.29

ABOUT THE AUTHORS

Veteran travel writers **Darwin Porter** and **Danforth Prince** have written many popular guides in the Frommer's series, including books on the Caribbean, France, England, Germany, and Italy. This travel team wrote the first-ever Frommer's guide to The Bahamas, and also a number of other Frommer's guides to island destinations such as Bermuda, Puerto Rico, Jamaica, Barbados, Dominican Republic, and the Cayman Islands. Porter is also a Hollywood biographer, film critic, broadcaster, and columnist. Prince was formerly employed in the Paris bureau of the New York Times and is the president of Blood Moon Productions.

HOW TO CONTACT US

In researching this book, we discovered many wonderful places—hotels, restaurants, shops, and more. We're sure you'll find others. Please tell us about them, so we can share the information with your fellow travelers in upcoming editions. If you were disappointed with a recommendation, we'd love to know that, too. Please write to:

Frommer's Portable Bahamas, 8th Edition
John Wiley & Sons, Inc. • 111 River St. • Hoboken, NJ 07030-5774
frommersfeedback@wiley.com

ADVISORY & DISCLAIMER

Travel information can change quickly and unexpectedly, and we strongly advise you to confirm important details locally before traveling, including information on visas, health and safety, traffic and transport, accommodations, shopping, and eating out. We also encourage you to stay alert while traveling and to remain aware of your surroundings. Avoid civil disturbances, and keep a close eye on cameras, purses, wallets, and other valuables.

While we have endeavored to ensure that the information contained within this guide is accurate and up-to-date at the time of publication, we make no representations or warranties with respect to the accuracy or completeness of the contents of this work and specifically disclaim all warranties, including without limitation warranties of fitness for a particular purpose. We accept no responsibility or liability for any inaccuracy or errors or omissions, or for any inconvenience, loss, damage, costs, or expenses of any nature whatsoever incurred or suffered by anyone as a result of any advice or information contained in this guide.

The inclusion of a company, organization, or website in this guide as a service provider and/or potential source of further information does not mean that we endorse them or the information they provide. Be aware that information provided through some websites may be unreliable and can change without notice. Neither the publisher nor author shall be liable for any damages arising herefrom.

FROMMER'S STAR RATINGS, ICONS & ABBREVIATIONS

Every hotel, restaurant, and attraction listing in this guide has been ranked for quality, value, service, amenities, and special features using a star-rating system. In country, state, and regional guides, we also rate towns and regions to help you narrow down your choices and budget your time accordingly. Hotels and restaurants are rated on a scale of zero (recommended) to three stars (exceptional). Attractions, shopping, nightlife, towns, and regions are rated according to the following scale: zero stars (recommended), one star (highly recommended), two stars (very highly recommended), and three stars (must-see).

In addition to the star-rating system, we also use seven feature icons that point you to the great deals, in-the-know advice, and unique experiences that separate travelers from tourists. Throughout the book, look for:

special finds—those places only insiders know about

fun facts—details that make travelers more informed and their trips more fun

kids—best bets for kids and advice for the whole family

special moments—those experiences that memories are made of

overrated—places or experiences not worth your time or money

insider tips—great ways to save time and money

great values—where to get the best deals

The following abbreviations are used for credit cards:

AE	American Express	DISC	Discover	V	Visa
DC	Diners Club	MC	MasterCard		

TRAVEL RESOURCES AT FROMMERS.COM

Frommer's travel resources don't end with this guide. Frommer's website, **www.frommers.com**, has travel information on more than 4,000 destinations. We update features regularly, giving you access to the most current trip-planning information and the best airfare, lodging, and car-rental bargains. You can also listen to podcasts, connect with other Frommers.com members through our active-reader forums, share your travel photos, read blogs from guidebook editors and fellow travelers, and much more.

THE BEST OF THE BAHAMAS

I f you've decided that The Bahamas sounds like the perfect place to relax, feel free to start unwinding right now, because we've done all the legwork for you. Below you'll find our carefully compiled lists of the best that The Bahamas has to offer, from beaches and dive sites to resorts, restaurants, and sightseeing—and nearly everything else you'll want to see and do.

THE best BEACHES

o **Cable Beach** (New Providence Island) The glittering shoreline of Cable Beach proffers easy access to shops, casinos, restaurants, watersports, and bars. It's a sandy 6.5km-long (4-mile) strip, with a great array of facilities and activities. See p. 12.

o **Cabbage Beach** (Paradise Island) Think Vegas in the Tropics. It seems as though most of the sunbathers dozing on the sands here are recovering from the previous night's partying, and it's likely to be crowded near the mega-hotels, but you can find more solitude on the beach's northwestern extension (Paradise Beach), which is accessible only by boat or on foot. Lined with palms, sea grapes, and casuarinas, the sands are broad and stretch for at least 3km (1¾ miles). See p. 12.

o **Xanadu Beach** (Grand Bahama Island) Grand Bahama has 97km (60 miles) of sandy shoreline, but Xanadu Beach is most convenient to Freeport's hotels, several of which offer shuttle service here. There's more than a kilometer (⅔ mile) of white sand and (usually) gentle surf. Don't expect to have it to yourself, but if you want more quiet and privacy, try any of the beaches that stretch from Xanadu for many miles in either direction. See p. 141.

THE best DIVING

o **New Providence Island** Many ships have sunk near Nassau in the past 300 years, and all the dive outfitters here know the most scenic wreck sites. Other underwater attractions are gardens of elkhorn coral and dozens of reefs packed with life. The most spectacular dive site is **Shark Wall,** 16km (10 miles) off New Providence's southwest coast; it's blessed with incredible, colorful sea life and the healthiest coral offshore. You'll even get to swim with sharks (not as bait, of course). See p. 73.

o **Grand Bahama Island** The island is ringed with reefs, and dive sites are plentiful, including the **Wall,** the **Caves** (site of a long-ago disaster known as Theo's Wreck), and **Treasure Reef.** Other popular dive sites include **Spit City** (yes, that's right), **Ben Blue Hole,** and the **Rose Garden** (no one knows how this one got its name). What makes Grand Bahama a cut above the others is the presence of a world-class dive operator, **UNEXSO,** the Underwater Explorer Society (© **800/992-DIVE** [3483] or 242/373-1244; www.unexso.com). See p. 146.

o **Lucayan National Park** This park on Grand Bahama is the site of a 9.5km-long (6-mile) underground freshwater cave system, the longest of its type in the world. The largest cave contains spiral staircases that lead visitors into a freshwater world inhabited by shrimp, mosquito fish, fruit bats, freshwater eels, and a species of crustacean (*Spelionectes lucayensis*) that has never been documented elsewhere. In the 16-hectare (40-acre) preserve are examples of the island's five ecosystems—pine forests, rocky coppice, mangrove swamps, whiteland coppice, and sand dunes. Pause to sunbathe on a lovely stretch of sandy beach or hike along paths accented by orchids, hummingbirds, and barn owls. See p. 148.

THE best SNORKELING

o **New Providence and Paradise Islands** The waters that ring densely populated New Providence and nearby Paradise Island are easy to explore. Most people head for the **Rose Island Reefs,** the **Gambier Deep Reef,** the **Booby Rock Channel,** the **Goulding Reef Cays,** and some easily seen, well-known underwater wrecks that lie in shallow water. Virtually every hotel on the island offers equipment and can book you onto a snorkel cruise to sites farther offshore. See p. 73 and 110.

o **Grand Bahama Island**   Resort hotels can hook you up with snorkeling excursions, such as the ones offered by **Reef Tours** (© 242/373-5880; www.bahamasvacationguide.com/reef tours), the best snorkeling outfitter, which can also arrange any kind of watersport from banana-boating to water-skiing. The clear waters around Grand Bahama are wonderful for snorkeling because they have a rich marine life. Snorkelers are fond of exploring **Ben's Cave,** a stunning cavern that's part of Lucayan Caves, as well as the coral beds at places like **Silver Point Reef** and **Gold Rock.** See p. 146.

THE best FISHING

o **New Providence Island**   The waters around New Providence teem with game fish. In-the-know fishermen long ago learned the best months to pursue their catch: November to February for wahoo found in the reefs, June and July for blue marlin, and May to August for the oceanic bonito and blackfin tuna. Nassau, in particular, is ideal for sportfishing. Most boat charters allow passengers to start fishing within 15 minutes after leaving the dock. The best outfitter is **Born Free Charters** (© 242/393-4144; www.bornfreefishing.com). Anchoring and bottom-fishing are also options. See p. 72.

o **Grand Bahama Island**   The tropical waters along Grand Bahama lure anglers in search of "the big one" because this is home to some of the biggest game fish on earth. Off the coast, the clear waters are good hunting grounds for snapper, grouper, yellowtail, wahoo, barracuda, and kingfish. Many fishermen catch dolphin (the mahimahi kind, not Flipper). And Deep Water Cay is a fishing hot spot. The best outfitter is **Reef Tours** (© 242/373-5880; www.bahamasvacationguide.com/reef tours). See p. 144.

THE best SAILING

o **New Providence Island**   A greater number of organized boating excursions is offered in New Providence than anywhere else in The Bahamas, especially by outfitters such as **Barefoot Sailing Cruises** (© 242/393-0820; www.barefootsailingcruises. com) and **Majestic Tours** (© 242/322-2606; www.majestic holidays.com). You can also choose from an array of sunset cruises, such as the ones the *Flying Cloud* (© 242/394-5067; www.flyingcloud.info) offers aboard its fleet of catamarans. The most popular—and the most scenic—trip is to tranquil **Rose Island,** 13km (8 miles) east of the center of Nassau and reached after sailing past several small uninhabited cays. (The drawbacks to this island, however, are that cruise-ship passengers flock here and many beach buffs like to come on day trips.) In addition, **Blue Lagoon Island,** 5km (3 miles) northeast of Paradise Island, is a magnet for boaters, offering seven white-sand beaches with seaside hammocks. See p. 71.

o **Grand Bahama Island** On the beautiful waters off this large island, you can go sailing aboard the *Ocean Wonder* (© 242/373-5880), which is supposedly the world's largest twin-diesel-engine glass-bottom boat. This vessel offers the best and most panoramic picture of underwater life off the coast of Grand Bahama—a view most often reserved for scuba divers. You can also sail with **Superior Watersports** (© 242/373-7863; www.superiorwatersports.com), which operates the two-deck 22m (72-ft.) *Bahama Mama* catamaran, offering a Robinson Crusoe Beach Party as well as a shorter sunset Booze Cruise. See p. 143.

THE best GOLF COURSES

o **New Providence Island** The main draw is the 18-hole **Cable Beach Golf Club** (© 242/677-4175; http://crystalpalace vacations.com). The oldest golf course in The Bahamas, this par-71 green was the private retreat of British expatriates in the 1930s. Today, it's owned by Cable Beach casino marketers. Small ponds and water traps heighten the challenge, amid more than 5,901m (6,453 yd.) of well-maintained greens and fairways. See p. 73.

o **Paradise Island** Tom Weiskopf designed the **Ocean Club Golf Course** (© 242/363-2510; www.oneandonlyresorts. com), an 18-hole, par-72 course, and it's a stunner. With challenges that include the world's largest sand trap and water hazards (mainly the Atlantic Ocean) on three sides, the course has received praise from Jack Nicklaus and Gary Player. For the best panoramic ocean view—good enough to take your mind off your game—play the par-3 14th hole. See p. 110.

o **Grand Bahama Island** The Lucayan Country Club now boasts two separate courses. The **Reef Golf Course** (© 242/373-1333; www.ourlucaya.com), a sandy course with links-style greens designed by Robert Trent Jones, Jr., opened in 2000. The Bahamian press called it a bit like a Scottish course, "but a lot warmer." The **Lucayan Golf Course** (© 242/373-1333; www.ourlucaya.com) is a well-respected, renovated, tree-lined course originally laid out in 1964. Both courses have 18 holes and a par of 72. Though they aren't immediately adjacent, shuttle buses carry golfers from one course to the other at frequent intervals. See p. 144.

THE best TENNIS FACILITIES

o **Paradise Island** Well-heeled tennis buffs check into the **One&Only Ocean Club** (☎ **242/363-2501**; www.oneand onlyresorts.com). In fact, many visitors come here just for the tennis, which can be played day or night on the six Har-Tru courts. Although beginners and intermediate players are welcome, the courts are often filled with top-notch competitors. The tennis complex at **Atlantis** (☎ **242/363-3000**; www. atlantis.com) is more accessible to the general public, with six courts (three clay and three hard surface), some lit for night games. See p. 110.

o **Grand Bahama Island** Freeport/Lucaya is another top choice for tennis buffs. The island's best tennis is at the **Ace Tennis Center** at the **Radisson at Our Lucaya Beach & Golf Resort,** Royal Palm Way (☎ **242/350-5294**; www.ourlucaya. com). It has four courts with different playing surfaces. See p. 128.

THE best HONEYMOON RESORTS

o **Sandals Royal Bahamian** (Cable Beach, New Providence Island; ☎ **800/SANDALS** [726-3257]; www.sandals.com) is one branch of a Jamaica-based chain of couples-only, all-inclusive hotels popular among honeymooners. This property is more upscale than many of its Jamaican counterparts and offers 27 secluded honeymoon suites with semiprivate plunge pools. Staff members lend their experience and talent to on-site wedding celebrations: Sandals will provide everything from a preacher to flowers, as well as champagne and a cake. It's more expensive than most Sandals resorts, but you can usually get better prices than the official rack rates through a travel agent or a package deal. See p. 50.

o **One&Only Ocean Club** (Paradise Island; ☎ **888/528-7157**; www.oneandonlyresorts.com) is elegant, low-key, low-rise, and exclusive. Guests include many older honeymoon couples. With waterfalls, fountains, reflecting pools, and a stone gazebo, its formal terraced gardens were inspired by the club's founder (an heir to the A&P grocery fortune) and are the most impressive in The Bahamas. At the center is a French cloister, with carvings from the 12th century. See p. 98.

o **Old Bahama Bay by Ginn sur Mer** (Grand Bahama Island; ☎ **888/800-8959**; www.oldbahamabay.com) is perfect for honeymooners seeking a hideaway in a boutique-style hotel with cottages adjacent to a marina. The entertainment, shopping, and dining of Freeport/Lucaya are 40km (25 miles) away, so it's ideal for quiet luxury, solitude, and romance. See p. 132.

THE best FAMILY VACATIONS

o **Sheraton Nassau Beach Resort** (Cable Beach, New Providence Island; © 800/325-3535; www.starwoodhotels.com) could keep a family occupied for their entire vacation. On the grounds of this vast resort is a pool area that features the most lavish artificial waterfall this side of Tahiti; Camp Junkanoo, with supervised play for kids 3 through 12; and a long list of in-house activities such as dancing lessons. See p. 53.

o **Atlantis Paradise Island** (Paradise Island; © 800/285-2684; www.atlantis.com) is one of the world's largest hotel complexes, with endless rows of shops and watersports galore. Both children and adults will enjoy the sprawling sea world with water slides, a lagoon, white-sand beaches, and underground grottoes, plus an underwater viewing tunnel and 240m (787 ft.) of cascading waterfalls. Its children's menus and innovative, creative kids' programs are the best in The Bahamas and perhaps even in the Caribbean. See p. 93.

o **Castaways Resort & Suites** (Grand Bahama Island; © 866/410-9676; www.castaways-resort.com) is a good choice for families on a budget. The pagoda-capped lobby is set a very short walk from the ice-cream stands, souvenir shops, and fountains of the International Bazaar. Children under 11 and under stay free, and the in-house lounge presents limbo and fire-eating shows several evenings a month. The hotel also offers babysitting service and a free shuttle to William's Town Beach. See p. 126

THE best RESTAURANTS

o **Sun and . . .** (Nassau, New Providence Island; © 242/393-1205; www.sun-and.com) has made a comeback after being closed for many years. Once again, it is the leading independent choice on New Providence, serving a finely honed international cuisine. It's a throwback to Nassau in its grand heyday. Originally built in the 1930s as a private residence, it lies in an upscale residential neighborhood east of Nassau's center. See p. 59.

o **Moso** (Wyndham Nassau Resort, Cable Beach, New Providence Island; © 242/327-6200; www.wyndhamnassauresort.com) is New Providence Island's best Asian restaurant. Its well-trained staff has learned the secrets of the cuisines of the Far East, and they dispense an array of some of the best-known and tastiest dishes, including teriyaki specialties. See p. 65.

o **Dune** (One&Only Ocean Club, Paradise Island; © 242/363-2501, ext. 64739; www.oneandonlyresorts.com) is the most cutting-edge restaurant in Paradise Island/Nassau. It's the creation of French-born restaurant guru Jean-Georges Vongerichten, the moving force behind several of New York City's top dining spots. Everything that comes out of the kitchen benefits from a special touch—witness the chicken and coconut-milk soup accompanied by shiitake cakes. See p. 105.

o **Nobu** (Atlantis, Paradise Island; © 242/363-3000; www.atlantis.com) has opened a branch of this celebrated Japanese restaurant in The Bahamas. It's the island's most-talked-about—and arguably its best, attracting a string of celebrities. The setting is glamorous, and the cuisine is top-rated, prepared with either market-fresh ingredients or exotic imported ingredients. See p. 107.

THE best NIGHTLIFE

o **Cable Beach** has a lot more splash and excitement than Nassau, its neighbor on New Providence Island. Wandering around Cable Beach is also much safer than exploring Nassau's back streets at night. The main attraction is the **Wyndham Nassau Resort & Crystal Palace Casino** (© 242/327-6200; www.wyndhamnassauresort.com), with an 800-seat theater known for staging glitzy extravaganzas and a gaming room that will make you think you're smack-dab in the middle of Vegas. One of the largest casinos in the islands, the Crystal Palace features blackjack tables, roulette wheels, craps tables, hundreds of slot machines, and a baccarat table. (We think the Paradise Island casino has more class, though.) Despite all the glitter, you can still find cozy bars and nooks throughout the resort, if you'd prefer a tranquil evening. See p. 88.

o **Paradise Island** offers the flashiest nightlife in all of The Bahamas, hands down. Not even nearby Nassau and Cable Beach can come close. Nearly all of the action takes place at the incredible **Atlantis Paradise Island** (© 242/363-3000; www.atlantis.com), where you'll find high rollers from Vegas and Atlantic City alongside grandmothers from Iowa who play the slots when the family isn't looking. It's all gloss, glitter, and showbiz, with good gambling (though savvy locals say your odds of beating the house are better in Vegas). For a quieter night out, you can also find intimate bars, discos, a comedy club, and lots more in this sprawling behemoth of a resort. See p. 114.

PLANNING YOUR TRIP TO THE BAHAMAS

Y ou can be in The Bahamas after a quick 35-minute jet hop from Miami. And it's never been easier to take advantage of great package deals that can make these islands a terrific value.

If your papers are in order, flying to The Bahamas is like flying to Florida if you live on the Eastern Seaboard. Unless you run into transportation delays because of bad weather, you should encounter no hassle at all before landing on a beach strip.

For additional assistance in planning your trip and for further on-the-ground resources in The Bahamas, please see chapter 6, "Fast Facts."

THE LAY OF THE LAND

With more than 700 islands and some 2,000 cays, The Bahamas spreads over 259,000 sq. km (100,000 sq. miles) of the Atlantic Ocean and encompasses countless natural attractions, including underwater reefs that stretch 1,220km (758 miles) from the Abacos in the northeast to Long Island in the southeast.

The Bahamas is the largest oceanic archipelago nation in the tropical Atlantic, with miles of crystal-clear waters rich in fish and other marine resources. Although New Providence is heavily populated, the rest of the Out Islands, including Grand Bahama, have relatively small populations. Unlike Puerto Rico, Jamaica, Barbados, and other Caribbean island nations, The Bahamas has large areas of undeveloped natural land. The islands also have the most extensive ocean-hole and limestone cave systems in the world.

The country's approximately 2,330 sq. km (900 sq. miles) of coral reefs include the world's third-largest barrier reef, off the coast of Andros. Reef marine life includes green moray eels, cinnamon clownfish, and Nassau grouper. The Bahamas was one of the first Caribbean countries to outlaw long-line fishing, recognizing it as a threat to regional ecology.

The **Bahamas National Trust** administers 12 national parks and protected areas covering more than 97,100 hectares (239,939 acres). Its headquarters, which is home to one of the Western Hemisphere's finest collections of wild palms, is in Nassau at the Retreat Gardens on Village Road (✆ **242/393-1317;** www.bnt. bs). Volunteers help arrange visits to the islands' national parks. For more information about the ecotourism highlights of The Bahamas, also contact the **Ecotourism Association of Grand Bahama** (✆ **242/373-2485**).

Islands in Brief

The most developed islands for tourism are **New Providence,** site of Cable Beach and Nassau (the capital); **Paradise Island;** and **Grand Bahama,** home of Freeport and Lucaya. If you're after glitz, gambling, bustling restaurants, nightclubs, and a beach-party scene, these big three islands are where you'll want to be. Package deals are easily found.

Set sail (or hop on a short commuter flight) for one of the **Out Islands,** such as Andros, the Exumas, or the Abacos, and you'll find fewer crowds—and often lower prices, too. Though some of the Out Islands are accessible mainly (or only) by boat, it's still worth your while to make the trip if you like the idea of having an entire beach to yourself. These are really the places to get away from it all. For coverage of the Out Islands, pick up a copy of *Frommer's Bahamas.*

New Providence Island (Nassau/Cable Beach) New Providence isn't the largest Bahamian island, but it's the nation's historic heart, with a strong maritime tradition and the country's largest population (125,000). It offers groves of palms and casuarinas; sandy, flat soil; the closest thing in The Bahamas to urban sprawl; and superb anchorages sheltered from rough seas by nearby Paradise Island. New Providence also has the country's busiest airport and is dotted with hundreds of villas owned by foreign investors. Its two major resort areas are Cable Beach and Nassau.

Cable Beach is a glittering beachfront strip of hotels, restaurants, and casinos; only Paradise Island has been more developed. Its center is the Wyndham Nassau Resort & Crystal Palace Casino. Often, deciding between Cable Beach and Paradise Island isn't so much a choice of which island you prefer as a choice of which hotel you prefer. But it's easy to sample both, since it takes only about 30 minutes to drive between the two.

Nassau, the Bahamian capital, isn't on a great stretch of shoreline and doesn't have as many first-rate hotels as either Paradise Island or Cable Beach—with the exception of the British Colonial Hilton, which has a small private beach. The main advantages of Nassau are its colonial charm and lower price point. Its accommodations may not be ideally located, but they are relatively inexpensive, sometimes even during the winter high season. You can base yourself here and commute easily to the beaches at Paradise Island or Cable Beach. Some travelers even prefer Nassau because it's the seat of Bahamian culture and history—not to mention the shopping mecca of The Bahamas.

Paradise Island   If high-rise hotels and glittering casinos are what you want, alongside some of the best beaches in The Bahamas, there is no better choice than Paradise Island, directly off Nassau's coast. It has the best food, entertainment, hotels, and terrific beaches and casinos. Its major drawbacks are that it's expensive and often overcrowded. With its colorful history but unremarkable architecture, Paradise Island remains one of the most intensely marketed pieces of real estate in the world. The sands and shoals of the long, narrow island protect Nassau's wharves and piers, which rise across a narrow channel only 180m (591 ft.) away.

Owners of the 277-hectare (684-acre) island have included brokerage mogul Joseph Lynch (of Merrill Lynch) and Huntington Hartford (heir to the A&P supermarket fortune). More recent investors have included Merv Griffin. The island today is a carefully landscaped residential and commercial complex with good beaches, lots of glitter (some of it tasteful, some of it way too over-the-top), and many diversions.

Grand Bahama Island (Freeport/Lucaya)   The island's name derives from the Spanish term *gran bajamar* ("great shallows"), which refers to the shallow reefs and sandbars that, over the centuries, have destroyed everything from Spanish galleons to English clippers on these shores. Thanks to the development schemes of U.S. financiers such as Howard Hughes, Grand Bahama boasts a well-developed tourist infrastructure. Casinos, beaches, and restaurants are now plentiful.

Grand Bahama's **Freeport/Lucaya** resort area is another popular destination for American tourists, though it has a lot more tackiness than Paradise Island or Cable Beach. The compensation for that is a lower price tag on just about everything. Freeport/Lucaya offers plenty of opportunities for fine dining, entertainment, and gambling.

This island, especially popular with families, also offers the best hiking in The Bahamas and some of the finest sandy beaches. Its golf courses attract players from all over the globe and host major tournaments several times a year. You'll find some of the world's best diving here, as well as UNEXSO, the internationally famous diving school.

beaches 101: **PARADISE ISLAND, CABLE BEACH & MORE**

In The Bahamas, the issue about public access to beaches is a hot and controversial subject. Recognizing this, the government has made efforts to place public beaches near private ones, where access would otherwise be impeded. Although mega-resorts restrict nonguests from having easy access to their individual beaches, there are so many public beaches on New Providence Island and Paradise Island that all a beach lover has to do is stop the car at, or walk to, many of the unmarked, unnamed beaches that flank these islands.

If you stay in one of the large beachfront resorts, just head for the ocean via the sand in front the resort. Otherwise, below are a few details that will come in handy if your accommodations aren't oceanfront, or if you want to explore another beach:

Cabbage Beach ★★ (also called **West Beach**) On Paradise Island, this is the real showcase, with broad, white sands that stretch for at least 3km (1¾ miles). Casuarinas, palms, and sea grapes border it. While it's likely to be crowded in winter, you can find a little more elbowroom by walking to its northwestern stretch. You can reach Paradise Island from downtown Nassau by walking over the bridge, taking a taxi, or boarding a ferryboat at Prince George Wharf. Cabbage Beach does not have public facilities, but if you patronize one of the handful of bars and restaurants nearby, you can use its restrooms.

Cable Beach ★★ No particular beach is actually called Cable Beach, yet this is New Providence Island's most popular beachfront destination. The 6.5km (4-mile) stretch of resorts and white-sand beaches in the central northern coast has calypso music floating to the sand from hotel pool patios and vendors making their way between sunblock-slathered bodies. There are no public toilets here because guests of the resorts use their hotels' restrooms. If you're not a hotel guest or customer, you're not supposed to use the facilities. The Cable Beach resorts begin 5km (3 miles) west of downtown Nassau.

Caves Beach On the north shore, past Cable Beach, Caves Beach, which has soft sands, lies some 11km (6¾ miles) west of Nassau. It stands near Rock Point, right before the turnoff along Blake Road that

WHEN TO GO
The Weather

The temperature in The Bahamas averages between 75°F and 84°F (24°C–29°C) in both winter and summer, although it can get leads to the airport. Since visitors often don't know of this beach, it's a good spot at which to escape the hordes. There are no toilets or changing facilities.

Delaporte Beach   Just west of the busiest section of Cable Beach, Delaporte is a public-access beach where you can go to escape the crowds. It opens onto clear waters and boasts white sands, although it has no facilities.

Goodman's Bay   This public beach lies east of Cable Beach on the way toward Nassau's center. Goodman's Bay and Saunders Beach (see below) often host local fund-raising cookouts, at which vendors sell fish, chicken, conch, peas 'n' rice, and macaroni and cheese. People swim and socialize to blaring reggae and calypso music. To find out when one of these beach parties is happening, ask the staff at your hotel or pick up a local newspaper. There is a playground here, too, and toilet facilities.

Paradise Beach ★★   This beach, on Paradise Island, is one of the best in the entire area. White and sandy, it's dotted with *chikees* (thatched huts), which are perfect when you've had too much sun. Mainly used by guests of the Atlantis Resort (p. 93), it lies at the island's far western tip. If you're not a guest, access is difficult. If you're staying at a hotel in Nassau and want to come to Paradise Island for a day at the beach, it's better to go to Cabbage Beach (see above).

Saunders Beach   East of Cable Beach, this is where many island-ers head on their weekends off. To reach it, take West Bay Street from Nassau toward Coral Island. The beach is across from Fort Charlotte, just west of Arawak Cay. Like Goodman's Bay (see above), it often hosts local fund-raising cookouts that are open to the public. These can be a lot of fun. There are no public facilities.

Western Esplanade (also called **Junkanoo Beach** or **Lighthouse Beach**)   If you're staying at a hotel in downtown Nassau, such as the British Colonial Hilton (p. 44), this is a good beach to patronize close to town. The narrow strip of sand is convenient to Nassau and has toilets, changing facilities, and a snack bar.

chilly in the early morning and at night. The Bahamian winter is usually like a perpetual late spring—naturally, the high season for North Americans rushing to escape snow and ice. Summer brings broiling hot sun and humidity. There's a much greater chance of rain during the summer and fall.

The Hurricane Season

The curse of Bahamian weather, the hurricane season, lasts (officially) from June 1 to November 30. But there is no cause for panic. More tropical cyclones pound the U.S. mainland than The Bahamas. Hurricanes are actually fairly infrequent here, and when one does come, satellite forecasts generally give adequate advance warning so that precautions can be taken.

If you're heading for The Bahamas during the hurricane season, you might want to visit the National Weather Service at www.nws.noaa.gov.

For an online 10-day forecast, check the Weather Channel at www.weather.com.

Average Temperatures & Rainfall (in.) in The Bahamas

MONTH	JAN	FEB	MAR	APR	MAY	JUNE	JULY	AUG	SEPT	OCT	NOV	DEC
TEMP. °F	70	70	72	75	77	81	81	82	81	79	73	72
TEMP. °C	21	21	22	24	25	27	27	28	27	26	23	22
RAINFALL (IN.)	1.9	1.6	1.4	1.9	4.8	9.2	6.1	6.3	7.5	8.3	2.3	1.5

Note that these numbers are daily averages, so expect temperatures to climb significantly higher in the noonday sun and to drop a good deal in the evening.

The "Season"

In The Bahamas, hotels charge their highest prices during the peak winter period from mid-December to mid-April, when visitors fleeing from cold north winds flock to the islands. Winter is the driest season.

If you plan to visit during the winter, try to make reservations at least 2 to 3 months in advance. At some hotels, it's impossible to book accommodations for Christmas and the month of February without even more lead time.

SAVING MONEY IN THE OFF SEASON

The Bahamas is a year-round destination. The islands' "off season" runs from late spring to late fall, when tolerable temperatures (see "The Weather," above) prevail throughout most of the region. Trade winds ensure comfortable days and nights, even in accommodations without air-conditioning. Although the noonday sun may raise temperatures to uncomfortable levels, cool breezes usually make the morning, late afternoon, and evening more pleasant here than in many parts of the U.S. mainland.

Dollar for dollar, you'll spend less money by renting a summer house or fully equipped unit in The Bahamas than you would on Cape Cod, Fire Island, Laguna Beach, or the coast of Maine.

Avoiding Spring Break

Throughout March and into mid-April, it's spring-break season in the Caribbean for vacationing college and high-school students. Expect beach parties, sports events, and musical entertainment; if the idea of hundreds of partying fraternity kids doesn't appeal to you, beware. When you make your reservations, ask if your hotel is planning to host any big groups of kids.

The off season—roughly from mid-April to mid-December (rate schedules vary from hotel to hotel)—amounts to a summer sale. In most cases, hotel rates are slashed from 20% to a startling 60%. It's a bonanza for cost-conscious travelers, especially families who like to go on vacations together. In the chapters ahead, we'll spell out in dollars the specific amounts hotels charge during the off season.

OTHER OFF-SEASON ADVANTAGES

Although The Bahamas may appear inviting in the winter to those who live in northern climates, your trip may be more enjoyable if you go in the off season. Here's why:

o After the winter hordes have left, a less hurried way of life prevails.
o Swimming pools and beaches are less crowded—perhaps not crowded at all.
o To survive, resort boutiques often feature summer sales.
o You can often appear without a reservation at a top restaurant and get a table for dinner.
o The endless waiting game is over: no waiting for a rented car, no long wait for a golf course tee time, and quicker access to tennis courts and watersports.
o The atmosphere is more cosmopolitan than it is in winter, mainly because of the influx of Europeans.
o Some package-tour fares are as much as 20% lower, and individual excursion fares may be reduced from 5% to 10%.
o Accommodations and flights are much easier to book.
o Summer is an excellent time for family travel, which is not always possible during the winter season.
o Finally, the best Bahamian attractions—sea, sand, surf, and lots of sunshine—remain absolutely undiminished.

OFF-SEASON DISADVANTAGES

Let's not paint too rosy a picture. Although the advantages of off-season travel far outweigh the disadvantages, there are nevertheless some drawbacks to traveling here in summer:

- You might be staying at a construction site. Hoteliers save their major renovations until the off season. You may wake up to the sound of hammers.
- Single tourists find the dating scene better in winter when there are more visitors, especially unattached ones.
- Services are often reduced. In the peak of winter, everything is fully operational. But in summer, many programs (such as watersports) might be curtailed in spite of fine weather.

The Bahamas Calendar of Events

For an exhaustive list of events beyond those listed here, check http://events.frommers.com, where you'll find a searchable, up-to-the-minute roster of what's happening in cities all over the world. For specific events, you can call your nearest branch of **The Bahamas Tourist Office** (see "Visitor Information," p. 38) at ℭ **800/BAHAMAS** (224-2627) or check their website at www.bahamas.com or http://eventguide.com/bahamas.

JANUARY

Junkanoo. This Mardi Gras–style festival begins 2 or 3 hours before dawn on New Year's Day. Throngs of cavorting, costumed figures prance through Nassau, Freeport/Lucaya, and the Out Islands. Jubilant men, women, and children wear elaborate headdresses and festive apparel as they celebrate their African heritage with music and dance. Mini-Junkanoos, in which visitors can participate, are regular events. Local tourist offices will advise the best locations to see the festivities.

New Year's Day Sailing Regatta, Nassau and Paradise Island. Three dozen or more sailing sloops, ranging from 5 to 8.5m (16–28 ft.), converge off Montagu Bay in a battle for bragging rights. For information, call ℭ **242/394-0445.**

MARCH

Bacardi Billfish Tournament, Freeport. A weeklong tournament attracting the who's who of deep-sea fishing. Headquarters is the Port Lucaya Resort & Yacht Club. For more information, call ℭ **242/373-9090,** or visit www.portlucaya.com. Mid-March.

JUNE

Bahamas Summer Boating Fling/Flotilla. Boating enthusiasts and yachters make the 1-day crossing from Florida to The Bahamas (Port Lucaya's marina on Grand Bahama Island) in a flotilla of boats guided by a lead boat. All "flings" depart from the Radisson Bahia Mar Resort & Yacht Center in Fort Lauderdale. For more information, contact the **Bahamas Tourism Center** in Florida at ℭ **800/327-7678** or 954/236-9292. End of June to beginning of August.

JULY

Independence Week. Independence celebrations are marked throughout the islands by festivities, parades, and fireworks. It all culminates on Independence Day. Call ✆ **242/322-1312.** July 10.

AUGUST

Emancipation Day. The first Monday in August commemorates the emancipation of slaves in 1834. A highlight of this holiday is an early morning "Junkanoo Rushout" starting at 4am in Fox Hill Village in Nassau, followed by an afternoon of "cookouts," cultural events such as climbing a greased pole, and the plaiting of the Maypole. First Monday in August.

OCTOBER

Discovery Day. The New World landing of Christopher Columbus, traditionally said to be on the island of San Salvador, is celebrated throughout The Bahamas. Naturally, San Salvador has a parade every year on October 12.

Great Bahamas Seafood and Heritage Festival, Heritage Village, Arawak Cay. A cultural affair, this festival held in October showcases authentic Bahamian cuisine, traditional music, and storytelling. For more information, exact times, and a schedule of events, contact the **Ministry of Tourism** at ✆ **242/302-2000.**

NOVEMBER

Guy Fawkes Day. The best celebrations are in Nassau. Nighttime parades through the streets are held on many of the islands, culminating in the hanging and burning of Guy Fawkes, an effigy of the British malefactor who was involved in the Gunpowder Plot of 1605 in London. It usually takes place around November 5, but check with island tourist offices.

Annual One Bahamas Music & Heritage Festival. This 3-day celebration is staged at both Nassau and Paradise Island to celebrate national unity. Highlights include concerts featuring top Bahamian performing artists, "fun walks," and other activities. For details, contact the **Nassau/Paradise Island Office** at the Ministry of Tourism, ✆ **242/302-2000.** Last week of November.

DECEMBER

Junkanoo Boxing Day. High-energy Junkanoo parades and celebrations are held throughout the islands on December 26. Many of these activities are repeated on New Year's Day (see "January," above). December 26.

Holidays

Banks, government offices, post offices, and many stores and restaurants are closed on the following public holidays in The Bahamas: **New Year's Day** (January 1), **Good Friday, Easter Sunday,**

Easter Monday, Whit Monday (7 weeks after Easter), Labour Day (the first Friday in June), Independence Day (July 10), Emancipation Day (the first Monday in August), Discovery Day (October 12), Christmas (December 25), and Boxing Day (December 26). When a holiday falls on a Saturday or Sunday, stores and offices are usually closed on the following Monday, too.

ENTRY REQUIREMENTS

To enter The Bahamas, citizens of Britain and Canada coming in as visitors *must* bring a passport to demonstrate proof of citizenship. Under new Homeland Security regulations that started December 31, 2005, U.S. travelers were required to have a valid passport to re-enter the United States by January 1, 2008.

Onward or return tickets must be shown to immigration officials in The Bahamas. Citizens of other countries, including Australia, Ireland, and New Zealand, should carry a valid passport.

For information about how to get a passport, see "Passports" in chapter 6. The websites listed provide downloadable passport applications as well as the current fees for processing passport applications. For an up-to-date, country-by-country listing of passport requirements around the world, go to the "Foreign Entry Requirement" Web page of the U.S. State Department at **http://travel.state.gov**.

The Commonwealth of The Bahamas does not require visas. On entry to The Bahamas, you'll be given an immigration card to complete and sign. The card has a carbon copy that you must keep until departure, at which time it must be turned in. You'll also have to pay a departure tax before you can exit the country.

Unless you're coming from an area suffering from an epidemic, inoculations or vaccinations are not required for entry into The Bahamas.

For information about what you can bring with you to The Bahamas (and what you can bring home with you), see "Customs" in chapter 6.

GETTING THERE

Lying off the east coast of Florida, the archipelago of The Bahamas is the easiest and most convenient foreign destination Americans can fly to unless they live close to the Canadian or Mexican borders.

Nassau is the busiest and most popular point of entry (this is where you'll fly if you're staying on Paradise Island). Freeport, on Grand Bahama, also has its own airport, which is served by flights from the U.S. mainland, too.

Security Measures

Because of increased security measures, the Transportation Security Administration has made changes to the prohibited items list. In carry-on baggage, all liquids and gels—including shampoo, toothpaste, perfume, hair gel, suntan lotion, and all other items with similar consistency—must be in individual containers of 3 ounces or less, all of which must be packed in a 1-quart bag. Items that do not fulfill these requirements must be packed in checked baggage.

With the ever-changing security measures, we recommend that you check the **Transportation Security Administration**'s website, www.tsa.gov, as near to your departure date as possible to make sure that no other restrictions have been imposed.

Flight time to Nassau from Miami is about 35 minutes; from New York, 2½ hours; from Atlanta, 2 hours and 5 minutes; from Philadelphia, 2 hours and 45 minutes; from Charlotte, 2 hours and 10 minutes; from central Florida, 1 hour and 10 minutes; and from Toronto, 3 hours.

By Plane

From the U.S. mainland, about a half-dozen carriers fly nonstop to the country's major point of entry and busiest airline hub, **Lynden Pindling International Airport** (© 242/377-1759 or 377-0209; www.nas.bs), outside of Nassau on New Providence Island. Some also fly to the archipelago's second-most-populous city of Freeport, on Grand Bahama.

American Airlines (© 800/433-7300; www.aa.com) has several flights per day from Miami to Nassau, as well as four daily flights from Fort Lauderdale to Nassau. In addition, the carrier flies three times daily from Miami to Freeport.

Delta (© 800/221-1212; www.delta.com) has several connections to The Bahamas, with service from Atlanta, Orlando, and New York's LaGuardia.

The national airline of The Bahamas, **Bahamasair** (© 800/222-4262 or 242/377-8451; www.bahamasair.com), flies to The Bahamas from Miami and Fort Lauderdale, landing at either Nassau (with seven nonstop flights daily) or Freeport (with two nonstop flights daily).

US Airways (© 800/428-4322; www.usairways.com) offers daily direct flights to Nassau from Philadelphia and Charlotte, North Carolina.

JetBlue (✆ **800/JET-BLUE** [538-2583]; www.jetblue.com) has one direct flight daily to Nassau, from JFK in New York.

Continental Airlines (✆ **800/231-0856;** www.continental. com) has greatly expanded its connections to The Bahamas through South Florida through its regional affiliate, Gulfstream International.

Air Canada (✆ **888/247-2262;** www.aircanada.com) is the only carrier offering scheduled service to Nassau from Canada. Direct flights from Toronto and Montreal leave daily; other flights from Toronto and Montreal, as well as other Canadian cities, make connections in the U.S.

British travelers opt for transatlantic passage aboard **British Airways** (✆ **800/AIR-WAYS** [247-9297] in the U.S. or 0844/493-0787 in the U.K.; www.britishairways.com), which offers four weekly direct flights from London to Nassau. The airline also has at least one flight daily to Miami. From here, many connections are available to Nassau and many other points within the archipelago on several carriers.

GETTING AROUND
By Rental Car

Many travelers don't really need to rent a car in The Bahamas, especially those who are coming for a few days of soaking in the sun at their resort's own beach. In Nassau and Freeport, you can easily rely on public transportation or taxis.

Most visitors need transportation only from the airport to their hotel; perhaps you can arrange an island tour later, and an expensive private car won't be necessary. Your hotel can always arrange a taxi for you if you want to venture out.

You may decide that you want a car to explore beyond the tourist areas of New Providence Island, and you're very likely to want one on Grand Bahama Island.

Just remember: Road rules are much the same as those in the U.S., but you *drive on the left*.

The major U.S. car-rental companies operate in The Bahamas. We always prefer to do business with one of the major firms if they're present because you can call ahead and reserve from home via a toll-free number, they tend to offer better-maintained vehicles, and it's easier to resolve any disputes after the fact. Call **Budget** (✆ **800/472-3325;** www.budget.com), **Hertz** (✆ **800/654-3001;** www.hertz.com), **Dollar** (✆ **800/800-4000;** www.dollar.com), or **Avis** (✆ **800/331-1212;** www.avis. com).

"Petrol" is easily available in Nassau and Freeport, though quite expensive. You should have no problems finding adequate service stations on New Providence or Grand Bahama Island unless you start out with a nearly empty tank.

Visitors may drive with their home driver's license for up to 3 months. For longer stays, you'll need to secure a Bahamian driver's license.

By Taxi

Once you've reached your destination, you'll find that taxis are plentiful in the Nassau/Cable Beach/Paradise Island area and in the Freeport/Lucaya area on Grand Bahama Island. These cabs, for the most part, are metered—but they take cash only, no credit cards. See "Getting Around" in the chapters on each island for further details.

Taxis are usually shared, often with the local residents. Cars are often old and badly maintained, so be prepared for a bumpy ride over some rough roads if you've selected a particularly remote hotel.

MONEY & COSTS

THE VALUE OF THE BAHAMIAN DOLLAR VS. OTHER CURRENCIES

B$	US$	C$	£	€	A$	NZ$
1.00	1.00	0.98	0.62	0.69	0.94	1.23

Frommer's lists exact prices in U.S. dollars throughout this guide, as they are widely accepted throughout The Bahamas. The currency conversions quoted above were correct at press time. However, rates fluctuate, so before departing consult a currency exchange website such as **www.xe.com** or **www.oanda.com/convert/classic** to check up-to-the-minute rates.

It's always advisable to bring money in a variety of forms on a vacation: a mix of cash, credit cards, and traveler's checks. You should also exchange enough petty cash to cover airport incidentals, tipping, and transportation to your hotel before you leave home, or withdraw money upon arrival at an airport ATM.

In many international destinations, ATMs offer the best exchange rates. Avoid exchanging money at commercial exchange bureaus and hotels, which often have the highest transaction fees.

Currency

The currency is the **Bahamian dollar (B$1),** pegged to the U.S. dollar so that they're always equivalent. There is no restriction on bringing foreign currency into The Bahamas. Most large hotels and stores accept traveler's checks, but you may have trouble using a personal check. It's a good idea to exchange enough money to cover airport incidentals and transportation to your hotel before you leave home.

Be sure to carry some small bills or loose change when traveling. Petty cash will come in handy for tipping and public transportation. Consider keeping the change separate from your larger bills so that it's readily accessible and you'll be less of a target for theft. In general, prices are about the same as in urban America, but they are less expensive than costs in the U.K. Food is often more expensive, however, since so much of it has to be imported.

ATMs

The easiest way to get cash away from home is from an ATM (automated teller machine). The **Cirrus** (© 800/424-7787; www.mastercard.com) and **PLUS** (www.visa.com) networks span the globe; look at the back of your bank card to see which network you're on and then call or check online for ATM locations at your destination. Know your personal identification number (PIN) and your daily withdrawal limit. Ask your card carrier if your current PIN works on the island you'll be visiting. Every card is different, but some need a four-digit rather than a six-digit PIN to withdraw cash abroad.

Many banks impose a fee every time a card is used at a different bank's ATM, and that fee can be higher for international transactions (up to $5 or more) than for domestic ones. On top of this, the bank from which you withdraw cash may charge its own fee. To compare banks' ATM fees within the U.S., use **www.bankrate.com**. For international withdrawal fees, ask your bank. You can also get cash advances on your credit card at an ATM. Credit card companies do try to protect themselves from theft by limiting the funds someone can withdraw outside their home country, so notify your credit card company before you leave home. And keep in mind that you'll pay interest from the moment of your withdrawal, even if you pay your monthly bills on time.

On New Providence Island and Paradise Island, there are plenty of ATMs, including one at the Nassau International Airport. There are far fewer ATMs on Grand Bahama Island (Freeport/Lucaya), but those that are there are strategically located—including ones at the airport and the casino (of course).

Credit Cards

Credit cards are another safe way to carry money, though establishments in The Bahamas are becoming increasingly cautious about which cards they accept (see below). Cards provide a convenient record of all your expenses, and they generally offer relatively good exchange rates. You can usually withdraw cash advances from your credit cards at banks or ATMs, provided you know your PIN. Keep in mind that you'll pay interest from the moment of your withdrawal, even if you pay your monthly bills on time. Also, note that many banks now assess a 1% to 3% "transaction fee" on **all** charges you incur abroad (whether you're using the local currency or your native currency).

Be aware: Some establishments in The Bahamas might not accept your credit card unless you have a computer chip embedded in it. The reason? To cut down on credit card fraud. (The same is true of debit cards.)

Chip and PIN represents a change in the way that credit and debit cards are used. The program is designed to cut down on the fraudulent use of credit cards. More and more banks are issuing customers chip-and-PIN versions of their debit or credit cards. In the future, more and more vendors will be asking for a four-digit personal identification number, or PIN, which will be entered into a keypad near the cash register. In some cases, a waiter will bring a hand-held model to your table to verify your credit card.

More and more places in The Bahamas are moving from the magnetic-strip credit card to the chip-and-PIN system. In the changeover in technology, some retailers have falsely concluded that they can no longer take swipe cards, or can't take signature cards that don't have PINs anymore.

For the time being, both the new and old cards are used in shops, hotels, and restaurants regardless of whether they have the old credit and debit card machines or the new chip-and-PIN machines installed.

Beware of hidden credit card fees while traveling. Check with your credit or debit card issuer to see what fees, if any, will be charged for overseas transactions. Recent reform legislation in the U.S., for example, has curbed some exploitative lending practices. But many banks have responded by increasing fees in other areas, including fees for customers who use credit and debit cards while out of the country—even if those charges were made in U.S. dollars. Fees can amount to 3% or more of the purchase price. Check with your bank before departing to avoid any surprise charges on your statement.

Traveler's Checks

You can buy traveler's checks at most banks. They are offered in denominations of $20, $50, $100, $500, and sometimes $1,000. Generally, you'll pay a service charge ranging from 1% to 4%.

The most popular traveler's checks are offered by **American Express** (© 800/528-4800 or 221-7282 for cardholders—this number accepts collect calls, offers service in several foreign languages, and exempts Amex gold and platinum cardholders from the 1% fee), **Visa** (www.visa.com; AAA members can obtain Visa checks for a $9.95 fee—for checks up to US$1,500—at most AAA offices or by calling © 866/339-3378), and **MasterCard** (© 800/223-9920).

Be sure to keep a record of the traveler's checks' serial numbers separate from your checks in the event that they are stolen or lost. You'll get a refund faster if you know the numbers.

TIPS ON ACCOMMODATIONS

The Bahamas offers a wide selection of accommodations, ranging from small private guesthouses to large luxury resorts. Hotels vary in size and facilities, from deluxe (offering room service, sports, swimming pools, entertainment, and so on) to fairly simple inns.

There are package deals galore, and they are always cheaper than "rack rates." (A rack rate is what an individual pays if he or she literally walks in from the street. These are the rates we've listed in the chapters, though you can almost always do better—especially at the big resorts.) It's sometimes good to go to a reliable travel agent to find out what, if anything, is available in the way of a land-and-air package before booking particular accommodations. See "Special-Interest & Escorted Trips," later in this chapter, for details on a number of companies that usually offer good-value packages to The Bahamas.

There is no rigid classification of hotel properties in the islands. The label "deluxe" is often used (or misused) when "first class" might have been a more appropriate term. "First class" itself often isn't. For that and other reasons, we've presented fairly detailed descriptions of the properties so that you'll get an idea of what to expect. However, even in the deluxe and first-class resorts and hotels, don't expect top-rate service and efficiency. When you go to turn on the shower, sometimes you get water and sometimes you don't. You may even experience power failures.

The winter season in The Bahamas runs roughly from the middle of December to the middle of April, and hotels charge their highest prices during this peak period. Winter is generally the dry season in the islands, but there can be heavy rainfall regardless of the time of year. During the winter months, make reservations 2 months in advance if you can. You can't book early enough if you want to travel over Christmas or in February.

The off season in The Bahamas—roughly from mid-April to mid-December (although this varies from hotel to hotel)—amounts to a sale. In most cases, hotel rates are slashed a startling 20% to 60%. It's a bonanza for cost-conscious travelers, especially for families who can travel in the summer. Be prepared for very strong sun, though, plus a higher chance of rain. Also note that hurricane season runs through summer and fall.

MAP vs. AP, Or Do You Want to Go EP?

All Bahamian resorts offer a **European Plan (EP)** rate, which means that you pay for the price of a room. That leaves you free to dine around at night at various other resorts or restaurants without restriction. Another plan preferred by many is the **Continental Plan (CP),** which means you get a continental breakfast of juice, coffee, bread, and jam included in a set price. This plan is preferred by those who don't like to look around for a place to eat breakfast.

Another common option is the **Modified American Plan (MAP),** which includes breakfast and one main meal of the day, either lunch or dinner. The final choice is the **American Plan (AP),** which includes breakfast, lunch, and dinner. At certain resorts you will save money by choosing either the MAP or AP because discounts are granted. If you dine a la carte often for lunch and dinner, your dining costs will be much higher than if you stay on the MAP or AP.

Dining at your hotel at night cuts down on transportation costs. Taxis especially are expensive. Nonetheless, if dining out and having many different culinary experiences is your idea of a vacation and you're willing to pay the higher price, avoid AP plans or at least make sure the hotel where you're staying has more than one dining room.

One option is to ask if your hotel has a dine-around plan. You might still keep costs in check, but you can avoid a culinary rut by taking your meals in some other restaurants if your hotel has such a plan. Such plans are rare in The Bahamas, which does not specialize in all-inclusive resorts the way that Jamaica or some other islands do.

Before booking a room, check with a good travel agent or investigate on your own what you are likely to save by booking on a dining plan. Under certain circumstances in winter, you might not have a choice if MAP is dictated as a requirement for staying there. It pays to investigate, of course.

The Right Room at the Right Price

Ask detailed questions when booking a room. Specify your likes and dislikes. There are several logistics of getting the right room in a hotel. In general, back rooms cost less than oceanfront rooms, and lower rooms cost less than upper-floor units. If budget is a major consideration with you, opt for the cheaper rooms. You won't have a great view, but you'll save your money for something else. Just make sure that it isn't next to the all-night drummers.

Of course, all first-class or deluxe resorts feature air-conditioning, but many Bahamian inns do not. Cooling might be by ceiling fans or, in more modest places, the breeze from an open window, which also brings the mosquitoes. If sleeping in a climate-controlled environment is important to your vacation, check this out in advance.

If you're being your own travel agent, it pays to shop around by calling the local number given for a hotel and its toll-free number, if it has one. You can check online and call a travel agent to see where you can obtain the best price.

Another tip: Ask if you can get an upgrade or a free night's stay if you stay an extra few days. If you're traveling during the "shoulder" periods (between low and high season), you can sometimes get a substantial reduction by delaying your travel plans by a week or 10 days.

Transfers from the airports or the cruise dock are included in some hotel bookings, most often in a package plan but usually not in ordinary bookings. This is true of first-class and deluxe resorts, but rarely of medium-priced or budget accommodations. Always ascertain whether transfers (which can be expensive) are included.

When using the facilities at a resort, make sure that you know exactly what is free and what costs money. For example, swimming in the pool is nearly always free, but you might be charged for use of a tennis court. Nearly all watersports cost extra, unless you're booked on some special plan such as a scuba package. Some resorts seem to charge every time you breathe and might end up costing more than a deluxe hotel that includes most everything in the price.

Some hotels are right on the beach. Others involve transfers to the beach by taxi or bus, so factor in transportation costs, which can mount quickly if you stay 5 days to a week.

The All-Inclusives

A hugely popular option in Jamaica, the all-inclusive-resort hotel concept finally has a foothold in The Bahamas. At these resorts, everything is included—sometimes even drinks. You get your room and all meals, plus entertainment and many watersports (although some cost extra). Some people find the cost of this all-inclusive holiday cheaper than if they'd paid individually for each item, and some simply appreciate knowing in advance what their final bill will be.

The first all-inclusive resort hotel in The Bahamas was **Club Med** (© **888/WEB-CLUB** [932-2582]; www.clubmed.com) on Paradise Island. This is not a swinging-singles kind of place; it's popular with everybody, from honeymooners to families with kids along.

The biggest all-inclusive of them all, **Sandals** (© **888/SAN-DALS** [726-3257]; www.sandals.com), came to The Bahamas in 1995 on Cable Beach. This Jamaican company is now walking its sandals across the Caribbean, in Ocho Rios, Montego Bay, and Negril. This most famous of the all-inclusives (but not necessarily the best) recently ended its ban against same-sex couples. See p. 50.

Rental Villas & Vacation Homes

You might rent a big villa, a good-size apartment in someone's condo, or even a small beach cottage (more accurately called a cabana).

Private apartments come with or without maid service (ask upfront exactly what to expect). This is a more no-frills option than villas and condos. The apartments may not be in buildings with swimming pools, and they may not have a front desk to help you.

Many cottages or cabanas ideally open onto a beach, although others may be clustered around a communal swimming pool. Most of them are fairly simple, containing only a plain bedroom plus a small kitchen and bathroom. In the peak winter season, reservations should be made at least 5 or 6 months in advance.

Hideaways Aficionado (© **877/843-4433** in the U.S., or 603/430-4433; www.hideaways.com) publishes **Hideaways Life,** a 24-page pictorial directory of home rentals throughout the world, with full descriptions so you know what you're renting. Rentals range from cottages to staffed villas, to whole islands! On most rentals, you deal directly with owners. At condos and small resorts, Hideaways offers member discounts. Other services include specialty cruises, yacht charters, airline ticketing, car rentals, and hotel reservations. Annual membership costs $195.

Sometimes local tourist offices will also advise you on vacation-home rentals if you write or call them directly.

The Bahamian Guesthouse

Many Bahamians stay at a guesthouse when traveling in their own islands. In The Bahamas, however, the term *guesthouse* can mean anything. Sometimes so-called guesthouses are really like simple motels built around swimming pools. Others are small individual cottages with their own kitchenettes, constructed around a main building in which you'll often find a bar and restaurant serving local food.

RESPONSIBLE TRAVEL

The Bahamas is one of the most eco-friendly destinations in the Western Hemisphere. There are some, of course, who still eat endangered species like the turtle and pollute the environment, but the government is aware that the pristine beauty of the islands, both the sea and the land, is one of the main reasons their vital tourist industry exists. Officials want to preserve it for future generations.

For a rundown on what the **Bahamas National Trust** (www. bnt.bs) is doing to protect bird and animal life, see "The Lay of the Land," earlier in this chapter.

Conserving the wetlands has become of prime importance to the government. These wetlands are the source of potential for an expanded ecotourism industry and of vital importance to birds, animals, and fish.

The fishing industry is the third largest in The Bahamas, generating millions of dollars in exports because the vast coastal wetlands serve as marine nurseries.

Hurricanes, along with the destruction of wetlands by people, remain a constant threat to the environment. The flood-and-surge destruction from hurricanes alone can exceed $500 million in damage during a particularly destructive year when Mother Nature vents her fury on the archipelago.

Ecotours and adventures await you throughout The Bahamas. In Nassau and Paradise Island, **Bahamas Adventure Glass Bottom Kayaks** (📞 **800/688-5871;** http://bestonbahamas.com for bookings) allows you to sail the clear waters of New Providence Island while enjoying the marine life beneath you. Guided tours with equipment costs $77 or $40 for children 11 and under.

At the same number, you can also book a **Blackbeard Cay Stingray Adventure,** snorkeling and interacting with these gentle aquatic creatures. Prices are $42 or $37 for children 11 and under.

Nassau Segway Nature Tour takes you on a ride through Earth Village, a 162-acre preserve acclaimed by botanists as one of

GENERAL RESOURCES FOR
responsible TRAVEL

In addition to the resources for **The Bahamas** listed above, the following websites provide valuable wide-ranging information on sustainable travel.

○ **Responsible Travel** (www.responsibletravel.com) is a great source of sustainable travel ideas; the site is run by a spokesperson for ethical tourism in the travel industry. **Sustainable Travel International** (www.sustainabletravel international.org) promotes ethical tourism practices, and manages an extensive directory of sustainable properties and tour operators around the world.

○ **Carbonfund** (www.carbonfund.org), **TerraPass** (www. terrapass.org), and **Cool Climate** (http://coolclimate. berkeley.edu) provide info on "carbon offsetting," or offsetting the greenhouse gases emitted during flights.

○ **Greenhotels** (www.greenhotels.com) recommends green-rated member hotels around the world that fulfill the company's stringent environmental requirements. **Environmentally Friendly Hotels** (www.environmentally friendlyhotels.com) offers more green accommodations ratings.

○ For information on animal-friendly issues throughout the world, visit **Tread Lightly** (www.treadlightly.org). For information about the ethics of swimming with dolphins, visit the **Whale and Dolphin Conservation Society** (www.wdcs.org).

○ **Volunteer International** (www.volunteerinternational.org) has a list of questions to help you determine the intentions and the nature of a volunteer program. For general info on volunteer travel, visit **www.volunteerabroad.org** and **www. idealist.org**.

the most diverse ecosystems in The Bahamas. The cost is $75 for per person. For reservations, call the number above.

On Grand Bahama Island, you can experience ecotourism by taking the **Lucayana National Park and Cave Tour** (www. grandbahamanaturetours.com), discovering the pristine beauty of the 42-acre Lucayana National Park for $40 ($25 for children 10 and under). You can also take part in guided kayak expeditions through this tropical Eden for $79 per person. For reservations for both tours, call ℂ **866/440-4542.**

SPECIAL-INTEREST & ESCORTED TRIPS
Package Tours

Before you search for the lowest airfare on your own (see earlier in this chapter), you may want to consider booking your flight as part of a package deal—a way to travel independently but pay group rates.

A package tour is not an escorted tour, in which you're led around by a guide. Package tours are simply a way to buy the airfare, accommodations, and other elements of your trip (such as car rentals, airport transfers, and sometimes even activities) at the same time, often at discounted prices.

One good source of package deals is the airlines themselves. Most major airlines offer air/land packages, including **American Airlines Vacations** (© 800/321-2121; www.aavacations.com), **Delta Vacations** (© 800/654-6559; www.deltavacations.com), **Continental Airlines Vacations** (© 800/829-7777; www.covacations.com), and **United Vacations** (© 888/854-3899; www.unitedvacations.com). Several big **online travel agencies**—Expedia, Travelocity, Orbitz, Site59, and Lastminute.com—also do a brisk business in packages.

Liberty Travel (© 888/271-1584; www.libertytravel.com) is one of the biggest packagers in the U.S. Northeast, and it usually boasts a full-page ad in Sunday papers. There's also **TourScan, Inc.,** 1051 Boston Post Rd., Darien, CT 06820 (© 800/962-2080 in the U.S.; www.tourscan.com), which researches the best-value vacation at each hotel and condo.

For British travelers, package tours to The Bahamas can be booked through **Kuoni Travel,** Kuoni House, Dorking, Surrey RH5 4AZ (© 01306/747-002; www.kuoni.co.uk), which offers both land and air packages to destinations such as Nassau and Freeport. They also offer packages for self-catering villas on Paradise Island.

For an all-inclusive package, **Just-A-Vacation, Inc.,** 15501 Ebbynside Ct., Bowie, MD 20716 (© 301/559-0510), specializes in all-inclusive resorts on the islands of The Bahamas, plus other destinations in the Caribbean. **Club Med** (© 888/WEB-CLUB [932-2582]; www.clubmed.com) has various all-inclusive options throughout the Caribbean and The Bahamas.

Travel packages are also listed in the travel section of your local Sunday newspaper. Or check ads in the national travel magazines, such as *Arthur Frommer's Budget Travel Magazine, Travel + Leisure, National Geographic Traveler,* and *Condé Nast Traveler.*

Active Vacations

The more than 700 islands in the Bahamian archipelago (fewer than 30 of which are inhabited) are surrounded by warm, clear waters—ideal for fishing, sailing, and scuba diving. (Detailed recommendations and the costs of these activities are previewed under the individual destinations listings.) The country's perfect weather and its many cooperative local entrepreneurs allow easy access to more than 30 sports throughout the islands.

WATERSPORTS

FISHING   The shallow waters between the hundreds of cays and islands of The Bahamas are some of the most fertile fishing grounds in the world. Even waters where marine traffic is relatively congested have yielded impressive catches in the past, although overfishing has depleted schools of fish, especially big-game fish. Grouper, billfish, wahoo, tuna, and dozens of other species thrive in Bahamian waters, and dozens of charter boats are available for deep-sea fishing.

Frontiers International (✆ **800/245-1950** or 724/935-1577; www.frontierstravel.com) features fly- and spin-fishing tours of The Bahamas and is a specialist in saltwater-fishing destinations. In addition, reef fishing, either from small boats or from shorelines, is popular everywhere, with grouper, snapper, and barracuda being the most commonly caught species.

SAILING   The Bahamas is one of the top yachting destinations in the Atlantic. Its more than 700 islands and well-developed marinas provide a spectacular and practical backdrop for sailing enthusiasts.

Don't be dismayed if you don't own a yacht. All sizes and types of crafts, from dinghies to blue-water cruisers, are available for charter, and crew and captain are optional for experienced sailors. If your dreams involve experiencing the seagoing life for an afternoon or less, many hotels offer sightseeing cruises aboard catamarans or glass-bottom boats, often with the opportunity to snorkel or swim in the wide-open sea.

SCUBA DIVING   The unusual marine topography of The Bahamas offers an astonishing variety of options for divers. Throughout the more than 700 islands are innumerable reefs, drop-offs, coral gardens, caves, and shipwrecks. In many locations, you may feel that you are the first human ever to explore the site. Since fewer than 30 of the Bahamian islands are inhabited, you can usually dive in pristine and uncrowded splendor.

Freeport, on Grand Bahama Island, is home to the country's most famous and complete diving operation, **UNEXSO** (✆ **800/992-DIVE** [3483] or 242/373-1244; www.unexso.com).

It offers a 5.2m-deep (17-ft.) swimming pool where divers can work toward certification, and the popular "Dolphin Experience," in which visitors are allowed to pet, swim, snorkel, and dive with these remarkable animals.

You can easily learn to dive for the first time in The Bahamas. Lots of Bahamian hotels offer resort courses for novices, usually enabling a beginner to dive with a guide after several hours of instruction. You'll probably start out in the swimming pool for your initial instruction and then go out with a guide from the beach. A license (called a certification card, or "C" card) proving the successful completion of a designated program of scuba study is legally required for solo divers. Many resort hotels and dive shops offer the necessary 5-day training course. Participants who successfully complete the courses are awarded certifications by diving organizations such as PADI or NAUI.

For useful information, check out the website of the **Professional Association of Diving Instructors (PADI)** at www.padi. com. You'll find a description of the best dive sites and a list of PADI-certified dive operators. *Rodale's Scuba Diving Magazine* also has a helpful website at www.scubadiving.com. Both sites list dive-package specials and display gorgeous color photos of some of the most beautiful dive spots in the world.

BIKE & SCOOTER RENTALS   Most biking or scooter riding is done either on New Providence Island (Nassau) or on Grand Bahama Island; both have relatively flat terrain. Biking is best on Grand Bahama Island because it's bigger, with better roads and more places to go. Getting around New Providence Island is relatively easy once you're out of the congestion of Nassau and Cable Beach. In Nassau many hotels will rent you a bike or motor scooter.

On Grand Bahama Island, you can rent bikes at most big hotels (see chapter 5 for phone numbers and addresses of hotels). You can also rent motor scooters starting at about $60 per day. The tourist office at Freeport/Lucaya will outline on a map the best biking routes.

GOLF   The richest pickings are on Grand Bahama Island. The **Reef Course** is the first new golf course to open in The Bahamas since 1969. Designed by Robert Trent Jones, Jr., it features water along 13 of its 18 holes. The oldest course on Grand Bahama Island is the **Lucayan Golf Course,** a wooded course with elevated greens and numerous water hazards designed for precision golf. See chapter 5 for details, and also refer to "The Best Golf Courses," in chapter 1.

Special-Interest & Escorted Trips

PLANNING YOUR TRIP TO THE BAHAMAS

Quality golf in The Bahamas, however, is not restricted to Grand Bahama Island. The **Cable Beach Golf Course** is the oldest golf course in the country. The widely publicized **Ocean Club Golf Club** has unusual obstacles—a lion's den and a windmill—which have challenged the skill of both Gary Player and Jack Nicklaus. It also boasts the world's largest sand trap. See chapters 3 and 4 for more information, and also refer to "The Best Golf Courses," in chapter 1.

HIKING   The Bahamas isn't the greatest destination for serious hikers. The best hiking is on Grand Bahama Island, especially in **Lucayan National Park,** which spreads across 16 hectares (40 acres) and is some 32km (20 miles) from Lucaya. A large map at the entrance to the park outlines the trails. The park is laced with trails and elevated walkways. The highlight of the park is what may be the largest underground cave system in the world, some 11km (6¾ miles) long. Spiral steps let you descend into an eerie underground world.

Also on Grand Bahama Island, the **Rand Memorial Nature Centre** is the second-best place for hiking. It offers some 40 wooded hectares (99 acres) that you can explore on your own or with a tour guide. A .8km (.5 mile) stretch of winding trails acquaints you with the flora and fauna that call Grand Bahama home, everything from a native boa constrictor to the Cuban emerald hummingbird, whose favorite food is the nectar of the hibiscus.

HORSEBACK RIDING   The best riding possibilities are at **Pinetree Stables** on Grand Bahama Island (© **242/373-3600** or 305/433-4809; www.pinetree-stables.com). Its escorted ecotour trail rides are especially interesting. Rides are offered two times a day Tuesday through Sunday; be sure to book rides a few days in advance. See chapter 5 for more information.

Virtually the only place on New Providence Island (Nassau) that offers horseback riding is **Windsor Equestrian Centre & Happy Trails Stables,** Coral Harbour (© **242/362-1820;** www.windsorequestriancentre.com), which features both morning and afternoon trail rides and requires a reservation. These tours include transportation to and from your hotel. The trail rides are guided through the woods and along the beach. See chapter 4 for more information.

TENNIS   Most tennis courts are part of large resorts and are usually free for the use of registered guests during the day. Charges are imposed to light the courts at night. Nonguests are welcome but are charged a player's fee; they should call in advance to reserve. Larger resorts usually offer on-site pro shops and professional instructors. Court surfaces range from clay or asphalt to such technologically advanced substances as Flexipave and Har-Tru.

New Providence, with more than 80 tennis courts, wins points for offering the greatest number of choices. At least 21 of these lie on Paradise Island. See chapter 3. After New Providence, Grand Bahama has the largest number of courts available for play—almost 40 in all. See chapter 4.

NEW PROVIDENCE (NASSAU/ CABLE BEACH)

New Providence could almost be England—but for the weather, that is, and for the staunch sense of Bahamian nationalism. The shops draw a lot more business than the museums, but no other city in the Bahamas is as rich in history. You can climb up the 18th-century Queen's Staircase to Fort Fincastle or learn about the traditions of the Junkanoo festival at the Junkanoo Expo. It's an intoxicating, laid-back city, one that offers a good dose of British colonial charm, where tropical foliage lines streets and horse-drawn surreys trot by.

THINGS TO DO **Cable Beach** is perfect for families with its soft white sand, gentle waves and children's clubs. Away from the beach, take a swashbuckling trip back in time at the interactive **Pirates of Nassau** museum. Examine religious and folklore paintings at Nassau's **National Art Gallery of The Bahamas** or learn about the rich history and colorful costumes of the Junkanoo festival at the **Junkanoo Expo.** In Nassau's harbor, numerous **glass-bottom boats** wait to take you through the colorful sea gardens off New Providence Island.

SHOPPING Most of New Providence shopping is on **Bay Street** in Nassau. Look for cut-price jewelry, cosmetics, and hand-rolled cigars, as well as a plethora of T-shirts and souvenirs. The **Nassau International Bazaar,** with its cobbled alleyways and garreted storefronts, houses some 30 shops in its idyllic waterfront location. Hotel arcades are also worth browsing, as well as duty-free antique shops. Junkanoo carnival masks from artists' studios bring a little Caribbean flavor into your home.

NIGHTLIFE & ENTERTAINMENT As the sun goes down, **Cable Beach** offers fine dining, glitzy casinos, cabaret shows, moonlight cruises, romantic evening strolls, and parties on the sand. In the old town of **Nassau,** you can dance to *soca* and calypso in intimate clubs, or rattle your ribcage with pounding techno on **Paradise Island.** At local joints around the island, you can enjoy favorites such as "Funky Nassau" and older, more nostalgic tunes like "Goin' Down Burma Road" or "Get Involved."

RESTAURANTS & DINING New Providence accents its Bahamian fare with ethnic specialties such as Asian, Latin, and European cuisine. Thus, you can expect to find everything from steak and kidney pie (dating from the days of British colonial rule) in the celebrity-chef dining rooms of **Nassau** to the favorite **conch salad,** served at roadside shacks on the way to **Cable Beach.** Fresh seafood should not be missed, especially grouper, snapper, and conch.

ORIENTATION
Arriving

BY PLANE Flights land at **Lynden Pindling International Airport** (© **242/377-0209;** www.nas.bs), formerly known as Nassau International Airport, 13km (8 miles) west of Nassau, in the pine forests beside Lake Killarney.

No bus service goes from the airport to Nassau, Cable Beach, or Paradise Island. Your hotel may provide **airport transfers** if you've made arrangements in advance; these are often included in package deals. You'll find any number of **car-rental** offices here (p. 20), though we don't really think you need one.

If you don't have a lift arranged, take a **taxi** to your hotel. From the airport to the center of Nassau, expect to pay around $27; to Cable Beach, $18; and to Paradise Island, $34, a rate that includes the bridge toll for passage between New Providence and Paradise islands. Drivers expect to be tipped 15%, and some will remind you should you "forget." You don't need to exchange currency before departing the airport: U.S. dollars are fine for these (and any other) transactions.

BY CRUISE SHIP Nassau has spent millions of dollars expanding its port so that a number of cruise ships can dock at once. Sounds great in theory, but practically speaking, facilities in

New Providence Island

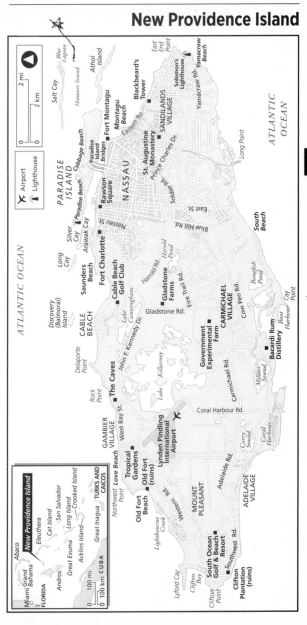

Nassau, Cable Beach, and Paradise Island become extremely over-crowded as soon as the big boats arrive. You'll have to stake out your space on the beach, and you'll find downtown streets, shops, and attractions overrun with visitors every day you're in port.

Cruise ships dock near Rawson Square, the heart of the city and the shopping area—and the best place to begin a tour of Nassau. Unless you want to go to one of the beach strips along Cable Beach or Paradise Island, you won't need a taxi. You can go on a shopping expedition near where you dock: The Straw Market is at nearby Market Plaza; Bay Street, the main shopping artery, is also close; and the Nassau International Bazaar is at the intersection of Woodes Rogers Walk and Charlotte Street.

The government has added **Festival Place** (© 242/323-3182) to the Prince George Wharf (where cruise ships arrive). Designed as a welcome point and service center for cruise-ship visitors, it's a multicolored structure with about 45 shops selling sundries, gift items, duty-free luxury goods, and Bahamian-themed arts, crafts, and souvenirs. There's also a tourist information booth (© **242/323-3182** or 323-3183) and various snack bars and cafes. You can lounge and have a daiquiri while you listen to the live calypso entertainment, or get your hair braided. This mall-like facility is open daily from 8am to 8pm, but if cruise ships are in port, closing may be extended to as late as 10pm. From a point nearby, you can catch a ride by horse and surrey, or take a water taxi across the channel to Paradise Island (p. 90).

Visitor Information

The Bahamas Ministry of Tourism maintains a tourist information booth at **Lynden Pindling International Airport** in the arrivals terminal (© **800/BAHAMAS** [224-2627] or 242/377-6806; www.bahamas.com). Hours are daily from 9am to 10pm.

You can also stop by the information desk at the offices of the **Ministry of Tourism,** Bolam House, George Street (© **242/302-2000**), open Monday through Friday from 9am to 5pm, or the information booth at **Festival Place** (© **242/323-3182** or 323-3183), where the cruise ships dock. This kiosk is usually open daily 8am to 7pm.

The Lay of the Land

Most of Nassau's hotels are city hotels and are not on the water. To stay right on the sands, choose a hotel in Cable Beach (described later in this chapter) or on Paradise Island (see chapter 4).

Rawson Square is the heart of Nassau, positioned just a short walk from **Prince George Wharf,** where the big cruise ships,

favorite NEW PROVIDENCE EXPERIENCES

Listening to the sounds of Goombay   At local joints—
such as Club Fluid and Da Tambrin Tree—you can enjoy an intoxicating beat and such island favorites as Andros-born Elon Moxey's
"Catch the Crab" and K.B.'s "Civil Servants" (a satire of the sometimes pervasive governmental bureaucracy in The Bahamas). Deeply
ingrained in the Bahamian musical psyche is a song that eventually
became a huge international hit, "Funky Nassau." Older, more nostalgic tunes include "Goin' Down Burma Road," "Get Involved," and
"John B. Sail."

Taking a glass-bottom boat ride   Right in the middle of
Nassau's harbor, numerous boats wait to take you through the colorful sea gardens off New Providence Island. In the teeming reefs,
you'll meet all sorts of sea creatures that inhabit this underwater
wonderland.

Spending a day on Blue Lagoon Island   It's like an old
Hollywood fantasy of a tropical island. Located off Paradise Island's
eastern end, Blue Lagoon Island boasts seven sandy beaches. Boats
from the ferryboat docks will take you there and back.

many of them originating in Florida, berth. Here you'll see the
Churchill Building, which contains the offices of the Bahamian
prime minister, along with other government ministries.

Busy **Bay Street,** the main shopping artery, begins on the south
side of Rawson Square. This was the turf of the infamous Bay
Street Boys, a group of rich, white Bahamians who once controlled
political and economic activity on New Providence.

On the opposite side of Rawson Square is **Parliament Square,**
with its government houses, House of Assembly, and statue of a
youthful Queen Victoria. These are Georgian and Neo-Georgian
buildings, some from the late 1700s.

The courthouse is separated by a little square from the **Nassau
Public Library and Museum,** which opens onto Bank Lane. It
was the former Nassau Gaol (jail). South of the library, across
Shirley Street, are the remains of the **Royal Victoria Hotel,**
which opened the same year the American Civil War began (1861)
and hosted many a blockade runner and Confederate spy.

A walk down Parliament Street leads to the **post office.** Philat-
elists may want to stop in—some Bahamian stamps are true collec-
tors' items.

Moving southward, farther away from the water, Elizabeth Avenue takes you to the **Queen's Staircase.** One of the major landmarks of Nassau, it climbs to Bennet's Hill and Fort Fincastle.

If you return to Bay Street, you'll discover the oversized tent that contains the **Straw Market,** a handicrafts emporium where you can buy all sorts of souvenirs.

GETTING AROUND
By Taxi

You can easily rely on taxis and skip renting a car. The rates for New Providence, including Nassau, are set by the government. Although working meters are required in all taxis, some of them don't work. Consequently, the government has established a well-defined roster of rates for passage between the airport and various points around the island. When you get in, the fixed rate is $3, plus 40¢ for each additional quarter-mile. Each passenger 2 years and older pays an extra $3. For sightseeing purposes, taxis can also be hired at the hourly rate of $50 for a five-passenger cab. Luggage is carried at a surcharge of $1 extra per piece, although the first two pieces are free. To call a cab, dial © **242/323-5111.** It's easy to get a taxi at the airport or at any of the big hotels.

If you'd like a personalized tour of the island, your best bet is to use **Romeo's Executive Limousine & Taxi Service** (© **242/363-4728;** www.romeoslimos.com). Romeo Farrington is quite informative about the island, its legends and lore. He personalizes all tours. A typical island tour, lasting from 2½ to 3 hours, costs $80 per hour for two passengers.

By Rental Car

You really don't need to rent a car. It's a lot easier to rely on taxis when you're ready to leave the beach and do some exploring.

 On Your Own Sturdy Feet

This is the only way to see Old Nassau, unless you rent a horse and carriage. All the major attractions and principal stores are within walking distance. You can even walk to Cable Beach or Paradise Island, although it's a hike in the hot sun.

Confine your walking to the daytime, and beware of the occasional pickpocket or purse snatcher. In the evening, avoid walking the streets of downtown Nassau, where, from time to time, muggings have been reported.

However, if you choose to drive (perhaps for a day of touring the whole island), some of the biggest U.S. car-rental companies maintain branches at the airport, in downtown Nassau, in Cable Beach, and on Paradise Island. **Avis** (🕿 **800/331-1212** or 242/377-7121; www.avis.com), maintains a downtown office at Bay Street and Cumberland Street across from the British Colonial Hilton (🕿 **242/326-6380**). **Budget** (🕿 **800/527-0700** or 242/377-9000; www.budget.com) has a desk at the airport and a branch downtown on Shirley Street (🕿 **242/323-7191**). **Dollar/Thrifty** (🕿 **800/800-3665** or 242/377-8300; www.dollar.com) also has a desk at the airport and another one at the British Colonial Hilton (🕿 **242/325-3716**). Finally, **Hertz** (🕿 **800/654-3131** or 242/377-6321; www.hertz.com) is only at the airport.

Remember: Drive on the left!

By Bus

The least expensive means of transport is via any of the buses (some locals refer to them as "jitneys") that make runs from downtown Nassau to outposts all over New Providence. The fare is $1, and the exact amount, in coins or with a dollar bill, is required. The jitneys operate daily from 6:30am to 7pm.

Buses to the Cable Beach area and points west of that include the much-used **no. 10,** the **no. 10A,** and **"the Western bus."** They depart from the corner of Bay Street and George Street, with stops at various clearly designated spots along Bay Street. Buses headed to the eastern (mostly residential and rarely accessed by short-term visitors) part of New Providence Island depart from the Frederick Street North depot.

By Boat

Water taxis operate daily from 9am to 6pm at 20-minute intervals between Paradise Island and Prince George Wharf.

Ferryboats link the wharves at the end of Casuarina Drive on Paradise Island to Rawson Square, which lies across the channel on New Providence Island. The ferry operates daily from 9am to 6pm, with departures every half-hour from both sides of the harbor.

Both the ferryboats and the water taxis charge the same fixed rate: $6 per person, each way, for passage across the channel.

By Moped

Lots of visitors like to rent mopeds to explore the island. Unless you're an experienced rider, stay on quiet roads until you feel at ease; don't start out in all the congestion on Bay Street. Some hotels maintain rental kiosks on their premises. If yours doesn't, try **Bowcar Scooter Rental** (🕿 **242/328-7300**) at Festival Place near the cruise-ship dock. It charges $60 per day, which includes insurance and mandatory helmets for both drivers and passengers. Mopeds are rented daily between 8am and 5pm.

[FastFACTS] NEW PROVIDENCE

ATMs Major banks with ATMs in Nassau include the **Royal Bank of Canada** (℃ 242/322-8700; www.rbcroyalbank.com), **Scotia Bank** (℃ 242/356-1517; http://scotiabank.com), and **First Caribbean Bank** (℃ 242/356-8000; www.firstcaribbeanbank.com). Some accept cards only in the **Cirrus** network (℃ 800/424-7787; www.mastercard.com), while others take only **PLUS** (www.visa.com). ATMs at the Paradise Island and Cable Beach casinos dispense quick cash. Be aware that, whereas ATMs within large hotels and casinos tend to dispense U.S. dollars, ATMs within banks and at the airport dispense Bahamian dollars. Since both U.S. and Bahamian currencies are readily accepted anywhere, it's not a crucial issue, but it's a good idea to read the information on the individual ATM before proceeding with your transaction.

Babysitting Hotel staff can help you hire an experienced sitter. Expect to pay between $12 and $15 per hour, plus $4 per hour for each additional child.

Dentists The **Princess Margaret Hospital,** on Sands Road (℃ 242/322-2861; www.phabahamas.org), has a dentistry department.

Doctors For the best service, go to the **Princess Margaret Hospital,** on Sands Road (℃ 242/322-2861; www.phabahamas.org).

Drugstores In the center of Nassau, **Lowes Pharmacy** at Palm Dale (℃ 242/322-8594), is your best bet, and it's open Monday to Saturday 8am to 6:30pm. The location is at the Palmdale Shopping Centre between Madeira Street and Alexander Street. Another Lowes Pharmacy is at the Harbour Bay Shopping Centre (℃ 242/393-4813), open Monday to Saturday 8am to 8:30pm and Sunday 9am to 5pm. The location is on East Bay Street (east of the center of Nassau by Fort Montagu and the Nassau Yacht Club).

Emergencies Call ℃ **911** or 919.

Eyeglass Repair The **Optique Shoppe,** 22 Parliament St., at Shirley Street (℃ 242/322-3910), is convenient to the center of Nassau. Hours are Monday through Friday from 9am to 5pm and Saturday from 9am to noon.

Hospitals The government-operated **Princess Margaret Hospital,** on Sands Road (☎ **242/322-2861;** www.phabahamas.org), is one of the country's major hospitals. The privately owned **Doctors Hospital,** 1 Collins Ave. (☎ **242/322-8411**), is the region's most modern private healthcare facility.

Hot Lines For assistance of any kind, call ☎ **242/326-HELP** (4357).

Internet Access Check out **Cyberjack** at the **Mall on Marathon Road** (☎ **242/394-6254**), which charges 15¢ per minute to get online using one of its computers or your own laptop. The mall, lying at the intersection with Robinson Road, is 3 miles south of the center of Nassau. Take Mackey Street to Wuff Road, which leads to Marathon Road. If you're on Cable Beach, take the Tonique Williams-Darling Highway and the East West Highway north to the intersection of Marathon Road and Robinson Road. Most of the larger hotels offer guests Internet access for a fee, which can in some cases be as high as 50¢ per minute.

Laundry & Dry Cleaning Superwash, at Nassau Street and Boyd Road (☎ **242/323-4018**), offers coin-operated machines 24 hours a day, 7 days a week. Drop-off service is available for a small additional fee. In the same building is the **New Oriental Dry Cleaner** (☎ **242/323-7249**).

Newspapers & Magazines The *Tribune* and the *Nassau Guardian,* both published in the morning, are the country's two competing daily newspapers. Hotels and tourist information desks distribute various helpful magazines, brochures, and booklets.

Police Dial ☎ 911 or 919.

Post Office The Nassau General Post Office, at the top of Parliament Street on East Hill Street (☎ **242/322-3344**), is open Monday through Friday from 9am to 5pm and Saturday from 8:30am to 12:30pm. Note that you can also buy stamps from most postcard kiosks. A postcard sent airmail to the U.S. or Canada costs 50¢; a letter to the same destinations costs 65¢ per half-ounce.

Safety Avoid walking along lonely side streets in downtown Nassau at night, when robberies and muggings sometimes occur. Because the local government is particularly punitive against crimes against tourists, most visitors from outside The Bahamas are never affected—but it's always better to be safe than sorry. Cable Beach and Paradise Island tend to be safer than downtown Nassau after dark.

Taxes There is no sales tax on any purchase made within The Bahamas, though there is a 12% hotel tax. Visitors leaving The Bahamas pay a $20 departure tax, a tariff that's automatically included in the price of any airline or cruise-ship ticket.

WHERE TO STAY

In the hotel descriptions that follow, we've listed regular room prices, or "rack rates," but these are simply for ease of comparison. They are likely to be accurate for smaller properties, but you can almost always get a better price at the larger hotels and resorts.

See the section entitled "Special-Interest & Escorted Trips," in chapter 2, before booking a hotel separately from your airfare. If you do book your own reservations, always inquire about honeymoon specials, golf packages, summer weeks, and other potential discounts. In many cases, a travel agent can get you a package deal that would be cheaper than the official rates.

Hotels add a 12% tax to your rate. Sometimes this is quoted in advance as part of the net price; other times, it's added as an unexpected afterthought to your final bill. When you are quoted a rate, always ask if the tax is included. Many hotels also add a 15% service charge to your bill. Be sure to ask about these charges in advance so you won't be shocked when you receive the final tab. Taxes and service charges are not included in the reviews below.

We lead off with a selection of hotels within the heart of Nassau, followed by accommodations in Cable Beach. Most visitors prefer to stay in Cable Beach because its resorts are right on the sand. But you can also stay in Nassau and commute to the beaches in Cable Beach or Paradise Island; it's less convenient but cheaper. Those who prefer the ambience of Old Nassau's historic district and convenience to the best shops may decide to stay in town.

Nassau

EXPENSIVE

British Colonial Hilton   This restored hotel exudes a palpable air of the long-ago days when The Bahamas was firmly within Britain's political and social orbit. This landmark seven-story structure has seen its share of ups and downs, despite a major renovation completed in 1999. Don't expect the glitz and glitter of Cable Beach or Paradise Island here—the Hilton is after business travelers rather than the casino crowd. It also lacks the aristocratic credentials of Graycliff (see below). Nonetheless, the hotel is dignified and friendly, though rather sedate. Bedrooms are on the small side but have a discreetly upscale decor. There's a small beach a few steps away, but it's not very appealing, as it's on the narrow channel separating New Providence from Paradise Island, with no wave action at all.

1 Bay St., Nassau, The Bahamas. ⓒ **800/HILTONS** (445-8667) in the U.S. and Canada, or 242/322-3301. Fax 242/302-9009. http://hiltoncaribbean.com. 288

units. Year-round $295–$465 double; $505–$595 suite. AE, DC, DISC, MC, V. Bus: 10. **Amenities:** 2 restaurants (including Aqua, p. 59); 2 bars; babysitting; concierge; health club & spa; outdoor pool; room service; nearby watersports equipment/rentals. *In room:* A/C, TV, hair dryer, Wi-Fi ($9.95).

Graycliff ★★★   One of the most luxurious accommodations in The Bahamas is steeped in glamour and imbued with memories of its past guests—the Duke and Duchess of Windsor, Sir Winston Churchill, Aristotle Onassis, even the Beatles. Originally an 18th-century private home reflecting Georgian colonial architecture, it's now a compound of cottages and garden villas, in a setting of ponds, splashing fountains, and limestone patios. Even though it's not on the beach, guests who can afford to stay anywhere select this address because of its Old World style and grace. Beach lovers go by taxi to either nearby Goodman's Bay or the Western Esplanade Beach, adjacent to Arawak Cay.

  The historic garden rooms in the main house are spacious and individually decorated with antiques, though many prefer the more modern garden units. The Yellow Bird, Hibiscus, and Pool cottages are idyllic, but the most luxurious unit is the Mandarino Suite, with its private balcony. One of the pools evokes a Tuscan-inspired neoclassical fantasy.

8–12 W. Hill St., Nassau, The Bahamas. ✆ 800/476-0446, 242/302-9150. Fax 242/326-6188. www.graycliff.com. 20 units. Winter $375–$425 double, $475–$700 cottage; off-season $325–$370 double, $425–$550 cottage. AE, MC, V. Bus: 10, 15, or 21A. **Amenities:** 2 restaurants (Graycliff, p. 45; and Humidor Churrascaria p. 58); 2 bars; babysitting; Jacuzzi; 2 outdoor pools; room service; sauna. *In room:* A/C, TV, hair dryer, minibar, Wi-Fi (free).

MODERATE

El Greco Hotel   This well-managed bargain choice attracts many European travelers. The Greek owners and staff genuinely seem to care about their guests—in fact, the two-story hotel seems more like a small European B&B than your typical Bahamian hotel. The location is across the street from Junkanoo Beach/Lighthouse Beach/Western Esplanade and a short walk from Arawak Cay's sometimes raucous nightlife. It's also a quick walk from the shops and restaurants of downtown Nassau. The midsize rooms are set around a courtyard that contains bougainvillea-draped statues. Accommodations aren't that exciting, but they are clean and comfortable, with ceiling fans, carpeted floors, and a bright, Mediterranean-esque decor.

W. Bay St., Nassau, The Bahamas. ✆ **242/325-1121.** Fax 242/325-1124. http://hotels-nassau-bahamas.com. 30 units. Year-round $89–$120 double; $150–$200 suite. AE, MC, V. Free parking. Bus: 10. **Amenities:** Bar; babysitting; outdoor pool. *In room:* A/C, TV, hair dryer, Wi-Fi (free).

Hotels & Restaurants in Nassau

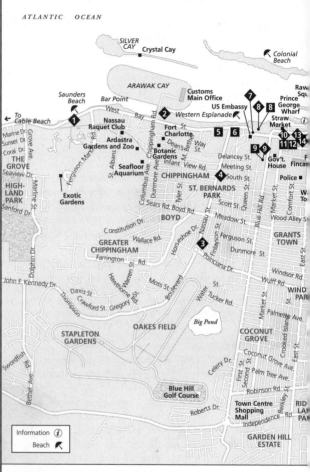

ATLANTIC OCEAN

HOTELS ■
British Colonial Hilton **8**
El Greco Hotel **6**
Grand Central Hotel **12**
Graycliff **9**
Nassau Palm Resort **5**
The Towne House **11**

RESTAURANTS ◆
Agua **8**
Bahamian Kitchen **4**
Café Matisse **13**
Café Skans **10**
Charlie's Place **18**
Chef Chea's **15**

Conch Fritters Bar & Grill **7**
Double Dragon **17**
Graycliff **9**
Humidor Churrascaria **9**
Luciano's of Chicago **16**
Poop Deck **19**

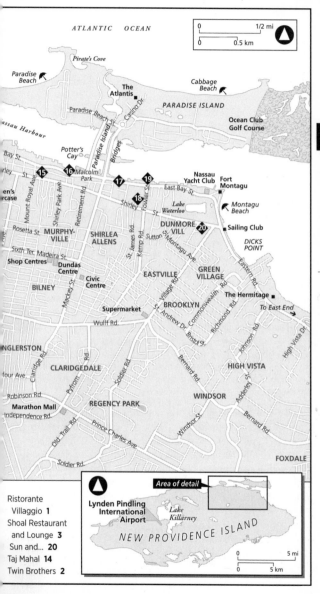

ATLANTIC OCEAN

0   1/2 mi
0   0.5 km

Pirate's Cove

Paradise
Beach

Cabbage
Beach

The
Atlantis

PARADISE ISLAND

Paradise Beach Rd

Casino Dr.

Ocean Club
Golf Course

Nassau Harbour

Potter's
Cay

Bay St.

Malcolm
Park

Nassau
Yacht Club

Fort
Montagu

15

16

17

19

East Bay St.

Bridges

Paradise Island Dr.

Montagu
Beach

en's
rcase

Shirley
St.

Mount Royal Ave.

Shirley Park Ave.

Retirement Rd.

18

Foster St.

Lake
Waterloo

Sailing Club

DUNMORE
VILL

20

Rosetta St.

MURPHY-
VILLE

SHIRLEA
ALLENS

St. James Rd.

Kemp Rd.

Sutton St.

Montagu Ave.

DICKS
POINT

Sixth Ter. Madeira St.

Shop Centres

Dundas
Centre

Civic
Centre

EASTVILLE

Village Rd.

GREEN
VILLAGE

Eastern Rd.

BILNEY

Supermarket

BROOKLYN

St. Andrew Dr.

Commonwealth Rd.

Bristol St.

Richmond Rd.

The Hermitage ■

Johnson Rd.

To East End →

Wulff Rd.

NGLERSTON

four Ave

Claridge Rd.

CLARIDGEDALE

Pyfrom Rd.

Soldier Rd.

Bernard Rd.

WINDSOR

HIGH VISTA

Adderley St.

High Vista Dr.

Robinson Rd.

Marathon Mall

Independence Rd.

REGENCY PARK

Prince Charles Ave.

Windsor St.

Bernard Rd.

Old Trail Rd.

Soldier Rd.

FOXDALE

3

NEW PROVIDENCE | Where to Stay

Ristorante
  Villaggio **1**
Shoal Restaurant
  and Lounge **3**
Sun and... **20**
Taj Mahal **14**
Twin Brothers **2**

Area of detail

Lynden Pindling
International
Airport

Lake
Killarney

NEW PROVIDENCE ISLAND

0   5 mi
0   5 km

47

INEXPENSIVE

Grand Central Hotel 🏷 This longtime favorite for frugal travelers dates back to the early 1940s. It is still going strong and has been much improved in recent years. There is no pool, and it's a bit of a walk to the beach, but this house and the adjoining former private home have much to recommend them. Bedrooms are midsize, well maintained, and comfortable, with pine furnishings. Some rooms have balconies, opening onto views of bustling Charlotte Street or the cruise ships beyond.

Charlotte St., Nassau, The Bahamas. ☎ **242/322-8356.** Fax 242/325-0218. www. grand-central-hotel.com. 35 units. Year-round $75–$90 double. AE, MC, V. *In room:* A/C, TV.

Nassau Palm Resort 🏷 A short walk west of downtown Nassau, within a cluster of other cost-conscious hotels that includes El Greco (see above), this hotel lies across busy West Bay Street from the relatively narrow confines of Junkanoo Beach (also known as Lighthouse Beach or the Western Esplanade). Though not as dramatic as Cable Beach, a few miles west, it's a safe urban beach with tranquil waters and a lot of shells. This place is a good value for those who don't demand particularly attentive service and who don't want to pay the higher prices charged by the more deluxe hotels along Cable Beach. Bedrooms are outfitted in a standard motel style, most with a view of Nassau Harbour, and come with extras you don't always find in a moderately priced choice, such as alarm clocks, two-line phones, and desks.

W. Bay St., Nassau, The Bahamas. ☎ **242/356-0000.** Fax 242/323-1408. www. nassau-hotel.com. 183 units. Year round $90–$110 double; $120 suite. AE, DISC, MC, V. Bus: 10 or 17. **Amenities:** Restaurant (breakfast only); bar; concierge; health club & spa; 2 outdoor pools. *In room:* A/C, TV, fridge, hair dryer, Wi-Fi ($16 per day).

The Towne House 🏷 If your demands aren't great, this modest hotel offers affordable rates, plus a location within walking distance of the center of Nassau and Lighthouse Beach. The hotel features simply but comfortably furnished midsize bedrooms, along with a swimming pool and a sun deck. If you don't want to go out at night, the Talking Stick Bar and Restaurant serves three meals a day, its menu mostly Bahamian with some international dishes.

40 George St., Nassau, The Bahamas. ☎ **242/322-8450.** Fax 242/328-1512. www.townehotel.com. 46 units. Winter $80 double, $90 suite; off-season $65 double, $80 suite. Rates include breakfast. MAP (lunch or dinner) $16 per person extra. AE, MC, V. **Amenities:** Restaurant; bar; Internet (free); outdoor pool. *In room:* A/C, TV.

Cable Beach

Cable Beach has always figured high in the consciousness of The Bahamas. Ever since Atlantis premiered on Paradise Island, Cable Beach has flourished, and occasionally suffered, in the shadow of its more dramatic counterpart.

Cable Beach derived its name from the underwater telephone and telegraph cable that brought electronic communications from the outside world. For years, it was a rural outpost of New Providence Island, flanked by private homes and a desirable shoreline that was a destination for local residents. Its first major tourist boost came with the construction of the Ambassador Beach Hotel, now the site of Breezes Bahamas. In the 1980s, a building boom added a string of condos, timeshares, and hotels, all designed to serve the needs of sun-seekers and casinogoers. The district now has a wide variety of restaurants and sports facilities, lots of glitz and glitter, and one of the country's two biggest casinos (in terms of square footage).

In 2005, a consortium of investors, coalescing under the name **Baha Mar Resorts** (© **242/677-9000;** www.bahamar.com), pinpointed Cable Beach as the eventual site of one of the Atlantic's most far-reaching resort developments. By 2014, expect big changes that might make Cable Beach one of the world's most talked-about casino and resort destinations—that is, if all phases of the redevelopment are completed as planned. Completed in 2010 was a radical upgrade of the beachfront, with the addition of sea-fronting boardwalks and gazebos along with a dance floor and a sophisticated sound system.

Major changes will include revising the layout of West Bay Street, one of New Providence's busiest arteries; dredging new lakes and marinas; creating water traps for a redesigned golf course; demolishing some older buildings within the Cable Beach compound; and enlarging the existing casino. The project also calls for constructing a new string of resort hotels, each catering to a different market. A W hotel, for example, will accent avant-garde design and, it's hoped, attract a youthful, trend-setting clientele. Another property will offer more conservative comforts geared to the haute bourgeoisie.

Even in its current form, Cable Beach has many loyal fans, some of whom find Paradise Island too expensive, too snobbish, too contrived, and too Disney-esque. Stay tuned for further developments—and expect endless delays, with investment money tight in these bad economic times.

VERY EXPENSIVE

Breezes Bahamas ★ In 1996, the SuperClubs chain spent $125 million transforming a tired old relic—the Ambassador Beach Hotel—into this all-inclusive resort. Today, its biggest competitor is the nearby Sandals Royal Bahamian (see below), which is more imposing, more stylish, more expensive, and more upscale. Rowdier and more raucous, however, and located on a prime 450m (1,476-ft.) beachfront along Cable Beach, Breezes attracts a more middle-of-the-road crowd; it's unpretentious and more affordable (though it isn't exactly cheap, and we think it's a bit overpriced for what it is).

The U-shaped resort has two wings of rooms plus a main clubhouse facing a large, sometimes overcrowded terrace with a swimming pool that serves as the social centerpiece. Couples and single travelers are equally accepted here, and the rate includes everything—the room, meals, snacks, unlimited wine (not the finest) with lunch and dinner, even premium-brand liquor at the bars, plus activities and airport transfers. Accommodations are not as luxurious as those at Sandals (picture pastel-painted furniture with Formica tops), but rates are deliberately lower.

Diners can sample unremarkable international fare at the food court, although the Italian restaurant serves better food. A beachside grill and snacks are available throughout the day. Entertainment includes a high-energy disco, a piano bar, and a nightclub. Karaoke is inevitable, but the professional Junkanoo live shows, which are presented every Saturday night, are more entertaining, and local bands often perform. For most of the year, there is a 7-night minimum stay required.

Cable Beach, Nassau, The Bahamas. © **877/BREEZES** (2733-937) or 242/327-5356. Fax 242/327-5155. www.breezes.com. 391 units. Year-round $264–$430 double; $368–$475 suite. Rates include all meals, drinks, tips, airport transfers, and most activities. AE, DISC, MC, V. Free parking. Bus: 10. No children 15 and under; no children 18 and under, unless accompanied by an adult 21 or older. **Amenities:** 4 restaurants; 4 bars; state-of-the-art health club; Internet ($18/hr.); 3 outdoor pools; 3 tennis courts (lit for night play); watersports equipment/rentals. *In room:* A/C, TV, CD player, hair dryer.

Sandals Royal Bahamian ★ This all-inclusive, couples-only property originated as a very posh hotel, the Balmoral Beach, in the 1940s. In 1996, the Jamaica-based Sandals chain poured $20 million into updating the resort. Everywhere, you'll find trappings of Edwardian England in the tropics: manicured gardens, neoclassical/Palladian architectural themes, and hidden courtyards tastefully accented with sculptures. The resort is located on a beach a short walk west of Cable Beach's more glittery mega-hotels.

Hotels & Restaurants in Cable Beach

HOTELS ◼

Breezes Bahamas **13**
Compass Point Beach Resort **5**
Marley Resort & Spa **12**
Orange Hill Beach Inn **4**
Sheraton Nassau Beach Resort **10**
Sandals Royal Bahamian **8**
A Stone's Throw Away **3**
Westwind II Club **9**
Wyndham Nassau Resort & Crystal Palace Casino **11**

RESTAURANTS ◆

Amici **10**
Black Angus Grille **11**
Goodfellow Farms **1**
Indigo **7**
Moso **12**
Poop Deck at Sandyport **6**
Provence **6**
Restaurant at Compass Point **5**
Slimmer Down **12**
Travellers Rest **2**

junkanoo FESTIVALS

No Bahamian celebration is as raucous as **Junkanoo.** Its special rituals originated during the colonial days of slavery, when African-born newcomers could legally drink and enjoy themselves only on certain strictly predetermined days of the year. In how it's celebrated, the Junkanoo festival closely resembles Carnival in Rio and Mardi Gras in New Orleans. Its major difference lies in the costumes and the timing (the major Junkanoo celebrations occur the day after Christmas, a legacy of the English celebration of Boxing Day on Dec 26, and on New Year's Day). A more touristy 2-month event, the **Junkanoo Summer Festival** (② 242/302-2007; www.bahamas.com), takes place in June and July every year.

In the old days, Junkanoo costumes were crafted from crepe paper, often in primary colors, stretched over wire frames. (One sinister offshoot of the celebrations was that Junkanoo costumes and masks were used to conceal the identity of anyone seeking vengeance on a white person, or on another slave.) Today, locals have more money to spend on costumes and festivals than they did in the past. The finest costumes can cost up to $15,000 and are sometimes sponsored by local bazaars, lotteries, church groups, and charity auctions. Everyday folks from all walks of Bahamian life join in, often with homemade costumes that are sensuous or humorous.

The best time and place to observe Junkanoo is New Year's Day in Nassau, when throngs of cavorting, music-making, and costumed figures prance through the streets. Find yourself a good viewing position on Bay Street. Less elaborate celebrations take place in major towns on the other islands, including Freeport on Grand Bahama Island.

You can learn more about Junkanoo at the **Educulture Museum** at Ivern House, 31 W. St. at Delancey (② 242/328-DRUM [3786]; www.educulturebahamas.com). The owner, Arlene Nash Ferguson, who has been joining in Junkanoo parades from the age of 4, is an expert on Bahamian culture and tradition and a font of information. She's one of the most gracious hosts in Nassau. This admission-free attraction can be visited Monday to Friday 9am to 5pm. The small museum is installed in the owner's childhood home. On display is the history of Junkanoo, with some of its more flamboyant costumes. This is a favorite with kids, too, since there's a room where they're given such instruments as drums and cowbells and told to create their own Junkanoo sounds.

A favorite for honeymooners, Sandals offers well-furnished and often elegant rooms, all classified as suites and positioned within either the resort's core Manor House or the 1998 Windsor Building. Others, including some of the most upscale, occupy outlying villas known collectively as the Royal Village. The villas are preferable thanks to their rigorously secluded settings and easy access to nearby semiprivate plunge pools. Bedrooms, regardless of their location, have thick cove moldings and formal English furniture. The rooms that face the ocean offer small terraces with views of an offshore sand spit, Sandals Key.

In addition to spectacular buffets, dining options include white-glove service and continental dishes at **Baccarat,** Japanese cuisine at **Kimonos,** and Italian fare at **Casanova.** The pool here is one of Nassau's most appealing, with touches of both Vegas and ancient Rome (outdoor murals and replicas of ancient Roman columns). Complimentary shuttle service goes to the casino and nightlife options at the nearby Wyndham Crystal Palace complex.

W. Bay St., Cable Beach, Nassau, The Bahamas. ℂ **888/SANDALS** (726-3257) or 242/327-6400. Fax 242/327-6961. www.sandals.com. 403 units. Year-round $3,647–$8,106 per couple for 7 days. Rates include all meals, drinks, and activities. AE, DISC, MC, V. Free parking. Bus: 10. Couples only; no children allowed. **Amenities:** 8 restaurants; 9 bars; concierge (for guests in higher-priced units); health club & spa; 7 outdoor pools; 2 tennis courts (lit for night play); watersports equipment/rentals. *In room:* A/C, TV, hair dryer, Wi-Fi ($14/day).

EXPENSIVE

Sheraton Nassau Beach Resort ★ ☺   Prominently visible in the center of Cable Beach (its best asset) is this seven-story high-rise, connected by a shopping arcade to the Crystal Palace Casino. The nearby Wyndham (p. 54) is glitzier and has better facilities, but the Sheraton is still one of the best choices for families (many of its rooms contain two double beds, so they can accommodate up to four). You'll think of Vegas when you see the rows of fountains in front, the acres of marble inside, and the hotel's propensity for hosting large wedding parties. The big, brassy building forms a horseshoe-shaped curve around a landscaped beachfront garden; its Aztec-inspired facade of sharp angles incorporates prominent balconies. Bedrooms are modern and comfortable, reflecting a lighthearted interpretation of Tommy Bahama style, replete with dark-wood furniture and understated tones completely devoid of the floral prints of yesteryear. Big windows open onto views of either the garden or the beach.

W. Bay St., Cable Beach, Nassau, The Bahamas. ℂ **800/325-3535** or 242/327-6000. Fax 242/327-5968. www.starwoodhotels.com. 694 units. Year round $269–$380 double; $400–$590 suite. AE, MC, V. Free parking. Bus: 10. **Amenities:** 4 restaurants, including Amici (p. 64); 3 bars; babysitting; kids' club; exercise room; 3 outdoor pools; room service; 2 tennis courts (lit for night play). *In room:* A/C, TV, hair dryer, Internet (free).

Westwind II Club ☺ Set on the western edge of Cable Beach's hotel strip, 9.5km (6 miles) from the center of Nassau, the West-wind II is a cluster of two-story buildings that contain two-bedroom, two-bathroom timeshare units made available to the public when not occupied by their investor-owners. The size and facilities of these units, including full kitchens (there's a grocery store nearby), make them ideal for families. All the diversions of the mega-hotels are nearby, but in the complex itself, you can enjoy privacy and a low-key atmosphere. (A masonry wall separates the compound from street traffic.) Each unit is pleasantly outfitted with white tile floors, rattan furniture, and a balcony or terrace. Price differences are based on whether the units face the beach, the pool, or the garden. Don't stay here if you expect resort luxuries or facilities; Westwind II is more for self-sufficient, do-it-yourself types.

W. Bay St., Cable Beach, Nassau, The Bahamas. ℂ **866/369-5921** or 242/327-7211. Fax 262/327-7529. www.westwind2.com. 52 units. Winter $240–$355 double; off-season $205–$320 double. MC, V. Bus: 10. **Amenities:** Bar; babysitting; 2 outdoor pools; 2 tennis courts (lit for night play). *In room:* A/C, TV, kitchen, Wi-Fi ($15/day).

Wyndham Nassau Resort & Crystal Palace Casino ★ ☺ This flashy mega-resort on the lovely sands of Cable Beach is so vast and all-encompassing that some of its guests never venture into Nassau during their stay on the island. The futuristic-looking complex incorporates three high-rise towers, a central core topped with massive greenhouse-style domes, and a cluster of beachfront gazebos—all linked by arcades, covered passageways, and mini-pavilions. Guest rooms come in several categories, ranging from standard island view to ocean vista, each with private balcony. Corner suites are the way to go, with lots of space, wraparound balconies, and water views through floor-to-ceiling glass.

The Art of Massage

The **Red Lane Spa**, at the Sandals Royal Bahamian in Nassau, has repeatedly made the top 10 list of spa resorts in the *Condé Nast Traveler* readers' choice survey. The decor features walls and floors of Italian Saturnia stone, rich mahogany doors, and a collection of pre-Raphaelite prints in gilded frames. One service offered, "In Each Other's Hands," allows couples to learn the art of massage from a professional so they can practice on each other in the comfort of their hotel room.

The Wyndham will be the centerpiece of a radical expansion of the hotel lineup here, as described in our introduction to Cable Beach (p. 49). Aside from the massive **Crystal Palace Casino** (p. 54), one of the two largest casinos in The Bahamas, the complex contains a wide array of dining and drinking facilities. Its restaurants are among New Providence's best; a particular favorite of ours is the appealingly experimental **Moso** (p. 65). Even if you're not a guest of the hotel, you might want to take advantage of the bars, restaurants, or casino action here.

W. Bay St., Cable Beach, Nassau, The Bahamas. ☏ **877/999-3223** in the U.S., or 242/327-6200. Fax 954/327-6818. www.wyndhamnassauresort.com. 559 units. Year-round $190–$270 double; $245–$325 suite. AE, DC, MC, V. Free self-parking; valet parking $5. Bus: 10. **Amenities:** 4 restaurants (including Black Angus Grille, p. 64; Moso, p. 65); 4 bars; babysitting; concierge; state-of-the-art health club; room service. *In room:* A/C, TV, fridge, hair dryer, Wi-Fi ($15).

MODERATE

Orange Hill Beach Inn ★ 🏨   This hotel, set on 1.4 landscaped hillside hectares (3½ acres), lies about 13km (8 miles) west of Nassau and 1.5km (1 mile) east of Love Beach, which has great snorkeling. It's perfect for those who want to escape the crowds and stay in a quieter part of New Providence; it's easy to catch a cab or jitney to Cable Beach or downtown Nassau. Many of the guests are Europeans, especially during summer.

Accommodations come in a variety of sizes, though most are small. Each room has a balcony or patio, and some have kitchenettes. An on-site bar serves sandwiches and salads throughout the day, while the restaurant offers simple but good dinners. Diving excursions along New Providence's southwestern coast are a popular activity, and the hotel provides free regular jitney service to and from local grocery stores, a fact that's much appreciated by guests who prepare meals within their kitchenettes.

W. Bay St. (just west of Blake Rd.), Nassau, The Bahamas. ☏ **888/399-3698** or 242/327-7157. Fax 242/327-5186. www.orangehill.com. 32 units. Winter $151–$170 double; off-season $131–$150 double. MC, V. Free parking. Bus: 10. **Amenities:** Restaurant; bar; outdoor pool; Wi-Fi (free in lobby). *In room:* A/C, TV.

West of Cable Beach
EXPENSIVE

Compass Point Beach Resort ★★   The whimsical Compass Point is self-consciously funky and out-of-the-way. The island's most westerly resort—directly beside Love Beach, several minutes' drive west from Cable Beach—is the closest thing to Jamaica in The Bahamas. In fact, it's associated with the Jamaica-based Island Outpost chain, owned by Christopher Blackwell, the music-industry entrepreneur who discovered and promoted Bob Marley's talent. Accommodations are within airy, old-fashioned, brightly painted wooden cottages, each simply but artfully furnished in a manner that encourages barefoot living if not altogether nudity. Prices vary according to the unit's view and size, and whether or not it's raised on stilts above the rocky landscape (units on stilts get more breezes and better views).

W. Bay St., Gambier, Nassau, The Bahamas. ℂ **866/431-2874** or 242/327-4500. Fax 242/327-9904. www.compasspointbeachresort.com. 18 units. Year round $350–$440 double; $530 2-bedroom apt for 4. AE, MC, V. Bus: 10. **Amenities:** Restaurant (p. 66); bar; outdoor pool; Wi-Fi (free in lobby). *In room:* A/C, TV/DVD, CD player, fridge, hair dryer.

Marley Resort & Spa ★★★ A pocket of posh, the former home of Bob Marley has been turned into New Providence's most elegant boutique hotel, with a Caribbean/African theme. The home is not only devoted to the good life but to the "life, legend, and inspiration" of the King of Reggae himself. As the managers so aptly put it, "Come embrace the feeling of One Love and One Heart in One Place."

The property was originally the governor's mansion until Rita Marley purchased it as a summer getaway for the Marleys, including Bob. The resort lies on a secluded stretch of Cable Beach, and is filled with sculpted hard-carved doors, mosaic tiles, intricate stonework, and limestone walls. Naturally, the memory of Marley is perpetuated in nostalgic mementos.

The names of the luxurious, spacious suites center on Marley song titles—"Kinky Reggae," "Talkin' Blues," and "Kaya," among others. The most spectacular way to stay here is to rent one of the three Royal Suites on the second floor, each with its own private balcony offering views of the water. Our favorite is "Royal Rita."

West Bay St., Cable Beach, The Bahamas. ℂ **866/737-1766** or 242/702-2800. Fax 242/327-4393. www.marleyresort.com. 16 suites. Winter $425 double, $545–$995 suite; off-season $295 double, $425–$865 suite. AE, MC, V. **Amenities:** Restaurant; room service; music gallery; "Natural Mystic Spa." *In room:* A/C, TV, hair dryer, Wi-Fi (free).

A Stone's Throw Away ★★ 🏠 At last, New Providence has a gourmet-level B&B, a secluded hideaway conceived by French and Belgian owners, 21km (13 miles) west of Nassau. This boutique hotel for discerning visitors has already been discovered by some celebrities (though, for privacy's sake, management doesn't name names). Surrounded by verandas, the colonial-style inn's public rooms evoke an old plantation home. On the ground floor, guest rooms open onto gardens and a pool area, while the upper two floors provide panoramic lake views. Accommodations are luxuriously furnished with plush towels, Indonesian teak beds, and mahogany antiques. The staff serves three meals a day, including finely honed continental dinners.

Tropical Garden Rd. and W. Bay St., Gambier, Nassau, The Bahamas. ℰ **242/327-7030.** Fax 242/327-7040. www.astonesthrowaway.com. 10 units. Nov–May $200–$290 double, $290 suite; off season $175–$235 double, $235 suite. AE, MC, V. **Amenities:** Restaurant; bar; outdoor pool; room service. *In room:* A/C, TV/DVD, Internet (free), minibar.

WHERE TO EAT
Nassau

Nassau restaurants open and close often. Even if reservations aren't required, it's a good idea to call first just to verify that a place is still in business and that the hours haven't changed. European and American cuisine are relatively easy to find. Surprisingly, it used to be difficult to find Bahamian cuisine, but in recent years, more restaurants have begun to offer authentic island fare.

EXPENSIVE

Chef Chea's ★ CONTINENTAL/BAHAMIAN   New since 2010, this dining room evokes the Nassau of years ago when the Duke of Windsor (King George VI's brother) ruled over the colony. Chef Christopher Chea is Le Cordon Bleu trained as reflected by his menu, which is more continental than local. You can peruse the menu by the soft glow of Art Deco chandeliers, in an elegant but subdued atmosphere. You can order tasty dishes such as oven-roasted duck, short ribs, or a juicy T-bone steak. Guests often begin with such starters as meaty portobello mushroom slices or a savory conch salad. Main courses often feature plump lobster ravioli or a classic and flavorful coq au vin. Whatever you order, save room for one of the best slices of cheesecake you'll encounter in The Bahamas. It's flavored with mango.

Dowdeswell & Armstrong sts. ℰ **242/323-3201.** Reservations recommended. Main courses $18–$35. AE, MC, V. Mon–Fri 11:30am–3pm; Mon–Sat 6–10pm. Bus: 10 or 17.

Graycliff ★★ CONTINENTAL   Part of the Graycliff Hotel, an antiques-filled colonial mansion located in Nassau's commercial core (opposite the Government House), this deeply entrenched restaurant retains a history and nostalgia for the old days of The Bahamas as a colonial outpost of Britain. The chefs use local Bahamian products whenever available and turn them into old-fashioned cuisine that appeals to tradition-minded visitors, many of whom return here year after year. Try such dishes, neither completely traditional nor regional, as grouper soup in puff pastry or plump, juicy pheasant cooked with pineapples grown on

Eleuthera. Lobster, another specialty, comes half in beurre blanc and half with a sauce prepared from the head of the lobster. Other options include escargots, foie gras, and lamb. The pricey wine list is praised as one of the finest in the country, with more than 250,000 bottles. This hotel and restaurant are managed by the same entrepreneurs who run a cigar-making facility; as such, its collection of Bahama-derived cigars is the world's most comprehensive.

Graycliff Hotel, 12 W. Hill St. ℰ 242/302-9150. www.graycliff.com. Reservations required. Jacket advised for men. Main courses $28-$68. AE, MC, V. Mon–Fri noon–2:45pm; daily 6:30–9:30pm. Bus: 10, 15, or 21A.

Humidor Churrascaria ★ BRAZILIAN Brazilian *rodizio,* the art of grilling large amounts of chicken, sausage, pork, and beef, has finally come to Nassau within this annex of the fabled Graycliff Hotel. Set in the same building as Graycliff's cigar factory and shop, within a generously proportioned, high-ceilinged enclave that's vaguely reminiscent of the long-ago British regime, it's fun, colorful, and filling. A staff wearing gaucho-inspired shirts invites you to the salad bar and then makes endless runs from the grill to your plate with skewers of assorted grilled meats—plus occasional *raciones* of grilled pineapple—as part of a ritual that evokes South America's pampas and plains. The only option available is the set-price dinner noted below. Vegetarians or the not-terribly-hungry can easily make do with a meal composed entirely from the salad bar.

Graycliff Hotel, 12 W. Hill St. ℰ 242/302-9150. www.graycliff.com. Reservations required. Fixed-price, all-you-can-eat *churrasco* dinner $40. Access to salad bar without any *churrasco* $25. AE, MC, V. Mon–Sat 6:30–10pm. Bus: 10, 10A, or 21A.

Ristorante Villaggio ★★ TUSCAN/CONTINENTAL One of the island's most appealing restaurants lies 3.2km (2 miles) west of Cable Beach, close enough to the gated residential enclave of Lyford Cay to ensure a steady flow of upscale locals. Set within an ochre-colored complex of shops and office buildings known as Caves Village at Caves Point, it's posh, a bit dilettantish, and charming. There's a cozy dining room, elaborate French Empire–style chandeliers, and rustic furniture that might have been pulled from a farmhouse in Tuscany. Even better is a sprawling covered terrace whose furniture—wrought-iron tables and deep armchairs—seems appropriate for someone's private library. Menu items are savory and artful; the lemon grass–poached lobster salad is fabulous, as are the *trenette* pasta with seafood, the clam linguine, and the Angus beef with arugula. Also delicious is the black sea bass atop a bed of truffle-studded creamed potatoes, bacon-braised organic leeks, and wild mushrooms. The place is run by slightly dotty English supervisors and a rather hip Bahamian and international staff.

At Caves Point, W. Bay St. at Blake Rd. ℰ **242/327-0965.** www.villaggio
restaurant.com. Reservations recommended. Main courses $26–$40. AE, MC, V.
Tues–Sat 6–9:30pm. Bus: "the Western bus."

Sun and . . . ★★ INTERNATIONAL This is a prominent
culinary landmark in Nassau, the best of a core of locally owned
restaurants valiantly holding their own against daunting competi-
tion from better-funded restaurants within the island's mega-
resorts. Today, under the hardworking leadership of Belgium-born
owner/chef Ronny Deryckere and his wife, Esther, it's more of an
inner sanctum than ever, occupying the premises of what was
originally built in the 1930s as a private residence, Red Mill
House, within an upscale, mostly residential neighborhood east of
downtown Nassau. You might start with a drink in the bar area,
which is a distinctly separate entity all its own, before heading into
one of several dining rooms, arranged around a courtyard containing tropical plants, shrubs, and a pool. Some of the dishes emerging from the kitchen are unique to New Providence and Paradise
Island: Examples include sweetbreads, prepared either with white
wine and mushroom sauce or with a demi-glacé and cognac; the
best Roquefort salad in town; a fabulous steak tartare served with
pommes frites; and grilled octopus with chopped onions and olive
tapenade. Of special note is the Bahamian fisher's platter, composed of artfully prepared fish caught in local waters.

Lakeview Rd. at E. Shirley St. ℰ **242/393-1205.** www.sun-and.com. Reservations required. Lunch platters $12–$18; dinner main courses $35–$60. AE, DC,
DISC, MC, V. Tues–Sat 11:30am–3pm and 6:30–10pm.

MODERATE

Aqua ★ INTERNATIONAL Anchor yourself at a window seat
in the British Colonial Hilton to watch the cruise ships from
Florida arrive or depart. This restaurant is best at night, when you
can enjoy lights along the harbor or from neighboring Paradise
Island. The chef shows imagination in creating unusual taste sen-
sations such a Bahamian lobster Wellington with a mushroom
tapenade, chili oil, and pimento coulis, or else a chicken satay with
an avocado salsa. The chef's specialties are a Bahamian conch
sampler—conch salad, conch chowder, and conch fritters. Two or
four diners can try the Aqua "Sample Tower," with marinated
squid, seaweed salad, conch fritters and salad, and honey sesame
shrimp among other ingredients.

British Colonial Hilton, 1 W. Bay St. ℰ **242/322-3301.** www.hiltoncaribbean.com.
Reservations recommended. Main courses $18–$27 lunch, $18–$42 dinner; lunch
buffet $24; dinner buffet (Fri–Sat) $39; breakfast buffet $22. AE, MC, V. Daily
6:30am–10:30pm.

Café Matisse ★ INTERNATIONAL/ITALIAN   Set directly behind Parliament House, in a mustard-colored building built a century ago as a private home, this restaurant is on everybody's short list of downtown Nassau favorites. It serves well-prepared Italian and international cuisine to businesspeople, government workers, and all kinds of dealmakers. Guests are seated in an enclosed courtyard and on two floors of the interior, which is decorated with colorful Matisse prints. The sophisticated Bahamian-Italian team of Greg and Gabriella Curry prepare menu items that include calamari with spicy chili-flavored jam, grilled filet of local grouper served with a light tomato-caper sauce, and spaghetti with lobster.

Bank Lane at Bay St., just north of Parliament Sq. ✆ **242/356-7012.** www.cafe-matisse.com. Reservations recommended. Main courses $17–$28 lunch; $24–$46 dinner. AE, DISC, MC, V. Tues–Sat noon–3pm and 6–11pm. Bus: 17 or 21.

Luciano's of Chicago ★ ITALIAN/SEAFOOD/STEAK   One of Nassau's best upscale restaurants lies within a low-slung, red-painted building. A branch of a successful Chicago-based franchise, it emphasizes stiff drinks, two-fisted portions, and macho charm. Many visitors prefer the terrace, which affords a view of the towers and glittering lights of Atlantis just across the water. There's also a smoothly upscale dining room, air-conditioned and outfitted in tones of beige and brown. The menu includes a tempting roster of steaks, a romaine salad topped with basil-and-garlic-marinated sweet peppers, pot-roasted and marinated chicken served with sautéed garlic and kalamata olives, and country-style rigatoni with sweet Italian sausage, pancetta, and a light tomato-flavored cream sauce.

E. Bay St., just before the northbound entrance to the Paradise Island Bridge. ✆ **242/323-7770.** www.lucianosnassau.com. Reservations recommended. Main courses $11–$30 lunch; $23–$46 dinner. AE, DC, DISC, MC, V. Mon–Fri 11:30am–3:30pm; daily 6–10pm. Bus: 10.

Poop Deck BAHAMIAN/SEAFOOD   Raffish and informal, this is the older version of a restaurant that has expanded with another branch in Cable Beach. This original is less touristy, hosting a clientele of sailors, yachties, and workers from the nearby marinas and boatyards. Many of them find perches on the second-floor terrace, which overlooks the harbor and Paradise Island. If you like dining with a view, you won't find a better spot in the heart of Nassau. At lunch, order the perfectly seasoned conch chowder or a juicy beef burger. The waiters are friendly, the crowd is convivial, and the festivities continue into the evening, usually with lots of drinking. Native grouper fingers served with peas 'n' rice is the Bahamian soul-food dish. Two of the best seafood selections are the fresh lobster and the stuffed mushrooms with crabmeat. The creamy linguine with crisp garlic bread is another fine choice.

Nassau Yacht Haven Marina, E. Bay St. © **242/393-8175.** www.thepoopdeck restaurants.com. Reservations recommended for dinner, not necessary at lunch. Main courses $12–$27 lunch; $19–$58 dinner. AE, DC, DISC, MC, V. Daily noon–4:30pm and 5–10:30pm. For the branch at the Nassau Yacht Haven: Bus 10, 19, or 23. For the branch on W. Bay St.: Bus 10 or "the Western bus."

Shoal Restaurant and Lounge ★ 🍴 BAHAMIAN   Many of our good friends in Nassau swear this is one of the best joints for authentic local food. We rank it near the top for a venue that's utterly without glamour, serving sensible down-home food at a spot far removed from the typical tourist path. After all, where else can you get a good bowl of okra soup these days? This may or may not be your fantasy, but to a Bahamian, it's like what pot liquor and turnip greens with corn bread are to a Southerner. Many diners follow a bowl of soup (either split pea or the above-mentioned okra) with conch, either cracked or perhaps curried. But you can also order some unusual dishes, such as Bahamian-style curried mutton with native spices and herbs, stewed oxtail, or braised short ribs. Peas 'n' rice accompanies virtually everything served here.

Nassau St., near Poinciana Dr. © **242/323-4400.** Main courses $9–$28. AE, DISC, MC, V. Sun–Thurs 7:30am–10pm; Fri 7am–10:30pm. Closed Sat. Bus: 16.

Taj Mahal NORTHERN INDIAN   This is Nassau's best and most frequently recommended Indian restaurant. Within a room lined with Indian art and artifacts, you'll dine on a wide range of savory and zesty Punjabi, tandoori, and curried dishes. Some of the best choices are the lamb selections, though concessions to local culture, like curried or tandoori-style conch, have begun cropping up on the menu. Consider a tandoori mixed platter, which, with a side dish or two, might satisfy two diners. All of the *korma* dishes, which combine lamb, chicken, beef, or vegetables in a creamy curry sauce, are very successful. Take-out meals are also available.

48 Parliament St., at Bay St. © **242/356-3002.** Reservations recommended. Main courses $20–$35. AE, MC, V. Daily noon–3pm and 6:30–11pm. Bus: 10 or 17.

Twin Brothers ★ 🎁 BAHAMIAN   If you're visiting old Arawak Cay, you get not only the best daiquiris in The Bahamas, but fresh, well-prepared food in a convivial atmosphere that's "hopping," as the locals call it. The McCardy twins emigrated from Eleuthera at the age of 21, heading for Nassau where they began making dai-quiris—strawberry, banana, whatever—at the old Straw Market and earned a kind of local fame, especially with their sour sop daiquiri. Here, in a nautical setting, you can begin with one of Nassau's tastiest conch salads, and wash it down with a mango lemonade (a first for some visitors). Served with a side of potato salad, the fried shrimp is succulent. You can also order a meaty and juicy Bahamian lobster tail. The catch of the day can be grilled, fried, boiled, or steamed, and your conch can either be cracked or scorched. Sides include creamy coleslaw or cheesy macaroni or else fried plantains or peas 'n' rice.

Arawak Cay. ✆ **242/328-5033.** www.twinbrothersbahamas.com. Reservations recommended. Main courses $13–$38. DISC, MC, V. Daily 11:30am to midnight. Bus: 10.

INEXPENSIVE

Bahamian Kitchen 🍴 ☺ BAHAMIAN/INTERNATIONAL Located next to Trinity Church, in one of downtown's most congested neighborhoods, this is one of the best places for good Bahamian food at modest prices. Solid and unpretentious, it feels like the kind of restaurant you might find on a remote Out Island. Down-home dishes include Bahamian-style lobster, fried red snapper, conch salad, stewed fish, curried chicken, okra soup, and pea soup and dumplings. Most dishes are served with peas 'n' rice. You can also order such old-fashioned fare as stewed fish served with johnnycake. If you'd like to introduce your kids to Bahamian cuisine, this is an ideal choice. There's also take-out service, which is great if you're planning a picnic.

Trinity Place, off Market St. ✆ **242/325-0702.** www.bahamiankitchen.cbt.cc/index.html. Main courses $18–$32. AE, MC, V. Mon–Sat 11:30am–10pm. Bus: 10.

Café Skans 🍴 GREEK/AMERICAN/BAHAMIAN Owned and operated by a hardworking Greek family, this straightforward, Formica-clad diner offers flavorful food that's served without fanfare in generous portions. Set in the midst of Nassau's densest concentration of shops, it attracts local residents and office workers from the government buildings nearby. Menu items include Bahamian fried or barbecued chicken, conch chowder, bean soup with dumplings, souvlaki or gyros in pita bread, burgers, steaks, and seafood platters. This is also where workaday Nassau comes for breakfast.

Bay St., near Market St. ✆ **242/322-2486.** Reservations not accepted. Breakfast items $4–$13; sandwiches $6–$12; main-course platters $6–$24. MC, V. Mon–Sat 8am–5pm; Sun 8am–3pm. Bus: 10 or 17.

Charlie's Place ★ 🎒 BAHAMIAN In the old Nassau Stadium, this eatery is where locals go for food like Grandma Bahama used to cook. The specialty is Charlie's "cracked chicken;" it's his own invention, and he's not giving out the recipe. It's delectable. Sometimes the daily special is pig's feet, and the drink of the day is gin and coconut water. You can also feast on "sweet, sexy conch,"

Afternoon Tea with the Governor

The British tradition of afternoon tea is still observed on the last Friday of each month, from January to August, at the hilltop mansion of the governor-general in Nassau. You can spend a memorable afternoon here, enjoying musical numbers and sampling some local treats. For an invitation to tea, call the **People-to-People Unit of the Ministry of Tourism** at ✆ **242/323-1853.**

or else "stew fish"; both of these dishes come with a rich brown gravy. If you want to go really native, try the sheep-tongue souse. If all these dishes are a bit too adventurous for you, you can order a bowl of okra or crab soup, perhaps grilled red snapper or garlic shrimp for your main course.

Fowler St. ✆ **242/394-0300.** Reservations not needed. Main courses $12–$16. No credit cards. Daily 8am–4pm. Bus: 9A, 9B, 11, or 19.

Conch Fritters Bar & Grill ☺ BAHAMIAN/INTERNA-TIONAL   A true local hangout with real island atmosphere, this lighthearted, family-friendly restaurant changes its focus several times throughout the day. Lunches and dinners are high-volume, high-turnover affairs mitigated by attentive staff. Guests invariably include older diners and parents with young children in tow. Food choices are standard but quite good, including cracked conch, fried shrimp, grilled salmon, blackened rib-eye steak, burgers, sandwiches, and six different versions of chicken, including a combination platter with barbecued ribs. Specialty drinks from the always-active bar include the Goombay Smash. Musicians perform Thursday through Saturday from 7 to 10pm.

Marlborough St. (across from the British Colonial Hilton). ✆ **242/323-8801.** Burgers, sandwiches, and platters $10–$50. AE, MC, V. Daily 11am–11pm (until midnight Fri–Sat). Bus: 10.

Double Dragon CANTONESE/SZECHUAN   The chefs at this unpretentious eatery hail from the province of Canton in mainland China, so that locale inspires most of the food here. You'll find the place in an unscenic, raffish-looking waterfront neighborhood a short drive east of downtown Nassau. If you've ever wondered about the differences between Cantonese and Szechuan cuisine, a quick look at the menu will highlight them. Lobster, chicken, or beef, for example, can be prepared Cantonese style, with mild black-bean or ginger sauce; or in spicier Szechuan versions with red peppers, chilies, and garlic. Honey-garlic chicken and orange-flavored shrimp are always popular and succulent.

Overall, this place is a fine choice if you're eager for a change from grouper and burgers.

E. Bay St. (btw. Mackey St. and Williams Court). © **242/393-5718.** Main courses $10–$24. DISC, MC, V. Mon–Sat noon–3:30pm and 4:30–10:30pm. Bus: 10 or 19.

Cable Beach
VERY EXPENSIVE

Black Angus Grille ★ STEAK/SEAFOOD   This is a truly excellent steakhouse that's positioned amid a cluster of dining options immediately above Cable Beach's Crystal Palace Casino. Relaxed but macho-looking and undeniably upscale, it's Cable Beach's most consistently busy restaurant—a function of its good food and, according to its manager, of the predilection of gamblers for juicy steaks after a nerve-jangling session at the gaming tables. Those succulent steaks are well prepared and cooked to your specifications. There's prime rib, filet mignon, and pepper steak, along with grilled tuna with a white-bean salad, blackened conch filet, Caesar salad, and an array of dessert soufflés that includes versions with chocolate, praline, and orange.

Wyndham Nassau Resort, above the Crystal Palace Casino, W. Bay St. © **242/327-6200.** www.wyndhamnassauresort.com. Reservations recommended. Main courses $32–$48. AE, DC, DISC, MC, V. Daily 6–11pm. Bus: 10.

EXPENSIVE

Amici ★ ITALIAN   The most glamorous of the Sheraton's restaurants, the highly recommended Amici works hard to maintain its status as a culinary showcase for the flavorful Italian cuisine that many guests crave after too long an exposure to an all-Bahamian diet. Following a radical renovation in 2007, its two-story garden setting features ceiling fans, dark-wood furniture reminiscent of a trattoria in Italy, and big windows framing a beach view. Popular and long-enduring dishes here include scampi cocktails, Caesar salad, fettuccine alfredo, Florentine-style breast of chicken on a bed of spinach, spicy shrimp, and braised pork shank with olive oil, hot peppers, and angel-hair pasta.

Sheraton Nassau Beach Resort, W. Bay St. © **242/327-6000.** www.starwood hotels.com. Main courses $22–$48. AE, DC, DISC, MC, V. Daily 6–10:30pm. Bus: 10.

Indigo ★ ASIAN   Locals flock to this dive, and visitors find its funky atmosphere appealing as well. In the pre-dinner hours, the bar is bustling and animated. There's some Bahamian culture on show as well, as the walls are decorated with original oils, mostly of native island scenes. Friday and Saturday are the big nights here, when a steel-pan band is brought in. The joint can get classy, too: On some occasions, you're likely to hear a classical guitarist. The food, consisting of steaks, chicken, and fresh fish, is rather standard, except for the sushi, which comes as a surprise. Other Asian-style dishes are given a distinct Bahamian touch. The standard conch chowder has a South Seas flavor by the addition of coconut.

W. Bay St. (at the Sandals traffic circle). (C) **242/327-2524.** Reservations not necessary. Main courses $12–$36. AE, MC, V. Mon–Thurs 6–10pm; Fri–Sat 6–10:30pm.

Moso ★★ ASIAN This is one of the island's most experimental restaurants, and it deliberately prices meals several notches below the rates charged by other restaurants in the same resort. It's a hipster kind of place serving hipster cuisine—in fact, every dish you've ever liked from every Asian restaurant you've ever been to seems to have found its way onto the menu here. All of the Bahamian waiters have spent several months studying Asian food and Asian culture, and they'll guide you through a menu composed of many different small and medium-size dishes. The best items include aromatic crispy duck; Mongolian-style chicken and beef hot pot; fresh tofu stir-fried with minced pork, garlic, and chili; seared ahi tuna *tataki* with *yuzu* lemon sauce; and a succulent blend of octopus and local conch with cucumbers in rice vinegar. You can also order meticulously carved portions of chicken breast, shrimp, pork tenderloin, salmon, or mahimahi prepared in any of three different ways: Cantonese, Szechuan dry-rubbed, or teriyaki-style.

Wyndham Nassau Resort, above the Crystal Palace Casino, W. Bay St. (C) **242/327-6200.** www.wyndhamnassauresort.com. Reservations recommended. Small plates $11–$21; main courses $16–$37. AE, DC, DISC, MC, V. Thurs–Mon 6–10:30pm (opening days may vary). Bar daily 6pm–1am. Bus: 10.

Poop Deck at Sandyport INTERNATIONAL/SEAFOOD This is one of the three most imposing, desirable restaurants west of Cable Beach, convenient for the owners of the many upscale villas and condos, including those at Lyford Cay, that occupy New Providence's western edge. It's set within a peach-colored concrete building that's highly visible from West Bay Street. Despite the rosy exterior, it's a bit sterile-looking inside. This simple island restaurant evolved from a roughneck bar that occupied this site during the early 1970s. Lunch is usually devoted to well-prepared burgers, pastas, sandwiches, and salads. Dinners are more substantial, featuring filet mignon, seafood and steak combos, cracked conch, fried shrimp, and fresh fish. The house drink is a Bacardi Splish-Splash, an enticing blend of Bacardi Select, Nassau Royal Liqueur, pineapple juice, cream, and sugar-cane syrup.

Poop Deck Dr., off W. Bay St. (C) **242/327-DECK** (3325). www.thepoopdeck restaurants.com. Reservations recommended. Main courses $14–$36 lunch; $21–$50 dinner. AE, DISC, MC, V. Tues–Sat noon–10:30pm; Sun noon–10pm. Bus: 10 or "the Western bus."

Provence ★ MEDITERRANEAN Nassau's best Mediterranean cuisine is showcased within this sunny yellow restaurant. Lying near West Bay Street's western terminus, it's extremely popular with well-heeled locals (some of whom aren't particularly enchanted with the island's blockbuster casino hotels and their eateries). Decor includes big-windowed sea views and oil paintings of landscapes that evoke the southern French coast. Provence prepares its *cuisine du soleil* with superb simplicity—Atlantic salmon with citrus butter, for example—so as not to mar the natural flavor. Other dishes are heavily spiced, such as the rib-eye steak in a fire-breathing pepper sauce. The chefs also turn out a delightful bouillabaisse. Daily seafood specials may include pan-seared sea bass, our favorite, or black grouper filet. Everybody seems to like the lobster cocktails and the rack of lamb.

Old Towne Sandyport. ✆ **242/327-0985.** www.provencerestaurant.net. Reservations required. Main courses $8–$22 lunch; $28–$60 dinner. AE, DISC, MC, V. Mon–Fri 11:30am–3pm; Mon–Sat 6–10:30pm. Bus: 10 or "the Western bus."

West of Cable Beach

Goodfellow Farms ★ 🏠 BAHAMIAN A visit to this country store and open-air restaurant on the western end of the island is a journey back in time to the way The Bahamas used to be. This vegetable farm supplies fresh produce to Nassau restaurants and to visiting yachties, but you can sample it daily. The big event of the week is the Friday dinner buffet. Most visitors, however, show up for lunch, ordering from a menu that changes weekly. Our favorite items are the freshly grown gourmet greens and the large array of specialty vegetables, although you can also enjoy high-quality cuts of meat, ranging from lamb to organic chicken, as well as fresh seafood, especially mahimahi, sea bass, and jumbo lump crabmeat. An on-site retail shop is stocked with all sorts of delectable food items.

Nelson Rd., Mt. Pleasant Village. ✆ **242/377-5000.** www.goodfellowfarms.com. Reservations recommended, essential on Fri night. Lunch main courses $14–$21; Fri 3-course menu dinner $50. MC, V. Mon–Sat 9am–4pm; Sun 10am–3pm; Fri 6:30–8:30pm; Sun lunch 11am–2pm in winter. Drive west toward Old Fort Bay and Lyford Cay; at the traffic circle at Lyford Cay Plaza, exit up the hill toward Templeton. The farm is signposted.

Restaurant at Compass Point ★ BAHAMIAN Dining here might remind those who experienced the '60s of how they felt after ingesting one of those hallucinogenic brownies during their college years. The ceiling is orange, the bar is a study in marine blues, the view sweeps out over the sea, and everywhere you'll see the vivid Junkanoo, or reggae, colors of the West Indies. It's a charming and somewhat out-of-the-way retreat from the densely populated urban scenes of downtown Nassau and nearby Cable Beach. Lunches are simple and uncomplicated affairs, with turkey club sandwiches, meal-size salads, and burgers. Dinners are more elaborate and steeped in West Indian tradition, focusing on dishes such as cracked conch and pan-fried grouper with peas 'n' rice and plantains. Try the lobster stir-fried with mango and goat peppers. Because of its position facing the setting sun, the bar is a well-known spot from which to look for the elusive "green flash"; if that's your aim, the bartender can explain this to you and prepare you a bright-yellow Compass Bliss.

Compass Point Resort, W. Bay St., Gambier. © **242/327-4500.** www.compasspointbeachresort.com. Reservations recommended. Lunch platters $8–$18; dinner main courses $21–$39, more for lobster. AE, MC, V. Sun–Thurs 11am–10pm (last order); Fri–Sat 11am–11pm. Bar closes at midnight. Bus: 10 from Nassau and Cable Beach.

Simmer Down ★ CARIBBEAN   The Marley Resort's restaurant, Simmer Down, features a gourmet Caribbean cuisine with an emphasis on Jamaica, including some classic Marley family recipes and some of Bob's favorite dishes. Organic produce and fresh seafood highlight the tantalizing menu. Start with an appetizer of Bahamian crab cake or savory seafood and cheese terrine, followed by jerk chicken or spicy jerk fish (this was Bob's favorite). A specialty is roasted organic pineapple rum duck, or else you can try "Rita's Favorite," roasted rack of lamb. Desserts are sumptuous, including guava upside-down cake with brandy cream or chocolate banana pudding with vanilla ice cream and Jamaican rum.

You can not only eat here, but enjoy the spa or go shopping. On a stage in the courtyard, live entertainment, especially reggae, is often presented. On-site is Marley's Boutique, created by his daughter, Cedelia, a funky outlet selling arts and crafts by African, Jamaican, and Bahamian artisans. The boutique also sells high-end resort wear, designed by Cedelia, under the label "Catch a Fire."

In the Marley Resort & Spa, West Bay St., Cable Beach. © **272/702-2800.** www.marleyresort.com. Reservations required. Main courses $36–$52. AE, MC, V. Daily 7:30–10:30am, noon–3pm, and 6–10pm.

Travellers Rest ★ 🐟 BAHAMIAN/SEAFOOD   Set in an isolated spot about 2.5km (1½ miles) west of Cable Beach's megahotels, this restaurant feels far away from it all—like you're dining on a remote Out Island. The cozy cement-sided house, established as a restaurant in 1972, stands in a grove of sea-grape and palm trees facing the ocean. Because it's near the airport, travelers whose flights are delayed sometimes opt to chill out here until departure. You can dine outside, but if it's rainy (highly unlikely), go inside the tavern, with its small bar decorated with local paintings.

In this laid-back atmosphere, feast on well-prepared grouper fingers, barbecued ribs, curried chicken, steamed or cracked conch, or minced crayfish. Finish with guava cake, the best on the island. The conch salad served on weekends is said to increase men's virility.

W. Bay St., near Gambier (14km/8¾ miles west of the center of Nassau). ℂ 242/327-7633. Main courses $7.50–$29 lunch; $14–$28 dinner. AE, DISC, MC, V. Daily 11:30am–11pm. Bus: 10 or "the Western bus."

BEACHES & OUTDOOR PURSUITS

One of the great sports centers of the world, New Providence and the islands that surround it are marvelous places for swimming, sunning, snorkeling, scuba diving, boating, water-skiing, and deep-sea fishing, as well as playing tennis and golf.

You can learn more about available activities by contacting **The Bahamas Sports Tourist Office,** 1200 South Pine Island Rd., Ste. 750, Plantation, FL 33324 (ℂ **800/422-4262** in the continental U.S., or 954/236-9292; www.thebahamasguide.com/facts/sports.htm).

Hitting the Beach

In The Bahamas, as in Puerto Rico, the issue regarding public access to beaches is a hot and controversial subject. Recognizing this, the government has made efforts to intersperse public beaches with easy access between more private beaches where access may be impeded. Although mega-resorts discourage non-residents from accessing their individual beaches, there are so many local public beaches that all you'd have to do is drive or walk to any of the many unmarked, unnamed beaches.

Most visitors stay in one of the large beachfront resorts that have the ocean meeting the sand right outside of their doors. For those hoping to explore more of the coast, here's a list of recommended beaches that are absolutely accessible to the public:

CABLE BEACH ★★   No particular beach is actually called Cable Beach, yet this is the most popular stretch of sand on New Providence Island. Cable Beach is the name given not to a single beach, but to a string of resorts and beaches in the center of New Providence's northern coast, attracting the most visitors. This beachfront offers 6.5km (4 miles) of soft white sand, with many different types of restaurants, snack bars, and watersports offered by the hotels lining the waterfront. Calypso music floats to the sand from hotel pool patios. Vendors wend their way between sunscreen-slathered bodies selling armloads of shell jewelry, T-shirts, beach cover-ups, and fresh coconuts for sipping the sweet

THE ISLAND'S BEST picnic FARE

If you're keen on organizing a picnic and want to gather your provisions, consider heading about 3km (1¾ miles) west of Cable Beach. Within a shopping complex known as Caves Village, you'll find the **Gourmet Market** (✆ **242/327-1067;** www.gourmet marketnassau.com), the island's most upscale grocery store. Functioning like a magnet for villa owners within the nearby exclusive gated community of Lyford Cay, it sells fruits, cheeses, fish, wines, and pastries. And yes, they'll make sandwiches and even assemble, with or without strong guidance from you, picnic meals to go. It's open Monday to Saturday 8am to 7pm, Sunday 8am to 1pm.

"water" straight from the shell. Kiosks advertise parasailing, scuba-diving, and snorkeling trips, as well as party cruises to offshore islands. Waters can be rough and reefy, but then calm and clear a little farther along the shore. There are no public toilets here because guests of the resorts use their hotel facilities. If you're not a hotel guest and not a customer, you're not supposed to use the facilities. Cable Beach resorts begin 5km (3 miles) west of downtown Nassau, and even though they line much of this long swath of beach, there are various sections where public access is available without crossing through private hotel grounds.

CAVES BEACH   On the north shore, past the Cable Beach hotels, Caves Beach is 11km (6¾ miles) west of Nassau. It stands near Rock Point, right before the turnoff along Blake Road that leads to the airport. Since many visitors don't know of this place, it's a good spot to escape the hordes. It's also an attractive beach with soft sands. There are no toilets or changing facilities.

DELAPORTE BEACH   Just west of Cable Beach's busiest section is this public-access beach where you can escape the crowds. It opens onto clear waters and boasts white sands, although it has neither facilities nor toilets.

GOODMAN'S BAY   This public beach lies east of Cable Beach on the way toward Nassau's center. Goodman's Bay and Saunders Beach (see below) often host local fund-raising cookouts, during which vendors sell fish, chicken, conch, peas 'n' rice, and macaroni and cheese. People swim and socialize to blaring reggae and calypso tunes. To find out when one of these beach parties is

3

NEW PROVIDENCE

Beaches & Outdoor Pursuits

Continuing west along West Bay Street, you'll reach **Love Beach,** across from Sea Gardens, a nice stretch of sand lying east of Northwest Point. Love Beach, although not big, is a special favorite of lovers (hence the name). The snorkeling is superb, too. It's technically private, but no one bothers visitors, even though locals fervently hope it won't become overrun like Cable Beach.

3

happening, ask the staff at your hotel or pick up a local newspaper. There's a playground here, plus toilet facilities.

OLD FORT BEACH ★   To escape the crowds on weekdays, we often head here, a 15-minute drive west of Lynden Pindling International Airport (take W. Bay St. toward Lyford Cay). This lovely beach opens onto Old Fort Bay's turquoise waters, near western New Providence. The least developed of the island's beaches, it attracts many homeowners from the swanky Lyford Cay gated community. In winter, it can be quite windy, but in summer, it's as calm as the Caribbean.

SAUNDERS BEACH   East of Cable Beach, this is where many islanders go on the weekends. To reach it, take West Bay Street from Nassau toward Coral Island. This beach lies across from Fort Charlotte, just west of Arawak Cay. Like Goodman's Bay (see above), it often hosts local fund-raising cookouts open to the public. These can be a lot of fun. There are no public facilities.

WESTERN ESPLANADE   If you're staying at a hotel in downtown Nassau, such as the British Colonial, this is a good beach to patronize close to town. On this narrow strip of sand convenient to Nassau, you'll find toilets, changing facilities, and a snack bar. It's also known as Junkanoo Beach or Lighthouse Beach.

Biking

A half-day bicycle tour with **Bahamas Outdoors Ltd.** (✆ **242/362-1574;** www.bahamasoutdoors.com) takes you on a 5km (3-mile) ride along scenic forest and shoreline trails in the Coral Harbour area on the island's southwestern coast. New Providence resident Carolyn Wardle, an expert on the region's ecology, bird life, and history, provides ongoing commentary. The itinerary follows a series of easy trails, usually on hard-packed earth, along seashores and through pink forests. En route, you'll see sleepy Adelaide Village (settled by freed slaves in the 1830s) and spot local birds, either with the naked eye or aided by binoculars. Shorts and a T-shirt are the recommended attire. Tours rarely include more than a half-dozen participants at a time; most are morning events that last around 4 hours. The cost is $69 to $109 per person; there is a two-person minimum.

If you'd like to go it alone, know that some of the major hotels on Paradise Beach and Cable Beach rent bicycles to their guests. You can bike along Cable Beach or along the beachfront at Paradise Island, but roads through downtown Nassau are too narrow, and traffic too congested, to make the ride genuinely pleasant or even particularly safe.

Boat Cruises

A number of operators offer cruises from the harbors around New Providence, with trips ranging from daytime voyages—for snorkeling, picnicking, sunning, and swimming—to sunset and moonlight cruises.

Barefoot Sailing Cruises, Bay Shore Marina, on East Bay Street (© 242/393-0820; www.barefootsailingcruises.com), operates the 12m (41-ft.) *Wind Dance,* which leaves for all-day cruises involving many sailing and snorkeling possibilities. This is your best bet if you're seeking a more romantic cruise and don't want 100 people aboard. The cruises usually stop at Rose Island, a charming, picture-perfect spot with an uncrowded beach and palm trees. You can also sail on a ketch, the 17m (56-ft.) *Riding High.* Cruise options are plentiful, including sailing, snorkeling, and exploring for $75 per person for a half-day and $115 for a full day. A 2-hour sunset cruise, departing between 5 and 8pm two to three times a week (depending on the season, the weather, and advance bookings), costs $65 per person.

The *Flying Cloud,* Paradise Island West Dock (© 242/394-5067; www.flyingcloud.info), is a twin-hulled sailing catamaran that carries 50 people for day and sunset trips. It's a good bet for those who want a more intimate cruise and shy away from the heavy volume carried aboard the Majestic Tours catamarans (see below). Snorkeling equipment is included in the cost, which is $70 per person for a half-day charter. A 2½-hour sunset cruise also goes for $70. Evening bookings are on Monday, Wednesday, and Friday. On Sunday, a 5-hour cruise leaves at 10am and costs $85 per person.

Majestic Tours, Hillside Manor, Cumberland Street (© 242/322-2606; http://majestictoursbahamas.com), books 3-hour cruises on two of the biggest catamarans in the Atlantic, offering views of the water, sun, sand, and outlying reefs. It, too, makes stops at Rose Island. This is the biggest and most professionally run of the cruise boats, and it's an affordable option, but we feel there are just too many other passengers aboard. An onboard cash bar keeps the drinks flowing. The *Yellow Bird* (℃ **242/322-2606**) is suitable for up to 110 passengers and departs from Prince George Wharf in downtown Nassau, just behind the Straw Market; ask for the exact departure point when you make your reservation. The tour lasts 4 hours and includes lunch, drinks, and snorkel gear. The cost is $25 per adult and $8 ages 3 to 12. Another boat, the *Robinson Crusoe*, holds 200 passengers. On Wednesday, Friday, and Sunday, cruises run from 10am to 4:30pm, costing $60 for adults and $35 for kids 4 to 12. Sunset dinner cruises run from 7 to 10pm on Tuesday and Friday; the cost is $60 for adults, half-price for children.

Fishing

Fishing choices are plentiful: You can troll for wahoo, tuna, and marlin in the deep sea, or cast in the shallows for snapper, grouper, and yellowtail. Anchoring and bottom-fishing are calmer options. May to August are the best months to catch oceanic bonito and the blackfin tuna, June and July for blue marlin, and November through February for the wahoo found in reefy areas. Arrangements for fishing trips can be made at any of the big hotels, but unfortunately, there's a hefty price tag.

Born Free Charters (℃ **242/393-4144;** www.bornfreefishing.com), one of the most reliable companies, maintains a fleet of three vessels, each between 11 and 14m long (36–46 ft.), that can seat six comfortably. You can rent them for a half-day ($600–$800) or a full day ($1,200–$1,600). Each additional person pays $50. We recommend this company because it offers so many types of fishing and gives lots of leeway regarding where you want to fish and how much time you want to spend.

Occasionally, boat owners will configure themselves and their boats as businesses for deep-sea fishing. Unless you're dealing with a genuinely experienced guide, however, your fishing trip may or may not be a success. **John Pratt** has emerged over the years as one of the most consistently reliable deep-sea fishermen. He maintains a 14m (46-ft.) fishing boat, making it available for full- or half-day deep-sea fishing excursions. It docks every night at the island's largest marina, the 150-slip **Nassau Yacht Haven Marina,** on East Bay Street (℃ **242/393-8173** or 242/422-0364; www.nassauyachthaven.com), where a member of the staff will direct you. Alternatively, you can call ℃ **242/422-0364** to speak to Mr. Pratt directly. It takes about 20 minutes of boat travel to reach an offshore point where dolphin and wahoo may or may not be biting, depending on a raft of complicated seasonal factors. *Note:* These trips need to be booked several weeks in advance.

Golf

Some of the country's best golfing is in Nassau and on nearby Paradise Island (p. 110). Although "dormant," or storm-damaged, courses on the extreme western end of New Providence might one day be rejuvenated, at press time, the only functioning golf course on New Providence Island that is open to nonmembers is the **Cable Beach Golf Club ★★**, West Bay Street, Cable Beach (© 242/677-4175; http://crystalpalacevacations.com). An intricately designed 18-hole, 5,901m (6,453-yd.), par-71 championship course, it benefited from a major redesign between 2000 and 2003. The makeover reshaped the fairways, repositioned putting greens, and introduced new hazards and water-lined holes throughout two-thirds of its layout. Better year-round playing conditions were ensured by introducing a salt-tolerant grass (paspalum) that is greener, firmer, and more upright, withstanding the salty breezes and tropical heat while providing a premium putting surface. The alterations were overseen by veteran designer Fred M. Settle, Jr.

Many of the players who tee off are guests of hotels on Cable Beach. Year-round greens fees are $75 for guests of the Sheraton or Wyndham resorts, $100 to $130 for those staying elsewhere. Greens fees include the use of an electric golf cart.

Horseback Riding

Windsor Equestrian Centre & Happy Trails Stables, Coral Harbour, on the southwest shore (© 242/362-1820; www.bahamahorse.com or www.windsorequestriancentre.com), offers 90-minute horseback trail rides, which are limited to a maximum of eight riders at a time, for $150 per person. The price includes free transportation to and from your hotel. The stables are signposted from the Lynden Pindling International Airport, which is 3km (1¾ miles) away. Children must be 12 and older, riders must weigh less than 91kg (201 lb.), and reservations are required.

Snorkeling & Scuba Diving

There's great snorkeling off most of New Providence's shore, especially at **Love Beach.** Most hotels and resorts will rent or loan snorkeling equipment to guests. Several of the companies mentioned under "Boat Cruises" (p. 71) offer snorkel trips. Also see "Easy Side Trips to Nearby Islands" (p. 82) for descriptions of additional snorkeling excursions.

Our favorite snorkel site is **Goulding Cay,** off the island's western tip. Underwater, you'll find a field of hard corals, especially the elegant elkhorn. The clear waters and shallow coral heads make it ideal for filmmakers. In fact, it's been featured in many films, from a number of James Bond movies to *20,000 Leagues Under the Sea.* More elkhorn coral is found to the south at **Southwest Reef,** which also shelters stunning star coral in water less than 2.4m (8 ft.) deep. To the north is **Fish Hotel,** which is not much on coral but graced with large schools of fish, especially red snapper, jacks, and grunts.

There are more dive sites around New Providence than you can see in one visit, but a few of our recommendations are: the intriguing **Shark Wall ★★**, 16km (10 miles) off the coast; the **Rose Island Reefs;** the **Southwest Reef; Razorback;** and **Booby Rock Reef.** Dive outfitters can also lead you to many old shipwrecks off the coast, along with caves and cliffs. Wrecks include the *Mahoney* and *Alcora,* plus the wreck featured in the James Bond film *Never Say Never Again.* Divers can also explore the airplane propeller used in another Bond film, *Thunderball.* All outfitters will take you to one or more of these sites.

Bahamas Divers, Nassau Yacht Haven Marina, on East Bay Street (*C* **800/398-3483** in the U.S., or 242/393-5644; www. bahamadivers.com), offers packages that include a half-day of snorkeling at offshore reefs for $50 per person, or a half-day scuba trip with experienced, certified divers for between $70 and $129, depending on the destination. Half-day excursions for certified divers to deeper outlying reefs, drop-offs, and blue holes can be arranged, usually for $129 for a two-tank dive. Novice divers sometimes sign up for a carefully supervised course that includes instruction with scuba equipment in a swimming pool, followed by a shallow shorefront dive accompanied by an instructor, also for $109 per person. Participants receive free transportation from their hotel to the boats. Children must be 10 and older, and reservations are required, especially during the holiday season.

Stuart Cove's Dive Bahamas, on Southwest Bay Street, South Ocean (*C* **800/879-9832** in the U.S. or 242/362-4171; www.stuartcove.com), is about 10 minutes from top dive sites, including the coral reefs, wrecks, and underwater airplane structure featured in James Bond thrillers. For the island's most exciting underwater adventure, divers head to the *Caribe Breeze* **wreck,** depicted in the film *Open Water.* Here the staff feed reef sharks some 15m (49 ft.) below the water; from a position of safety, divers in full scuba gear witness the show. Steep sea walls and the Porpoise Pen Reefs (named for Flipper) are also on the agenda. A two-tank dive in the morning costs $109; an all-day program goes for $155. All prices for boat dives include tanks, weights, and belts. An open-water certification course starts at $960. Bring along two friends, and the price drops to $615 per person. Three-hour escorted boat snorkeling trips cost $65; children 11 and under are included for $30. A special feature is a series of shark-dive experiences priced at $150. At **Shark Arena,** divers kneel while a dive master feeds the toothsome predators off a long pole. On the **Shark Buoy** dive at a depth of about 9m (30 ft.), sharks swim among divers while the dive master feeds them.

SEEING THE SIGHTS

Most of Nassau can be explored on foot, beginning at **Rawson Square** in the center, where Bahamian fishers unload a variety of produce and seafood—crates of mangoes, oranges, tomatoes, and limes, plus lots of crimson-lipped conch. To experience this slice of Bahamian life, go any morning Monday through Saturday before noon.

The best way to see some of Nassau's major public buildings is to take a walking tour (p. 81), which will give you not only an overview of the historic highlights, but also an overall feel for the city. After that, concentrate on specific sights you'd like to take in; Ardastra Gardens and Coral Island Bahamas are notable options.

The Top Attractions

Ardastra Gardens, Zoo & Conservation Center ★ The main attraction of the Ardastra Gardens, almost 2 hectares (5 acres) of lush tropical plants about 1.5km (1 mile) west of downtown Nassau near Fort Charlotte, is the parading flock of **pink flamingos.** The Caribbean flamingo, national bird of The Bahamas, had almost disappeared by the early 1940s, but was brought back to significant numbers through the efforts of the National Trust. They now flourish in the rookery on Great Inagua. A flock of these exotic feathered creatures has been trained to march in drill formation, responding to human commands with long-legged precision. The flamingos perform daily at 10:30am, 2:10pm, and 4:10pm.

Other exotic wildlife here include boa constrictors (very tame), macaws, kinkajous (honey bears) from Central and South America, peacocks and peahens, capuchin monkeys, iguanas, lemurs, margays, brown-headed tamarins (monkeys), and a crocodile. There are also numerous waterfowl in Swan Lake, including black swans from Australia and several species of wild ducks. Parrot feedings take place at 11am, 1:30pm, and 3:30pm.

You can get a good look at Ardastra's flora by walking along the signposted paths. Many of the more interesting and exotic trees bear plaques listing their names.

Chippingham Rd. ℂ **242/323-5806.** www.ardastra.com. Admission $15 adults, $7.50 children 4-12. Daily 9am–4:15pm. Bus: 10.

Fifteen Miles of Great Scenery for a Buck

In Nassau, local tourism officials are promoting a bus route, the no. 10, that takes you on a road trip that covers 15 scenic miles along West Bay Street, passing historic forts, ocean vistas, well-to-do neighborhoods, secluded coves, and strands of golden-sand beaches. The cost is only $1 per ride, a super bargain compared to the other means of transport used by visitors—chauffeured limos, horse-and-carriage rides, loaded bus tours, rented cars, or even motor bikes.

National Art Gallery of The Bahamas ★   At long last, this archipelago nation has a showcase in which to display the works of its talented artists. In a restored 18th-century building in the center of Nassau, the gallery features Bahamian art, which, as an entity, has existed for only 50 years. Curators claim that the present collection is only the nucleus of a larger, long-range strategy to beef up the present number of works. Most of the paintings on exhibit are divided into historical and contemporary collections. Pioneering Bahamian artists are honored, as are younger and more modern painters. Among island artists, Amos Ferguson is one of the most acclaimed. His somewhat naïve yet sophisticated technique is at its best in the painting *Snowbirds:* He used house paint on cardboard to create a remarkable portrait. Maxwell Taylor and Antonius Roberts are two other heavily featured Bahamian painters.

Villa Doyle, W. Hill St. in downtown Nassau. ☎ **242/328-5800.** www.nagb.org. bs. Admission $5 adults, $3 seniors and students, free for children 12 and under. Tues–Sat 10am–4pm. Bus: 10.

Seaworld Explorer ★   If you're curious about life below the waves but aren't a strong swimmer, hop aboard this 45-person submarine. Tours last 90 minutes and include 45 to 55 minutes of actual underwater travel at depths of about 3.5m (11 ft.). Big windows allow big views of a protected ecology zone offshore from Paradise Island Airport. The remainder of the time is devoted to an above-water tour of landmarks on either side of the channel that separates Nassau from Paradise Island.

W. Bay St. at Elizabeth Ave. ☎ **242/356-2548.** www.seaworldtours.com. Reservations required. $45 adults, $25 children 2–12. Tours Tues, Wed, Fri, and Sat at 9:30am, 11:30am, and 1:30pm year-round; call for latest details. Bus: 10.

More Attractions

Balcony House   This landmark house's original design exemplifies late-18th-century Southeast American architecture. The pink

Nassau Sights

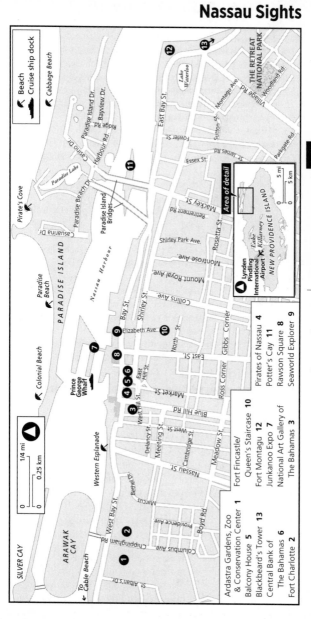

SILVER CAY

ARAWAK CAY

Cable Beach

Colonial Beach

Paradise Beach

PARADISE ISLAND

Cabbage Beach

Pirate's Cove

Paradise Lake

Nassau Harbour

Western Esplanade

Prince George Wharf

Casuarina Dr.

Casino Dr.

Paradise Island Dr.

Ridge Rd.

Harbour Rd.

Bayview Dr.

Paradise Beach Dr.

Paradise Island Bridges

East Bay St.

Fowler St.

Essex St.

St. James Rd.

Mackey St.

Retirement Rd.

Shirley Park Ave.

Rosetta St.

Montrose Ave.

Mount Royal Ave.

Collins Ave.

Shirley St.

Bay St.

Elizabeth Ave.

North St.

East St.

East Hill St.

Market St.

Blue Hill Rd.

West Hill St.

Delancy St.

Meeting St.

West St.

Cambridge St.

Meadow St.

Nassau St.

Marcus

Bethel Dr.

West Bay St.

Boyd Rd.

Providence Ave.

Chippingham Rd.

Columbus Ave.

St. Alban's Dr.

Gibbs Corner

Ross Corner

Village Rd.

Montagu Ave.

Sutton St.

Woodland Rd.

Parkgate Rd.

Lake Waterloo

THE RETREAT NATIONAL PARK

Key:
- Beach
- Cruise ship dock

Area of detail

NEW PROVIDENCE ISLAND

Lake Killarney

Lynden Pindling International Airport

0   5 mi
0   5 km

0   1/4 mi
0   0.25 km

Ardastra Gardens, Zoo & Conservation Center **1**
Balcony House **5**
Blackbeard's Tower **13**
Central Bank of The Bahamas **6**
Fort Charlotte **2**
Fort Fincastle/ Queen's Staircase **10**
Fort Montagu **12**
Junkanoo Expo **7**
National Art Gallery of The Bahamas **3**
Pirates of Nassau **4**
Potter's Cay **11**
Rawson Square **8**
Seaworld Explorer **9**

77

TO MARKET, TO MARKET AT
potter's cay

One of the liveliest places in Nassau during the day is **Potter's Cay,** a native market that thrives beneath the Paradise Island Bridge. From the Out Islands, fishing boats and heavily laden sloops arrive early in the morning to unload the day's catch. Spiny lobster is the most expensive seafood, but grouper reigns supreme along with fresh crab, jack, and mackerel.

If grouper is king, then "sweet, sexy conch," as the locals say, is queen. Vendors make the freshest conch salad right on the spot; if you haven't eaten the delicacy before, this is the place to try it.

What we don't like to see are fishmongers chopping up sea turtles, a highly endangered species. However, the vendors are not of the politically correct sort, and they're more interested in catering to the Bahamians' lifelong love of turtle flesh than they are in preserving the species for future generations.

Not just fish is sold here. Sloops from the Out Islands also bring in cartons of freshly harvested vegetables, including the fiery hot peppers so beloved by locals, along with an array of luscious exotic fruits. **Tip:** Many of these vendors have a wicked sense of humor and will offer you a taste of tamarind, claiming it's the "sweetest taste on God's earth." Invariably, tricked visitors spit it out: The taste is horrendously offensive.

You can also see mail boats leaving and coming to this quay. Watching their frenetic departure or arrival is one of the island's more amusing scenes.

two-story structure is named for its overhanging and much-photographed balcony. Restored in the 1990s, the house has been returned to its original design, recapturing a historic period. The mahogany staircase inside is thought to have been salvaged from a wrecked ship in the 1800s. At press time, the house was closed for renovations, but might be open by the time of your visit. Call in advance before you go.

Trinity Place and Market St. (📞 **242/302-2621.** Free admission, but donations advised. Mon–Wed and Fri 9:30am–1pm and 2–4:30pm; Thurs 10am–1pm. Bus: 10.

Blackbeard's Tower These crumbling remains of a watchtower are said to have been used by the infamous pirate Edward Teach in the 17th century. The ruins are only mildly interesting—there isn't much trace of buccaneering. What's interesting is the view: With a little imagination, you can almost see Blackbeard, who also purportedly lived here (though this is hardly well documented), peering out at unsuspecting ships.

8km/5 miles east of Fort Montagu. No phone. Free admission. Daily 24 hr. Reachable by jitney.

Central Bank of The Bahamas   The nerve center that governs the archipelago's financial transactions is also the venue for a year-round cycle of temporary exhibitions of paintings that represent the nation's multifaceted artistic talent. The cornerstone of the building was laid by Prince Charles on July 9, 1973, when the country became independent from Britain. Queen Elizabeth II officially inaugurated the bank in 1975.

Trinity Place and Frederick St. ☎ **242/302-2600.** www.centralbankbahamas.com. Free admission. Mon–Fri 9:30am–4:30pm. Bus: 10.

Fort Charlotte   Begun in 1787, Fort Charlotte is the largest of Nassau's three major defense buildings, built with plenty of dungeons. It used to command the western harbor. Named after King George III's consort, it was built by Gov. Lord Dunmore, who was also the last royal governor of New York and Virginia. Its 42 cannons (only seven remain on-site) never fired a shot—at least, not at an invader. Within the complex are underground passages, which can be viewed on a free tour (guides are very happy to accept a tip).

Off W. Bay St. on Chippingham Rd. ☎ **242/325-9186.** Free admission. Daily 8am–3pm. Bus: 10.

The Secret Garden

The **Retreat,** Village Road (☎ **242/393-1317;** www.bnt.bs), on the southern outskirts of downtown Nassau, is the home of The Bahamas National Trust. A clapboard-sided green-and-white building, it was originally conceived as the homestead of the Langlois family and purchased from them by the National Trust in 1925. Whereas there's nothing of particular interest inside the house (it contains mostly workaday offices), its gardens are worth a visit. They comprise 4.4 hectares (11 acres) of the most unspoiled greens on New Providence and contain about 200 species of exotic palm trees. The grounds, which are for the most part flat, can be navigated with a map available on-site. A gift shop sells books and memorabilia approved by and associated with the National Trust. Visit Monday through Friday from 9am to 5pm; admission is $2 for adults and $1 for children 5 to 12 and students up to 18.

MEET THE bahamians

The **People-to-People Program,** established by the Ministry of Tourism, provides an opportunity for visitors to learn more about the culture of The Bahamas by interacting with Bahamians themselves. The program matches visitors, often entire families, with more than 1,500 Bahamian volunteers of similar ages and interests for a day or evening activity, which could include boating, fishing, shopping at a local outdoor market, or visiting them in their home for a traditional meal. These encounters have resulted in lasting friendships. To participate in the program in Nassau/Paradise Island, e-mail peopletopeople@ bahamas.com. To participate in the program on Grand Bahama Island, e-mail peopletopeople@gbmot.com; www.bahamas.com/ bahamas/people-people.

Fort Fincastle   Reached by climbing the Queen's Staircase, this fort was constructed in 1793 by Lord Dunmore, the royal governor. You can take an elevator ride to the top and walk on the observation floor (a 38m-high/125-ft. water tower and lighthouse) for a panoramic view of the harbor. The tower is New Providence's highest point. This fort's so-called bow is patterned like a Mississippi paddle-wheel steamer; it was built to defend Nassau against a possible invasion, though no shot was ever fired.

Though the ruins hardly compete with the view, you can walk around on your own here. Be wary, however, of the very persistent young men who will try to show you around; they'll try to hustle you, but you really don't need a guide to see some old cannons.

Elizabeth Ave. ✆ **242/322-7500.** Free admission. Mon–Sat 8am–5pm. Bus: 10 or 17.

Fort Montagu   Built in 1741, this fort—the island's oldest— stands guard at the eastern entrance to Nassau's harbor. The Americans captured it in 1776 during the Revolutionary War. Less interesting than Fort Charlotte and Fort Fincastle (described above), the ruins of this place are mainly for fort buffs. Regrettably, it can be visited only from the outside, but many visitors find the nearby park, with well-maintained lawns, plenty of shade, and vendors peddling local handicrafts, more interesting than the fort itself.

Eastern Rd. No phone. Free admission. No regular hours. Bus: 10 or 17.

Junkanoo Expo   This museum is dedicated to Junkanoo—the colorful, musical, and surreal festival that takes place on December 26, when Nassau explodes into sounds, celebrations, and a sea of masks. It is the Bahamian equivalent of Mardi Gras in New Orleans. If you can't visit Nassau for Junkanoo, seeing this exhibition is the next best thing. You'll get a good idea of the lavish costumes and floats used by revelers during this annual celebration. The bright colors and costume designs are impressive, if for no other reason than their sheer size. Some of the costumes are nearly as big as the small parade floats—but the difference is that only one person wears and carries each one. The Expo is in an old Customs warehouse at the entrance to Nassau's wharf. A souvenir boutique sells a variety of Junkanoo handicrafts and paintings.

Prince George Wharf, Festival Place. ℭ **242/356-2731.** Admission $2. Mon–Sat 10am–4pm. Bus: 10.

Pirates of Nassau ☺   This museum, which opened in 2003, celebrates the dubious "golden age of piracy" (1690–1720). Nassau was once a bustling, robust town where buccaneers grew rich from gold and other goods plundered at sea. Known as a paradise for pirates, it also attracted various rogues and the wild women who flooded into the port to entertain them—for a price, of course. The museum re-creates those bawdy days in exhibits illustrating pirate lore. You can walk through the belly of a pirate ship, the *Revenge,* as you hear "pirates" plan their next attack, smell the dampness of a dungeon, and even hear the final prayer of an ill-fated victim before he walks the gangplank. It's fairly cheesy, but fun for kids. Exhibits also tell the saga of Capt. Woodes Rogers, who was sent by the English crown to suppress pirates in the Caribbean.

Marlborough and George sts. ℭ **242/356-3759.** www.pirates-of-nassau.com. Admission $12 adults, $6 children 4–17, free for children 3 and under. Mon–Sat 9am–6pm; Sun 9am–noon. Bus: 10.

Organized Tours

There's a lot to see in Nassau. Many tour options can be customized to suit your taste and take you through the colorful historic city and outlying sights of interest.

Walking tours, arranged by the Ministry of Tourism, leave from the tourist information booth at Festival Place every day intermittently and, depending on demand, at 10am. Tours last an hour and include descriptions of some of the city's most venerable buildings, with commentaries on Nassau's history, customs, and traditions. The cost is $10 per person for all ages. Call ℭ **242/395-8382** to confirm that tours are running. Reservations are helpful but not essential.

Majestic Tours, Hillside Manor, Cumberland Street (ℭ **242/322-2606;** http://majestictoursbahamas.com), offers a number of trips, both night and day. A 2½-hour city-and-country

Going Over the Hill

Few visitors make the trip anymore, but it used to be a tradition to go over the hill to Nassau's most colorful area. **"Over-the-Hill"** is the actual name of this poor residential district, where descendants of former slaves built rainbow-hued houses, leaving the most desirable lands around the harbor to the rich folk. This, not the historic core of Nassau around Rawson Square, is truly the heart of Bahamian-African culture. The thump of the Junkanoo-Goombay drum can be heard here day and night. The area never sleeps, or so it is said—and certainly not on Sunday morning, when you can drive by the churches and hear hell and damnation promised loudly to all sinners and backsliders.

This fascinating part of Nassau begins .5km (⅓ mile) south on Blue Hill Road, which starts at the exclusive Graycliff Hotel. But once you're "Over-the-Hill," you're a long way from the hotel's vintage wine and Cuban cigars. Some people—usually savvy store owners from abroad—come here to buy local handicrafts from individual vendors. The area can be explored on foot (during the day *only*), but many visitors prefer to drive. *Note:* This area is well worth a visit, but keep your eyes open; most of Nassau's criminal incidents happen in this part of town.

tour leaves daily at 2pm, visiting major points of interest, including forts, the Queen's Staircase, the water tower, and the former site of the Straw Market (passing but not entering it). The cost is $45 per person. An extended city-and-country tour also leaves daily at 2pm and includes the Ardastra Gardens; the cost is $55 per person, half-price for children 12 and under. Combination tours depart Tuesday to Thursday at 10am and include all the sights listed on the first tour above, plus the Retreat Gardens and lunch. These cost $70 per person, $48 for children 12 and under. Many hotels have a Majestic Tours Hospitality Desk in the lobby, where you can get information and make reservations for these tours. Other hotels have brochures and can tell you where to sign up.

Easy Side Trips to Nearby Islands

Remote **Rose Island** is a sliver of land poking out of the sea just northeast of Nassau's Prince George waterfront. Shelling is one of the lures of this little islet. If you want to escape the crowds of Nassau for an island retreat, you can take a boat here, relax in a hammock, snorkel among the coral reefs, and enjoy the white-sand beach before and after a sizzling barbecue lunch with white wine. Excursions to Rose Island are offered by **Barefoot Sailing**

Cruises, Bay Shore Marina, East Bay Street (𝒞 **242/393-0820;** www.barefootsailingcruises.com), and **Majestic Tours,** Hillside Manor, Cumberland Street (𝒞 **242/322-2606;** www.majestic holidays.com). With Majestic Tours, expect to pay $45 to $70 per adult for a trip lasting from 10am to 4:30pm. For more information on boat cruises, see p. 71.

If you want to see the Exuma island chain on a daylong excursion, try **Powerboat Adventures,** East Bay Street (𝒞 **242/363-1466;** www.powerboatadventures.com), which provides an excellent overview of the area. The boat departs Nassau Harbour at 9am and arrives in the Exuma Cays about an hour later. There are several stops, including snorkeling at a private cay (Ship Channel), visiting the iguanas on Allan's Cay, feeding stingrays along the shore, and enjoying a barbecue lunch. A full bar is available all day, and drinks are included in the cost, which is $199 for adults and $140 for children 2 to 12. Transportation from your hotel to the port of embarkation is included. The experience finishes around 5pm.

SHOPPING

Nassau's shopping options are more upscale than they once were, with the arrival of swanky jewelers and a burgeoning fashion scene. There are still plenty of T-shirts claiming that "It's Better in The Bahamas," but you can also find diamonds and platinum watches. The range of goods is staggering; in the midst of all the junk souvenirs, you'll see an increasing array of china, crystal, watches, and clothing from such names as Herend, Lalique, Baccarat, Bally, and Ferragamo.

But can you really save money compared to what you would pay stateside? The answer is "yes" on some items, "no" on others. If you're contemplating a major purchase, such as a Swiss watch or expensive perfume, it's best to do some research in your local discount outlets or online before you leave home. While the alleged 30% to 50% discount off stateside prices might apply in some cases, it's not true in others. Certain cameras and electronic equipment, for instance, are listed in The Bahamas at, say, 20% below the manufacturer's "suggested retail price." That sounds good, except the manufacturer's suggested price might be a lot higher than what you'd actually pay in retail stores back home.

There are no import duties on 11 categories of luxury goods, including china, crystal, fine linens, jewelry, leather goods, photographic equipment, watches, and fragrances. Antiques, of course, are exempt from import duty worldwide. But even though prices are "duty free," you can still end up spending more on an item in The Bahamas than you would back home; it's a tricky situation.

journey **INTO THE WILD**

Take a day off from the beach and join one of the wildlife tours offered by **Bahamas Outdoors** (✆ **242/362-1574** or 242/457-0329; www.bahamasoutdoors.com). Carolyn Wardle, president of the organization and a passionate conservationist, is a great source for insight into the best of the island's remaining wildlife habitats. Consider signing on for a half-day tour, priced at $69 per person, or a full-day tour, $109 per person. Tours rarely include more than a half-dozen participants and can be conducted either in a vehicle (with frequent stops along the way for closer observation) or on an all-terrain bike. Depending on your stated preferences, the focus of your island tour could include birds, native flora and fauna, butterflies, national parks, historic sites, or a combination. Access to binoculars and a battered collection of field guides is included. The full-day tours also include a picnic lunch.

It's advisable to make reservations at least a day in advance. Most tours begin in front of the participants' hotel at a prearranged time. Bird-watching tours tend to begin earlier (around 7am) than biking and/or historic and nature tours, which start just a bit later.

A lot of price-fixing seems to be going on in Nassau. For example, a bottle of Chanel perfume is likely to sell for pretty much the same price anywhere, regardless of the store. Don't try to bargain with the salespeople in Nassau stores as you would with merchants at the local market. The price marked is the price you must pay.

How much you can take home depends on your country of origin. For details about Customs requirements, see "Customs" in chapter 6.

The principal shopping areas are **Bay Street** and its side streets downtown, as well as the shops in the arcades of hotels. Not many street numbers are used along Bay Street; just look for store signs.

Brass & Copper

Brass & Leather Shops   With two branches on Charlotte Street, this local chain offers English brass, handbags, luggage, briefcases, belts, scarves, and ties from such designers as Furla, Tumi, Briggs & Riley, and others. If you look carefully, you can find some good buys here. 12 Charlotte St., btw. Bay and Shirley sts. ✆ **242/322-3806.** www.brass-leather.com.

Cigars

Remember, U.S. citizens are prohibited from bringing Cuban cigars back home because of the trade embargo. If you buy them, enjoy them in The Bahamas.

Graycliff Cigar Company ★ In 1994, an emigrant business-man from Lake Como, Italy, moved to Nassau to supervise his investment, the Graycliff Hotel, and liked it so much there that he decided to stay. Eventually, he established the country's best-known and most respected cigar factory. It employs about 16 mostly Cuban-expatriate cigar rollers, who, within full view, use non-Cuban tobacco to create 10 different styles of sought-after cigars. These are sold on the premises and priced around $5 to $30 each, depending on quality. There's also a 41cm (16-in.) "big bamboo," priced at $50, that makes whoever smokes it look almost like a caricature, and that is guaranteed to get its consumer very, very high. Best of all, these cigars, crafted with the finest techniques, are completely legal to import back into the U.S. 12 West Hill St. ℂ **242/302-9150.** www.graycliff.com.

Crystal, China & Gems

Solomon's Mines Evoking the title of a 1950s MGM flick, this is one grand shopping adventure. This flagship store, with many branches, is one of the largest duty-free retailers in the Caribbean, a tradition since 1908. Entering the store is like making a shopping trip to London or Paris. The amount of merchandise is staggering, from a $50,000 Patek Philippe watch to one of the largest collections of Herend china in the West. Most prices on timepieces, china, jewelry, crystal, Herend, Baccarat, Ferragamo, Bally, Lalique, and other names are discounted 15% to 30%—and some of the merchandise and oddities here are not available in the U.S., such as the stunning African diamonds. The selections of Italian, French, and American fragrances and skin-care products are the best in the archipelago. Bay St. ℂ 242/356-6920. A 2nd location is at Charlotte and Bay sts. ℂ **242/325-7554.**

Fashion

Cole's of Nassau This boutique offers the most extensive selection of designer fashions in Nassau. Women can find everything from swimwear to formal gowns, sportswear to hosiery. Cole's also sells gift items, sterling-silver designer and costume jewelry, hats, shoes, bags, scarves, and belts. Parliament St. ℂ **242/322-8393.**

Fendi This is Nassau's only outlet for the well-crafted accessories made by this famous luxe-goods company. With handbags, luggage, shoes, watches, wallets, and portfolios to choose from, the selection may well solve some of your gift-giving quandaries. Charlotte and Bay sts. ℂ **242/322-6300.**

Handicrafts

Sea Grape Boutique   This is one of the island's genuinely fine gift shops, with an inventory of exotic decorative items that you'll probably find fascinating. It includes jewelry crafted from fossilized coral, sometimes with sharks' teeth embedded inside, and clothing that's well suited to the sometimes-steamy climate. W. Bay St. (next to Travellers Rest). ℂ **242/327-1308.**

Jewelry

Colombian Emeralds   Famous around the Caribbean, this international outlet is not limited to emeralds, although its selection of that stone is the best in The Bahamas. Here you'll also find an impressive display of diamonds and other precious gems. The gold jewelry here sells for about half the price it does stateside, and many of the gems are discounted 20% to 30%. Ask about the "cybershopping" program. Bay St. ℂ **242/326-1661.** www.columbian emeralds.com.

John Bull   The jewelry department here offers classic selections from Tiffany & Co., cultured pearls from Mikimoto, the creations of David Yurman and Carrera y Carrera, Greek and Roman coin jewelry, and Spanish gold and silver pieces. It's the best name in the business. The store also features a wide selection of watches, cameras, perfumes, cosmetics, leather goods, and accessories. It is one of the country's best places to buy a Gucci or Cartier watch. Bay St. ℂ **242/322-4253.** www.johnbull.com.

Leather

In addition to the stores mentioned below, another good source for leather goods is the **Brass & Leather Shops,** described under "Brass & Copper," above.

Gucci   This shop, opposite Rawson Square, is the best place to buy leather goods in Nassau. The wide selection includes handbags, wallets, luggage, briefcases, gift items, scarves, ties, eveningwear for men and women, umbrellas, shoes, sandals, watches, and perfume, all by Italy's famous producer of luxury items. Saffrey Sq., Bay St., at Bank Lane. ℂ **242/325-0561.**

Leather Masters   This well-known retail outlet carries an internationally known collection of leather bags, luggage, and accessories

markets IN NASSAU

The **Nassau International Bazaar** consists of some 30 shops selling international goods in a new arcade. A pleasant place for browsing, the million-dollar complex runs from Bay Street down to the waterfront (near Prince George Wharf). With cobbled alleyways and garreted storefronts, it looks like a European village.

Prince George Plaza, on Bay Street, is popular with cruise-ship passengers. Many fine shops (Gucci, for example) occupy space here. When you get tired of shopping, dine at the open-air rooftop restaurant that overlooks Bay Street.

by Ted Lapidus, Lanvin, Lancel, Etienne Aigner, and I Santi of Italy, plus luggage by Piel and Travel Pro. Non-leather items include pens, lighters, watches by Colibri, silk scarves, neckties, and cigar accessories. 8 Parliament St. ✆ **242/322-7597.**

Linens

The Linen Shop This is Nassau's best outlet for linens, featuring beautifully embroidered bedding, Irish handkerchiefs, and tablecloths. Look also for the most exquisite children's clothing and christening gowns in town. Ironmongery Building, Bay St., near Charlotte St. ✆ **242/322-4266.**

Perfumes & Cosmetics

Nassau has several good perfume outlets, notably **John Bull** and **Little Switzerland,** which stock a variety of merchandise beyond just perfume.

Beauty Spot The country's largest cosmetics shop, this outlet sells duty-free cosmetics by Lancôme, Chanel, YSL, Elizabeth Arden, Estée Lauder, Clinique, Christian Dior, and Biotherm, among others. It also operates facial salons. Bay and Frederick sts. ✆ **242/322-5930.**

Perfume Bar This little gem has exclusive rights to market Boucheron. It also stocks the Clarins line (though not exclusively). Bay St. ✆ **242/322-7216.**

Perfume Shop In the heart of Nassau, within walking distance of the cruise ships, the Perfume Shop offers duty-free savings on world-famous perfumes for women and men, including Eternity, Obsession, and Chanel. Bay and Frederick sts. ✆ **242/322-2375.**

NEW PROVIDENCE AFTER DARK

Gone are the days when tuxedo-clad gentlemen and elegantly gowned ladies drank and danced the night away at such famous nightclubs as the Yellow Bird and the Big Bamboo. You can still find dancing, along with limbo and calypso, but for most visitors, the major attraction is gambling.

Cultural entertainment in Nassau is limited, though the **Dundas Centre for the Performing Arts** sometimes stages ballets, plays, and musicals. Call _C_ **242/393-3728** to find out what's scheduled during your visit.

Rolling the Dice

As another option, you can easily head over to Paradise Island and drop into the massive, spectacular casino at **Atlantis** (p. 114).

Wyndham Nassau Resort & Crystal Palace Casino This dazzling casino is the only one on New Providence Island and is now run by the Wyndham Nassau Resort. Thanks to constant improvements, it stacks up well against the other major casinos of the Caribbean. Incorporating more than 3,250 sq. m (34,983 sq. ft.) into its flashy-looking premises, it's animated, bustling, and filled with the serious business of people having fun with their money and temptations. The gaming room features hundreds of slot machines—only a few of which resemble the low-tech, one-armed bandits that were in vogue 20 years ago. You'll find blackjack tables, roulette wheels, craps tables, a baccarat table, and a sophisticated electronic link to Las Vegas that provides odds on most of the world's major sporting events. There's also a serious commitment to poker. W. Bay St., Cable Beach. _C_ **242/327-6200.** www.wyndham nassauresort.com.

The Club & Music Scene

Club Fluid Set within a two-story building in downtown Nassau, this basement-level nightclub features a baby-blue-and-white interior, dozens of mirrors that are much appreciated by narcissists, two bars, and a dance floor. It attracts an animated crowd of local residents, most of them between 20 and 45, who groove to the reggae, _soca,_ hip-hop, and R&B music. It's open Wednesday through Saturday from 9pm to 2am. W. Bay St., near Frederick St. _C_ **242/356-4691.** Cover $10–$25.

Da Tambrin Tree ★ 👜 If you'd like to escape from the tourist joints and experience a slice of Bahamian life as lived by the locals, head for this nighttime dive. It lies a 10- to 15-minute taxi ride from the center of Nassau. The music is loud and compelling, and the place is the most fun club in Nassau. Something is always happening here, everything from a Wednesday night karaoke and gong show to a jam session with the best DJs on the island. Happy hour begins at 5pm, and the club often stays open until dawn, depending on business. Summerwind Plaza, Harold Rd. ☎ **242/356-7200.** Cover ranges from free to $20 (includes 2 drinks).

Rainforest Theatre Accessible directly from the Crystal Palace Casino on Cable Beach, this 800-seat theater is a major nightlife attraction. Revues tend to be small-scale, relatively restrained, and very definitely on the safe and family-friendly side of the great cultural divide. Fake palm trees and touches of glitter set the scene for the onstage entertainment. Hours vary with the season, the act, and the number of guests booked into the hotel at the time. Billboards located prominently throughout the hotel hawk whoever is headlining at the moment. Crystal Palace Casino, W. Bay St., Cable Beach. ☎ **242/327-6200.** Tickets $32–$40.

The Bar Scene

Charlie's on the Beach/Cocktails & Dreams The focus at this sparsely decorated club is local gossip, calypso and reggae music, and stiff drinks, all of which make for a high-energy night out in Nassau. The setting is a simple warehouselike structure a few blocks west of the British Colonial Hilton, though management warns that during some particularly active weekends (including spring break), the entire venue might move, for the short term, to a larger, as-yet-undetermined location. Open Wednesday and Friday through Sunday from 9pm to 4am. W. Bay St., near Long Wharf Beach. ☎ **242/328-3745.** Free or $15 cover, depending on the night.

Señor Frog's How can you hate a bar that manages to satirize itself as richly as this one does? The interior is deliberately and somewhat claustrophobically overcrowded with frogs, faux palm trees, and battered wooden tables. Choices range from midday salsa and chips to "Let's sample all of the margaritas available on this menu" contests conducted informally among heavy-drinking cruise-ship drop-ins. Expect merengue music (especially on weekends, when tables are pushed aside to form an ersatz dance floor) and a menu loaded with burgers, fajitas, and tacos. W. Bay St., near the British Colonial Hilton. ☎ **242/323-1777.** www.senorfrogs.com. No cover.

PARADISE ISLAND

J ust off Nassau's north shore lies paradise, with a sweeping tropical beach
edged by a luxurious grove of casuarina
trees. Paradise Island's centerpiece is the mammoth
Atlantis Paradise Island Resort & Casino, a pulsing
nightlife mecca and a sightseeing attraction in its own
right. Think Vegas in the Tropics. Away from the resort's
lively casinos, sunsets at The Cloister and strolls in
beautiful Versailles Gardens provide peaceful respite.
Tired of paradise? Cross to Nassau on foot, by boat, or
by car for sightseeing and shopping.

THINGS TO DO Try your luck at the **Atlantis
Paradise Casino,** one of the most imaginatively decorated casinos in the Caribbean. Away from the glitz and
glamor, wander around the statues of the peaceful **Versailles Gardens,** a popular location for weddings. The
sugar-white sand of **Cabbage Beach** invites sunbath-
ing and swimming. For one of the most beautiful pink
and mauve sunsets in all The Bahamas, sit amid stone
remains of the 12th-century French monastery at **The
Cloister.**

SHOPPING The energy from the Atlantis Paradise
Casino spills over at the **Shops at the Atlantis,** an
impressive collection of high-end couture boutiques
and designer emporiums. All the top labels are here,
from Cartier to Versace, alongside fine jewelry, giftware
and perfume. For Bahamian handicrafts and artwork,
browse the shops at **Marina Village.** For cut-price
jewelry, cosmetics and hand-rolled cigars, as well as a
plethora of T-shirts and souvenirs, cross the Paradise
Island Bridge into Nassau and head to **Bay Street.**

NIGHTLIFE & ENTERTAINMENT The razzle-
dazzle of gaming tables and a thousand clanging slot

machines vie for your attention at the lavish **Atlantis Paradise Casino.** Away from the casino, sip cocktails and gawk at yachts in **Marina Village,** squeeze onto a packed dance floor in a flashy club or enjoy a late-night latte in the **Royal Towers**—the tallest and most imaginative edifice in The Bahamas. Dress casually but leave the beachwear in the hotel.

RESTAURANTS & DINING   Paradise Island offers the broadest mix of restaurants in The Bahamas, from elegant beachfront bistros with harbor views to earthy surf-and-turf spots clustered around the **Atlantis Paradise Island Casino.** If you want a brand name, **Nobu** and **Bobby Flay** have a presence. Enjoy gourmet takes on seafood fresh from the Atlantic, broiled grouper amandine, for instance, or Nassau conch chowder. Paradise is pricey, though. Budged-minded visitors may want to cross over the bridge into downtown Nassau.

ORIENTATION
Arriving

Most visitors to Paradise Island arrive in Nassau and commute to Paradise Island by ground transport.

When you arrive at **Lynden Pindling International Airport** (formerly known as Nassau International Airport; see chapter 3 for information on flying into Nassau), you won't find bus service to take you to Paradise Island. Many package deals include hotel transfers from the airport. Otherwise, if you're not renting a car, you'll need to take a taxi. Taxis in Nassau are metered and take cash only; it usually costs around $35 to go from the airport to your hotel. The driver will also ask you to pay the northbound one-way $1 bridge toll, a charge that will be added onto your metered fare at the end of the ride.

Visitor Information

Paradise Island does not have a visitor information office, so refer to the tourist facilities in downtown Nassau (see chapter 3). The concierge or guest-services staff at your hotel can also give you information about local attractions.

Island Layout

Paradise Island's finest beaches lie on the Atlantic (northern) coastline, while the docks, wharves, and marinas are on the southern side. Most of the island's largest and glossiest hotels and restaurants, as well as the casino and a lagoon with landscaped borders, lie west and north of the roundabout. The area east of the roundabout is less congested, with only a handful of smaller hotels, a golf course, the Versailles Gardens, The Cloister, the airport, and many of the island's privately owned villas.

GETTING AROUND

You don't need to rent a car here. Most visitors walk around Paradise Island's most densely developed sections and hire a taxi for the occasional longer haul.

The most popular way to reach nearby Nassau is to **walk across the toll bridge.** There is no charge for pedestrians.

To tour Paradise Island or New Providence by **taxi,** make arrangements with either a taxi driver or your hotel's reception desk. Taxis wait at the entrances to all the major hotels. The hourly rate is about $60 in cars or small vans.

If you are without a car and don't want to take a taxi or walk, you can hop one of the **ferryboats** to Nassau, which leave from the dock on Casino Drive every 30 minutes between 9am and 6pm daily; the 10-minute ride costs $6 one-way. Quicker and easier than a taxi, the ferry deposits you right at Prince George Wharf, in downtown Nassau.

Water taxis also operate between Paradise Island and Nassau's Prince George Wharf. They depart at 15- to 30-minute intervals from 8:30am to 6pm daily. Round-trip fare is $6.

If you're a guest at one of the properties associated with **Atlantis** (see below), hop aboard one of the complimentary **shuttle buses** for drop-offs at any of the resort's accommodations. Atlantis guests can also take a complimentary tour of the island, which departs daily at noon.

Unlike New Providence, no public buses are allowed on Paradise Island.

WHERE TO STAY

In the off season—from mid-April to mid-December—prices are slashed by at least 20% and sometimes a lot more, though the weather isn't as ideal. But because Paradise Island's summer business has increased dramatically, you'll never see some of the 60% reductions that might be offered by cheaper properties in the Greater Nassau area. For inexpensive accommodations, refer to the listings for New Providence Island in chapter 3. Paradise Island isn't cheap!

An Offshore Yoga Retreat

Ex-Beatle George Harrison and a host of other yoga devotees over the years have checked into **Sivananda Ashram Yoga Retreat** (✆ **800/441-2096** or 242/363-2902; fax 242/363-3783; www.sivananda.org), which is reached only by boat from Paradise Island. For some 40 years, it's been completely removed from the rest of Paradise Island's frantic gambling, heady lifestyle, and high prices. Today, the retreat teaches the healing arts and spiritual practices.

Lecturers from all over the world come here to give seminars and practice meditation. When not devoting their time to yoga, guests rest on a lovely sandy beach, all part of a compound that reaches from Nassau Harbour to the Atlantic. Guests attend two daily meditation sessions, the first starting at 5am. Two yoga classes per day are also required, but you're free daily from 10am to 4pm. A boat shuttles guests into Nassau so they can see its sights.

Participants are housed in the simple main house or in small one-room bungalows. The most desirable units, a dozen of them, front the beach. There are also 35 private single rooms, plus seven dormlike spaces. Vegetarian meals are included in the rate of $89 to $99 for a single, $79 to $129 for a double, or $69 to $79 for a three- or four-bed dormitory. Tent space is available for $69 per night.

roof gardens with views. *Tip:* Rooms near the center of the resort are closest to the pools and laundry facilities.

Bayview Dr., Paradise Island, The Bahamas. ✆ **800-WESTERN** (937-8376) or 800/757-1357 in the U.S., or 242/363-2555. Fax 242/363-2370. www.bwbayviewsuites.com. 75 units. Winter $271 1-bedroom suite, $425 town house (for 4), from $445 villa; off-season $200 1-bedroom suite, $335 town house (for 4), from $345 villa. Weekly rates are slightly lower. AE, DC, MC, V. **Amenities:** Lunch-only restaurant; bar; babysitting; 3 outdoor pools; tennis court (lit for night play). *In room:* A/C, TV, hair dryer, kitchen, Wi-Fi (free).

Comfort Suites Paradise Island 🔖 A favorite with honeymooners, this three-story all-suite hotel is across the street from Atlantis and makes a nice alternative to the behemoth. You get all the splash and wonder, but don't have to stay when the cruise-ship crowds descend. Though the hotel has its own pool bar and restaurant, guests are also granted signing privileges at Atlantis's drinking and dining spots, as well as the pool, beach, and sports facilities. Accommodations are priced according to their views: over the island, the pool, or the garden. Bedrooms are standard motel size; the medium-size bathrooms are stocked with beach towels.

Paradise Island Dr., Paradise Island, The Bahamas. ✆ **877/424-6423** in the U.S. or Canada, or 242/363-3680. Fax 242/363-2588. www.comfortsuitespi.com. 228

Very Expensive

Atlantis Paradise Island ★★★ ☺ This creatively designed mega-resort, the biggest in The Bahamas, functions as a vacation destination and theme park in its own right. It's the most recent incarnation of a resort that originated in the early days of Paradise Island's tourism industry, passing through rocky and sometimes less glamorous days before reaching its current form as a destination that appeals to adults (its gambling facilities are the largest in The Bahamas) and to ecologists (its focus on protecting marine life adds a welcome dose of "save the planet" to an otherwise relentlessly consumerist theme, and dozens of waterways crisscross the flat, sandy terrain on which the resort sits). Atlantis is also a potent lure for children, and the child that remains within many of us, thanks to its evocation of a "lost continent" whose replicated ruins evoke—you guessed it—Atlantis.

The entire sprawling compound opens onto a long stretch of sandy beach with a sheltered marina. Think Vegas in the Tropics, with a mythological theme and an interconnected series of lagoons, rivers, waterfalls, and water tubes thrown in, and you'll get the picture. One advantage to the place is that there's a lot of visual distraction and high-energy, upbeat stimulation; the downside is that it's huge, impersonal, and at times downright bureaucratic. The resort offers such a range of sports, dining, and entertainment options that many guests never venture off the property during their entire vacation. It's expensive, but for your money, you'll find yourself neck-deep in the diversions you might expect from a theme park.

Overall, it's an appropriate (albeit rather pricey) choice for a family vacation, since the price includes direct access to endless numbers of watery gimmicks. Children's programs are comprehensive and well choreographed, and many parents simply turn their kids loose onto the extensive grounds, understanding that a battalion of lifeguards and supervisors keep the show rolling and the safety levels up to par. Singles and young couples who want a lot of razzle-dazzle appreciate the place, too.

Accommodations feature distinctly different levels of opulence, based, for the most part, on where they're located. The most grand and expensive units lie in semi-secluded annexes whose facilities are not open to the hotel's general clientele. These include the **One&Only Ocean Club** and the **Cove Atlantis,** a 600-unit, all-suite hotel-within-a-hotel that opened in 2007. Both pockets of heightened posh were designed as separate and semi-independent entities within the resort, and each is described in separate reviews below.

Hotels & Restaurants on Paradise Island

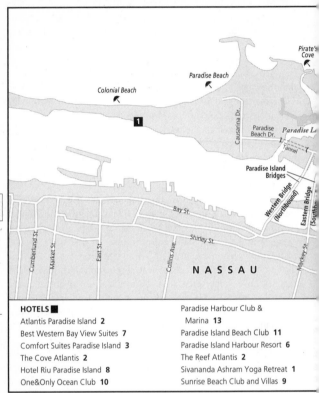

HOTELS ■

Atlantis Paradise Island **2**
Best Western Bay View Suites **7**
Comfort Suites Paradise Island **3**
The Cove Atlantis **2**
Hotel Riu Paradise Island **8**
One&Only Ocean Club **10**

Paradise Harbour Club & Marina **13**
Paradise Island Beach Club **11**
Paradise Island Harbour Resort **6**
The Reef Atlantis **2**
Sivananda Ashram Yoga Retreat **1**
Sunrise Beach Club and Villas **9**

As the resort has expanded, accommodations within its central core are emerging as more affordable options. And of those units, the plushest lie within the **Royal Towers**—the tallest and most imaginative edifice in The Bahamas, replete with decorative seahorses, winged dragons, and huge conch shells sprouting from cornices and rooflines. Rooms in the Royal Towers' **Imperial Club** come with concierge service and upgraded amenities. The most deluxe accommodations anywhere within the Atlantis fiefdom (going for $25,000 a night) are in the **Bridge Suite,** an architectural oddity that, many stories above ground level, links the two spires of the Royal Towers.

The Reef, in a category all its own, is a condo complex whose one-, two-, and three-bedroom units, each with full kitchen, are rented out as hotel accommodations according to a complicated

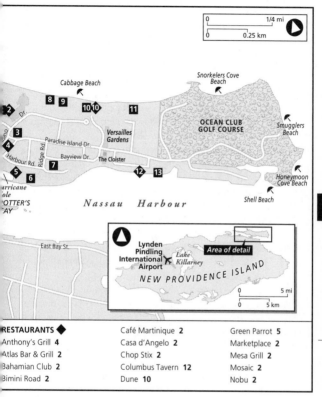

Map labels:

0 — 1/4 mi
0 — 0.25 km

Cabbage Beach

Snorkelers Cove Beach

8 9

10 10

11

OCEAN CLUB GOLF COURSE

Smugglers Beach

Dr.

2

3

Paradise Island Dr.

Versailles Gardens

4

Harbour Rd.

Ridge Rd.

Bayview Dr.

The Cloister

5

6

7

12 13

Honeymoon Cove Beach

Shell Beach

urricane
ole
OTTER'S
AY

Nassau Harbour

East Bay St.

Lynden Pindling International Airport

Lake Killarney

Area of detail

NEW PROVIDENCE ISLAND

0 — 5 mi
0 — 5 km

RESTAURANTS ◆		
Anthony's Grill **4**	Café Martinique **2**	Green Parrot **5**
Atlas Bar & Grill **2**	Casa d'Angelo **2**	Marketplace **2**
Bahamian Club **2**	Chop Stix **2**	Mesa Grill **2**
Bimini Road **2**	Columbus Tavern **12**	Mosaic **2**
	Dune **10**	Nobu **2**

schedule. Less posh and less plush are rooms within the **Coral Towers,** and least expensive of the entire lot are units within the still-serviceable but older **Beach Tower,** with a floor plan shaped like an airplane propeller, dating back to the dimly remembered 1980s. But even in the older, less pricey sections, accommodations are comfortable and well accessorized. Most units sport a balcony or terrace with water views.

Any old hotel might have tropical gardens, but Atlantis goes one better by featuring the world's largest collection of outdoor open-air marine habitats, each of them aesthetically stunning. A few of these were conceived for snorkelers and swimmers, but most were designed so that guests could observe the marine life from catwalks above and from glassed-in underwater viewing tunnels. Even folks who don't stay here, including thousands of cruise-ship passengers, can take part in orchestrated tours. These jaunts include 11 different exhibition lagoons, containing millions of gallons of water and at least 200 species of tropical fish. On-site marine habitats include separate lagoons for sharks, dolphins, and stingrays, plus individual habitats for lobsters, piranhas, and underwater exotica.

Swimmers can meander along an underwater snorkeling trail called **Paradise Lagoon** to explore a five-story replica of an ancient ziggurat-shaped Mayan temple, the sides of which incorporate water slides with slippery, wet, and wild runs, including an 18m (59-ft.) nearly vertical drop. Riders emerge from the sculpted mouths of giant Mayan gods like human sacrifices as they race giddily down the course of the water slide.

In 2007, additional water attractions, known collectively as **Aquaventure,** were added, bringing the surface area devoted to water features to 50 hectares (124 acres). The most visible monument within Aquaventure is a mythical-looking building called the **Power Tower,** site of even more imaginative water slides. Aquaventure is accessible, without charge, for guests staying at Atlantis. Nonresidents, however, are strictly barred from entering unless they buy a day pass, which costs $110 for adults, $80 for children 4 to 12. Day-pass holders get access to all marine habitats, water slides, beach and pool facilities, and Aquaventure.

One major entertainment venue within Atlantis that's open, without charge, to the general public is **Marina Village,** inspired by an old Bahamian harborfront with a string of clapboard-sided houses (think historic Key West, Florida, but with a lot more money). Flanking a marina that draws some of the world's most spectacular yachts, it's self-enclosed and has dozens of shops, bars, and restaurants, plus gazebos and live musicians.

The focal point of Atlantis's extravagance is the massive **Atlantis Casino,** the best-designed and most imaginatively conceived casino in The Bahamas. Set over a lagoon's watery depths, it contains three bars and two restaurants.

Within the diverse and scattered elements of this extended resort, you'll find some 40 separate food and beverage outlets, some of which open, close, and are reconfigured at dizzying rates. None of them comes cheap. For detailed descriptions of Atlantis's most worthy eateries, see "Where to Eat" and "Paradise Island After Dark," later in this chapter.

Casino Dr., Paradise Island, The Bahamas. ✆ **800/ATLANTIS** (285-2684) in the U.S., or 242/363-3000. Fax 242/363-6300. www.atlantis.com. 2,317 units. Rates in Beach Tower, Coral Towers, and Royal Towers: winter $430–$785 double, from $955 suite; off-season $270–$660 double, from $850 suite. AE, MC, V. **Amenities:** 20 restaurants; 18 lounges and clubs; babysitting; children's programs (ages 3-17); concierge; health club & spa; 17 outdoor pools; room service; 5 tennis courts (lit for night play). *In room:* A/C, TV, hair dryer, minibar, Wi-Fi ($15/day).

PROUDLY REMAINING adult AT ATLANTIS

Faced with increasing numbers of families with children, and with the perception that its acres of water slides and canals are a glorified summer camp for the offspring of parents who can afford it, there's an awareness that Atlantis needs quiet corners where grown-ups can be grown-ups.

If you fall into that category, we advise that you check into either the **Cove Atlantis,** the **Reef Atlantis,** the **One&Only Ocean Club,** or one of the more upscale rooms within the **Royal Towers.** None of these venues officially restricts children, but the Beach and Coral towers tend to house the greatest numbers of foursomes—usually a nuclear family with their kids or festive 20-somethings on reprieve from their lives in the frigid north. If you've opted for lodgings within the Cove, spend time at the **adults-only swimming pool.** Its staffers are hip, and 20 cabanas await you and your significant other.

On your first night at Atlantis, go for drinks and dinner at **Nobu.** We find the Asian food here delicious and fascinating— enough so that most North American kids will find it bizarre. The pre-dinner scene at the bar, where women look foxier than in the glaring sun of a Bahamian noon, is definitely not for children. Awaken, too, to the nocturnal charms of **Aura,** the appealingly permissive nightclub where celeb-gazing is something of an art form.

Finally, book a long session at **Mandara Spa.** If you see anyone inside who's 17 or under, it's likely they're in line to inherit a very substantial fortune. Otherwise, even though adults adore it, it's not the sort of place teeny-boppers necessarily crave.

The Cove Atlantis ★★★ Housed within a handsome turquoise-and-coral tower whose fanciful detailing matches the resort's mythical theme, this hotel was configured as a semiprivate hideaway. Don't expect anything conventional about this place: It serves partially (but not completely) as an adults-oriented venue, taking pains to dilute a growing perception that Atlantis has too much of a family emphasis. Inaugurated in 2007, it boasts an avant-garde design that combines the best of minimalist Japan and ultra-high-end postmodern Florida. All units are luxurious and high-tech, with step-down living rooms, personal butlers, and every imaginable amenity. Whereas one of the two pools reserved only for Cove guests is family-friendly, the adults-only social centerpiece is an 836-sq.-m (9,000-sq.-ft.) "ultrapool" that is strictly off-limits to anyone under 18. It's ringed by 20 private cabanas, which can be rented by the day for sybaritic adults seeking seclusion. On the lobby level, there's a branch of Bobby Flay's **Mesa Grill** (p. 106). Immediately adjacent to the Cove, and open to any Atlantis guest or day-pass holder, is **Mandara Spa,** whose design was inspired by the architecture of Bali and incorporates stone, bamboo, and tropical hardwoods.

Casino Dr., Paradise Island, The Bahamas. © **800/ATLANTIS** (285-2684) in the U.S., or 242/363-3000. Fax 242/363-6300. www.atlantis.com. 600 suites. Winter $789–$1,660 suite; off-season $505–$1,310 suite. AE, MC, V. **Amenities:** 2 restaurants; 2 bars; access to 18-hole golf course; health club & spa; 3 outdoor pools; room service. *In room:* A/C, TV, hair dryer, minibar, Wi-Fi ($15/day).

One&Only Ocean Club ★★★ Tranquil, secluded, and intimate, this is Paradise Island's most exclusive address, with sky-high prices to accompany the refined ambience and pampering service (the best in The Bahamas). Although it's owned by the same entity that controls the much larger Atlantis, huge efforts have been expended to separate it from the guests at the less personalized, more family-oriented mega-resort. In fact, though Atlantis's facilities are available to the residents here, that same privilege does not extend in the opposite direction. As such, you'll find a boutique-style hotel that, to a large degree, is cloistered from the much splashier venue nearby.

The resort's real heart and soul lie in the surrounding gardens, designed by the island's former owner, Huntington Hartford II, heir to the A&P grocery fortune. The formal gardens surround a rebuilt medieval French cloister set on 14 hectares (35 acres) of manicured lawns. Graceful 12th-century arcades are visible at the crest of a hill, across a stretch of terraced waterfalls, fountains, a stone gazebo, and rose gardens. Begin your tour of the gardens at the large swimming pool, which feeds a series of reflecting pools that stretch out toward the cloister. A kid-friendly pool is replete with aqua toys and a waterfall. This is also one of the best-developed tennis resorts in The Bahamas, and the white-sand beach adjacent to the hotel is the finest in the area. What could arguably be called Paradise Island's top restaurant is the resort's **Dune** (p. 105), created by culinary legend Jean-Georges Vongerichten.

Ocean Club Dr., Paradise Island, The Bahamas. © **888/528-7157** in the U.S., or 242/363-2501. Fax 242/363-2424. www.oneandonlyresorts.com. 105 units. Winter $795–$1,000 double, from $1,400 suite; off-season $495–$950 double, from $900 suite. AE, MC, V. Free parking. **Amenities:** 2 restaurants; 3 bars; babysitting; concierge; 18-hole golf course; health club & spa; 2 outdoor pools; room service; 6 tennis courts (lit for night play). *In room:* A/C, TV, hair dryer, kitchen, minibar, Internet (free).

On Top of the World

According to the lifestyle magazine *Elite Traveler,* The Bahamas rents one of the world's most coveted suites. At $10,000 a night, the Penthouse at the **Reef Atlantis,** Casino Drive (② **242/363-3000;** www.atlantis.com), was voted one of the most desirable places in the world to spend the night. (In case you're wondering, the top suite in the world is the Royal Penthouse Suite at the Hotel President Wilson in Geneva.)

The Reef Atlantis ★★★ Inaugurated in 2007, and purpose-built as a condominium complex in which the smallest unit is a fully self-sufficient one-bedroom apartment, this (along with the Cove) is Atlantis's tallest building. It's also the most flamboyantly state-of-the-art, permeated with the theme that defines virtually everything else around it. Although its decor most closely matches accommodations within the Cove, its level of contemporary comfort surpasses everything else at Atlantis. Opt for a room here if you're entertaining a group of four or more, if having a spectacularly high-tech kitchen is important to you, or if you have so much money that cost is absolutely no object. All of Atlantis's diversions and distractions are open to short-term residents of the Reef, and some renters have liked the place so much that they bought a unit.

Casino Dr., Paradise Island, The Bahamas. ② **800/ATLANTIS** (285-2684) in the U.S., or 242/363-3000. Fax 242/363-6300. www.atlantis.com. 550 suites. Winter $590–$810 double, from $890 suite; off-season $465–$680 double, from $670 suite. AE, MC, V. Rates include unrestricted access to all Atlantis attractions and amenities. *In room:* A/C, TV, hair dryer, kitchen, Wi-Fi (free).

Expensive

Hotel Riu Palace Paradise Island ★ ☺ In 2004, the Riu chain refurbished the old Sheraton Grand into this all-inclusive mega-resort. Opening onto a 5km (3-mile) stretch of beach, and within walking distance of Atlantis, this 14-story ecru-colored high-rise offers some of Paradise Island's most comfortably appointed bedrooms (many with balconies that afford sweeping water views). It's more understated than Atlantis, a lot cheaper, and more user-friendly and manageable in terms of size and layout. Your kids would likely be happier at Atlantis, but Riu is a viable runner-up for the family set.

Welcoming drinks are served in the lobby bar amid palm trees and tropical foliage. Guests can easily leave the shelter of the poolside terrace and settle onto one of the waterside chaise lounges on the beach. For an extra charge, you can skip the all-inclusive dinner fare and dine at Tengoku, a Japanese-themed restaurant, or Sir Alexander, for refined continental cuisine made with first-rate ingredients. Live entertainment is available 6 nights a week.

6307 Casino Dr., Paradise Island, The Bahamas. © **888/666-8816** in the U.S., or 242/363-3500. Fax 242/363-3900. www.riu.com. 379 units. Winter $310–$495 double, $556–$690 suite; off-season $254–$475 double, $330–$690 suite. Rates are all-inclusive. AE, DC, MC, V. **Amenities:** 4 restaurants; 3 bars; babysitting; concierge; health club & spa; outdoor pool; tennis court (lit for night play); watersports equipment/rentals; Wi-Fi (free in lobby). *In room:* A/C, TV, hair dryer, minibar.

Paradise Island Beach Club ★　This timeshare complex is set near Paradise Island's eastern tip, adjacent to a relatively isolated strip of spectacular beachfront. Managed by Marriott, it's more of a self-catering condo complex than a full-fledged resort. Many guests cook at least some meals in their own kitchens and head elsewhere, often to bigger hotels, for restaurants, watersports, gambling, and entertainment. Overall, the setting is comfortable and cozy—you'll feel like you have your own apartment with easy beach access. Accommodations have two bedrooms (for a maximum of six persons), with wicker and rattan furnishings, nice touches such as double basins in each bathroom, and views that may include ocean panoramas. The on-site pool bar opens for breakfast and serves drinks throughout the day until 5pm. The entertainment of the island's more densely developed sections lies just a short walk away.

Ocean Ridge Dr., Paradise Island, The Bahamas. © **242/363-2523.** Fax 242/363-2130. www.mypibc.com. 44 units. Winter $480 2-bedroom apt; off-season $380 2-bedroom apt. AE, MC, V. **Amenities:** Restaurant; bar; pool bar; exercise room; 2 outdoor pools; Wi-Fi (free in lobby). *In room:* A/C, TV, hair dryer, kitchen.

Paradise Island Harbour Resort ★ ☺　This older 12-floor property is adjacent to the waters of Nassau Harbour, opening onto a marina with very little beach. Just a short stroll from Atlantis with all its attractions, it has been turned into an all-inclusive resort. Bedrooms are midsize with twin or king-size beds, plus well-maintained bathrooms. The decor is comfortable, airy, and sunny, with tropically inspired colors and upholstery. The food served is palatable, though service can be slow. However, nightly live shows spice up the night, including fire dancing and Bahamian bands on occasion.

Harbour Dr., Paradise Island, The Bahamas. © **888/645-5550** or 242/363-2561. Fax 242/363-1220. www.paradiseislandbahama.com. 246 units. Winter $200–$320 double, $360–$430 suite; off-season $198–$270 double, $279–$385 suite. Rates are all-inclusive. AE, DC, DISC, MC, V. **Amenities:** 2 restaurants; 2 bars; babysitting; children's programs; concierge; health club with Jacuzzi; watersports equipment/rentals. *In room:* AC, TV, fridge, hair dryer, Wi-Fi ($10/day).

Sunrise Beach Club and Villas ★ ☺   Sunrise is a good bet for quieter families who want to avoid the circus at Atlantis and enjoy a more subdued, relaxed vacation. This cluster of Spanish-style low-rise town houses occupies one of the most desirable stretches of beachfront. Midway between Hotel Riu and the One&Only Ocean Club, it's a short walk from the casino and a variety of sports and dining options. The hotel is usually full of Germans, Swiss, and Austrians, many of whom stay for several weeks. Accommodations are clustered within five groupings of red-roofed town houses, each with access to the resort's two pools (one of which has a waterfall) and a simple snack bar. Expect pastel colors, summery furniture, a private patio or veranda, and a kitchen, plus king-size beds, floor-to-ceiling mirrored headboards, and average-size bathrooms. The best units are the three-bedroom apartments, situated directly on the beach.

Casino Dr., Paradise Island, The Bahamas. © **888/754-5315** or 242/363-2234. Fax 242/363-2308. www.sunrisebeachclub.com. 28 units. Winter $331–$426 1-bedroom unit, $579–$643 2-bedroom unit; off-season $221–$255 double, $463 2-bedroom unit. AE, MC, V. **Amenities:** Bar; babysitting; Internet ($11); 2 outdoor pools. *In room:* A/C, TV, hair dryer, kitchen.

Moderate

Best Western Bay View Suites ★   More than 20 kinds of hibiscus and many varieties of bougainvillea beautify this 1.6-hectare (4-acre) condo complex. The property is near the geographic center of Paradise Island, only a 10-minute walk to either the harbor or Cabbage Beach (the complex has no beach of its own). The dining options of Atlantis are only a few minutes away, but the modest Terrace restaurant here is nothing to be ashamed of. A shopping center is 3 minutes away, and a full-time personal cook can be arranged on request. Accommodations come in a variety of sizes—the largest can hold up to six—and some open onto views of the harbor. Each unit has its own kitchen with dishwasher, plus a patio or balcony and daily maid service. Penthouse suites have

Spa Serenity

Atlantis's 2,323-sq.-m (25,005-sq.-ft.) **Mandara Spa** (© **242/363-3000**; www.mandaraspa.com) is a Zen-inspired enclave of calm and serenity designed to make guests feel like gods and god-desses. Services include exotic body scrubs and wrap treatments with names like Caribbean Coffee Scrub, Tropical Coconut Scrub, and Sunburn Cooler.

An Offshore Yoga Retreat

Ex-Beatle George Harrison and a host of other yoga devotees over the years have checked into **Sivananda Ashram Yoga Retreat** (✆ **800/441-2096** or 242/363-2902; fax 242/363-3783; www.sivananda.org), which is reached only by boat from Paradise Island. For some 40 years, it's been completely removed from the rest of Paradise Island's frantic gambling, heady lifestyle, and high prices. Today, the retreat teaches the healing arts and spiritual practices.

Lecturers from all over the world come here to give seminars and practice meditation. When not devoting their time to yoga, guests rest on a lovely sandy beach, all part of a compound that reaches from Nassau Harbour to the Atlantic. Guests attend two daily meditation sessions, the first starting at 5am. Two yoga classes per day are also required, but you're free daily from 10am to 4pm. A boat shuttles guests into Nassau so they can see its sights.

Participants are housed in the simple main house or in small one-room bungalows. The most desirable units, a dozen of them, front the beach. There are also 35 private single rooms, plus seven dormlike spaces. Vegetarian meals are included in the rate of $89 to $99 for a single, $79 to $129 for a double, or $69 to $79 for a three- or four-bed dormitory. Tent space is available for $69 per night.

roof gardens with views. *Tip:* Rooms near the center of the resort are closest to the pools and laundry facilities.

Bayview Dr., Paradise Island, The Bahamas. ✆ **800-WESTERN** (937-8376) or 800/757-1357 in the U.S., or 242/363-2555. Fax 242/363-2370. www.bwbayview suites.com. 75 units. Winter $271 1-bedroom suite, $425 town house (for 4), from $445 villa; off-season $200 1-bedroom suite, $335 town house (for 4), from $345 villa. Weekly rates are slightly lower. AE, DC, MC, V. **Amenities:** Lunch-only restaurant; bar; babysitting; 3 outdoor pools; tennis court (lit for night play). *In room:* A/C, TV, hair dryer, kitchen, Wi-Fi (free).

Comfort Suites Paradise Island 🔖   A favorite with honeymooners, this three-story all-suite hotel is across the street from Atlantis and makes a nice alternative to the behemoth. You get all the splash and wonder, but don't have to stay when the cruise-ship crowds descend. Though the hotel has its own pool bar and restaurant, guests are also granted signing privileges at Atlantis's drinking and dining spots, as well as the pool, beach, and sports facilities. Accommodations are priced according to their views: over the island, the pool, or the garden. Bedrooms are standard motel size; the medium-size bathrooms are stocked with beach towels.

Paradise Island Dr., Paradise Island, The Bahamas. ✆ **877/424-6423** in the U.S. or Canada, or 242/363-3680. Fax 242/363-2588. www.comfortsuitespi.com. 228

Bellavia

Pickup By: August 8, 2019

Bellavia, Gerri

Bahamas

32126001213896

EMAIL

WilmLibrary.org

978-658-2967

facebook.com\WilmLibrary

twitter.com\WilmLibrary

units. Winter $279–$420 double; off-season $187–$399 double. Rates include continental breakfast. AE, DISC, MC, V. **Amenities:** Restaurant; bar; small health club; outdoor pool; tennis court (lit for night play). *In room:* A/C, TV, fridge, hair dryer, Wi-Fi (free).

Paradise Harbour Club & Marina   This place is noteworthy for its sense of isolation, despite being on heavily developed Paradise Island. Built in 1991 near the island's extreme eastern tip, the hotel has rambling upper hallways, terra-cotta tile floors, and clean, well-organized bedrooms. If available, opt for one of the top-floor units so you can enjoy the view. Some of the property's quaint services, all free, include a water taxi to downtown Nassau, a beach shuttle (albeit in a golf cart), and use of snorkeling gear and bikes.

Paradise Island Dr., Paradise Island, The Bahamas. ℂ **800/594-3495** or 242/363-2992. Fax 242/363-2840. www.festiva-paradise.com. 23 units. Winter $232 double, $270–$280 junior suite; $357 1-bedroom suite; off-season $143 double, $202 junior suite; $172–$263 1-bedroom suite. MC, V. **Amenities:** Restaurant; bar; babysitting; exercise room with Jacuzzi; room service; watersports equipment/rentals. *In room:* A/C, TV, hair dryer, kitchen (in some), minibar, Wi-Fi (free).

WHERE TO EAT

Paradise Island offers an array of the most dazzling, and the most expensive, restaurants in The Bahamas. If you're on a strict budget, cross over the bridge into downtown Nassau, which has far more affordable places to eat. Though pricey, meals on Paradise Island are often unimaginative—surf and turf appears on many a menu, so, unfortunately, you may not get what you pay for. The greatest concentration of restaurants is near the casino, but there are other good options outside the Atlantis complex, including Dune at the One&Only Ocean Club.

Expensive

Bahamian Club ★★ STEAK   With an upscale British colonial feel and an atmosphere like that of an elegant and somewhat macho country club, this is a big (but civilized) clubby spot, with spacious vistas, mirrors, gleaming mahogany, and forest-green walls. The excellent food is prepared with top-quality ingredients from the U.S. and served in two-fisted portions. Meat is king here, with all those old favorites like roasted prime rib and Cornish hen, plus the island's best T-bone, along with a selection of veal and lamb chops. The retro menu also lists the inevitable Dover sole, lobster Thermidor, and grilled salmon, as well as appetizers that hearken back to the good old days, such as fresh jumbo-shrimp cocktail and onion soup. Try the Bahamian conch chowder for some local flavor. Side dishes are excellent, especially the penne with fresh tomato sauce and the roasted shiitake mushrooms. Proper attire is required—that means no jeans or sneakers.

Coral Towers at Atlantis, Casino Dr. ℂ 242/363-3000. www.atlantis.com. Reservations required. Main courses $40-$68. AE, DC, DISC, MC, V. Usually Wed-Mon 6-11pm, though days and hours may vary.

Café Martinique ★★★ FRENCH   The most elegant and upscale restaurant on Paradise Island occupies a replica of the kind of town house that might belong to a billionaire who happened to live in, say, Martinique and happened to have imported art and antiques from Belle Epoque Paris. This mixture of haute Paris with a French Colonial twist is enormously appealing, as is the wrought-iron birdcage elevator that brings you upstairs to the dining room. Begin your evening in the supremely comfortable bar area, replete with French Caribbean carved mahogany antiques. In the tastefully posh dining area, masses of flowers and dessert trolleys await your pleasure—not to mention the cuisine of superchef Jean-Georges Vongerichten. Begin with such delectable items as caviar or smoked salmon. The main courses are sublime, especially the lobster Thermidor and the Dover sole meunière. The restaurant is known for its grills, everything from prime rib for two to a succulent veal chop.

In Marina Village at Atlantis, Casino Dr. ℂ **242/363-3000.** Reservations required. Main courses $42-$65. AE, DC, DISC, MC, V. Daily 6-11pm, though days and hours may vary.

Casa d'Angelo ★ ITALIAN   Posh, richly upholstered, and decorated with art and objects reminiscent of old-world Italy, Paradise Island's premier Italian restaurant creates classic dishes prepared with skill, served with flair, and comparable to the kind of elegant manicured cuisine you'd expect from a top-notch Italian restaurant in Florida. Some of the best main courses include sautéed Fra Diavolo–style calamari and clams served over crostini; tuna carpaccio with spinach, olives, artichoke hearts, and orange sauce; risotto with porcini mushrooms, truffle oil, goat cheese, and thyme; and grilled swordfish steak with garlic, white wine, tomatoes, capers, black olives, onions, and fresh oregano.

Coral Towers at Atlantis, Casino Dr. ℂ **242/363-3000.** www.atlantis.com. Reservations required. Main courses $34-$68. AE, DC, MC, V. Daily 6-10pm, though days and hours may vary.

Chop Stix CANTONESE   Many people come here just to hang out in the bar. But if you're in the mood for a good Chinese meal, you'll be ushered to a table in a circular dining room, engaging and stylish, with a ceiling draped with fabric that evokes a richly decorated tent. The sophisticated decor seems to encourage both your sense of humor and your sense of camp; it suggests Shanghai during the British colonial age. Some of the island's best appetizers are served here—try the steamed shrimp dumplings or the Thai chicken spring rolls. This might be followed by the wok-seared grouper with garlic sauce or the coconut curry chicken with mango.

Coral Towers at Atlantis, Casino Dr. © **242/363-3000.** www.atlantis.com. Reservations recommended. Main courses $28–$60. AE, DC, DISC, MC, V. Tues–Sat 6–10pm, though days and hours may vary.

Columbus Tavern ★ SEAFOOD   Through the large open windows of this restaurant, you can watch the boats in Nassau Harbour. At least some of them brought in the fresh catch of the day. The only native seaside restaurant and bar on Paradise Island is nestled between the Ocean Club Golf Course and the Paradise Harbour Club & Marina. Native-born owner Freddie Lightbourn is the guiding light here, ordering his staff to prepare your seafood dish as you like it—steamed, baked, whole, or fried. The chef's delectable specialties include lobster flambé or a steak Diane prepared tableside. But most guests gravitate to the "Fisherman's Fiesta," a combo platter that includes blackened lobster, fresh shrimp, or scallops in a tasty Creole sauce. Other classics are filet of Nassau grouper sautéed and topped with a creamy garlic, white wine, and shallot sauce, or else roasted Cornish hen glazed with a lemon pepper sauce. The Guava Duff, an old Bahamian dessert specialty, will win your heart.

Paradise Island Dr. © **242/363-2534.** www.columbustavernbahamas.com. Reservations recommended for dinner. Main courses $27–$43. AE, MC, V. Daily 11am–4pm and 4:30–10:30pm.

Dune ★★★ INTERNATIONAL   One of Paradise Island's most cutting-edge restaurants is a beachfront annex of the One&Only Ocean Club. It offers very attentive service, a sweeping view of the ocean, a teakwood floor that makes you feel like you're aboard a yacht, and a gray-and-black decor that looks like it was plucked from a chic enclave in Milan. Near the restaurant's entrance is a thriving herb garden from which many of the culinary flavorings are derived. The chefs here invariably select the finest ingredients and handle them with razor-sharp technique. Every dish has a special something, especially the shrimp dusted with orange powder and served with artichokes and arugula. The tuna spring rolls with soybean salsa are splendid, as is the chicken and coconut-milk soup served with shiitake cakes. The goat cheese and watermelon salad is an unexpected delight. Grouper filet—that Bahamian standard—is at its savory best here when served with zesty tomato sauce.

One&Only Ocean Club, Ocean Club Dr. ☏ **242/363-2501,** ext. 64739. www.oneandonlyresorts.com. Reservations required. Main courses $22–$39 lunch; $38–$60 dinner. AE, DC, DISC, MC, V. Daily 7–11am, noon–3pm, and 6–10:30pm, though days and hours may vary.

Marketplace ★ 🏷 BUFFET/INTERNATIONAL   Unless you're hopelessly jaded or blasé, you can't leave here without feeling amazed by how abundant and elaborate the buffets at a casino resort can really be. Decorated with old vases and terra-cotta tiles, this one evokes a sprawling market in which all the food just happens to be beautifully prepared, elegantly displayed, and showcased in breathtaking variety and quantity—making it the best buffet on Paradise Island. Before you start loading stuff onto your plate, browse your way past the various cooking stations and do some strategic planning. From fresh fruit to omelets, you can make breakfast as light or as heavy as you want. At lunch and dinner, you'll find everything from fresh seafood and made-to-order pastas to carved roast beef and lamb. No intimate affair, this place seats some 400 diners. Sit inside or on the patio overlooking a lagoon.

Royal Towers at Atlantis, Casino Dr. ☏ **242/363-3000.** www.atlantis.com. Reservations not needed. Buffets $25 breakfast, $30 lunch, $58 dinner. AE, DC, MC, V. Daily 7–11am, noon–3pm, and 5:30–10pm.

Mesa Grill ★★ SOUTHWESTERN   In 2007, Atlantis carved this Southwestern-chic enclave out of a beachfront spot on the lobby level of the Cove, its boutique-style hotel-within-a-hotel. Don't presume that this is a down-home joint for chili, beer, and barbecue. It's actually rather haute, distinctly gourmet, and run by celebrity chef Bobby Flay. Begin a meal here with a shrimp-and-roasted-garlic cornmeal tamale with fresh corn and cilantro sauce, or perhaps the raw tuna nachos with mango hot sauce and avocado cream. Follow that with the 16-spice chicken or honey-glazed salmon. There are at least three succulent preparations of grilled steaks, plus an excellent vegetarian main course: the cornmeal-crusted chili relleno filled with goat cheese, wild mushrooms, and a smoked red-pepper sauce. Well-flavored side dishes include collard greens, sweet-potato gratin, black-eyed peas with rice, and cilantro-pesto mashed potatoes. *Note:* Children 12 and under are discouraged from dining here.

The Cove Atlantis. ☏ **242/363-3000,** ext. 59250. www.atlantis.com. Reservations required. Main courses $32–$52. AE, DC, MC, V. Daily 5:30–10:30pm (last seating), though days and hours may vary.

Mosaic ★ 🏷 BAHAMIAN/MEDITERRANEAN   This is perhaps the best buffet restaurant in all the islands, and it serves a big spread for breakfast, lunch, and dinner. It's an all-you-can-eat type of establishment, and is popular with families. The restaurant changes from day to evening in its aura, using lighting to play off the polished chrome, Wedgewood, and limestone. A lot of the cuisine is inspired by the Mediterranean. Just because it's a buffet doesn't mean that all dishes are already prepared. Several cooking stations will prepare dishes on demand from the fresh catch of the day to churrasco grilled steaks.

Casino Dr. ☏ **242/363-3000.** www.atlantis.com. Reservations recommended. Buffets $32 at breakfast, $35 at lunch, $68 at dinner. AE, DC, MC, V. Daily 7–11am, noon–2:30pm, and 5:30–10pm.

Nobu ★★★ JAPANESE/ASIAN It's the most talked-about, hip, and sought-after restaurant in Atlantis, thanks to its avant-garde Asian food and its association with an ongoing round of celebrities. It's the culinary statement of chef Nobu Matsuhisa, whose New York City branch caused a sensation among the glitterati when it opened in the '90s. Some diners prefer to start with Nobu's special cold dishes, including lobster seviche—but since conch is queen in The Bahamas, you might opt instead for conch seviche. The best appetizer we've sampled is the yellowtail sashimi with jalapeño. If you like your dishes spicy, try the rock-shrimp tempura with a cream sauce or else the Chilean sea bass with black-bean sauce. The tempura selection is vast, ranging from pumpkin to shiitake. Most patrons order some items from the wide selection of sushi and sashimi, including exotica such as live conch, sea urchin, or freshwater eel. Of course, you can also order well-prepared standards such as tuna, octopus, and salmon. If you want Paradise Island's most lavish and exotic meal, request the *omakase*, the chef's signature fixed-price menu.

Atlantis Casino, Casino Dr. ☏ **242/363-3000.** www.atlantis.com. Reservations required. Main courses $10–$45; sushi and sashimi $4–$37; sushi or sashimi dinner $49; chef's special *omakase* menu $150. AE, DC, DISC, MC, V. Daily 6–11pm, though days and hours may vary.

Moderate

Bimini Road ★ BAHAMIAN/INTERNATIONAL The name refers to a mysterious underwater rock formation off the coast of Bimini that resembles a ruined triumphal boulevard. Partly because of its relatively reasonable prices and partly because it showcases Bahamian cuisine more proudly than any other restaurant at Atlantis, this eatery is among the most consistently popular and crowded dining spots. Start with specialties like scorched conch salad or Rum Bay boiled fish in a citrus broth. Other island favorites include the catch of the day, which can be grilled, blackened, or fried. The only problem with this place is the crowd of expectant diners who cluster, somewhat uncomfortably, near the entrance waiting for a table. A phone call in advance for information about wait times might help you avoid this inconvenience.

Marina Village at Atlantis, Casino Dr. (©) **242/363-3000.** www.atlantis.com. Reservations accepted only for parties of 6 or more. Main courses $13–$50. AE, DISC, MC, V. Daily noon–3pm and 6–11pm, though days and hours may vary.

Green Parrot AMERICAN   You might enjoy a panorama of the Nassau Harbour from your table at this informal open-air restaurant and bar, a fave of some expats and denizens of Nassau, along with a scattering of vacationers. During the day, it sells a lot of burgers and well-stuffed sandwiches, later gearing up for happy hour, karaoke, and a native group performing on Thursday and Saturday nights. Starters include typical sports-bar fare (buffalo wings, onion rings, chicken tenders). The most popular lunch item is the "Works Burger," a whopper with American and Swiss cheese along with grilled onions and mushrooms. The non-carnivore can opt for a veggie burger. At dinner, go for the catch of the day, which can be grilled or blackened. Other tasty mains include a grilled New York steak, cracked conch, and curried chicken.

Hurricane Hole Marina. (©) **242/322-9248.** www.greenparrotbar.com. Reservations not needed. Main courses $12–$15; burgers and sandwiches $8–$15. MC, V. Sun–Thurs 11:30am–11pm; Fri–Sat 11:30am–midnight.

Inexpensive

Anthony's Grill AMERICAN/CARIBBEAN   Its owners think of this place as an upscale version of Bennigan's or T.G.I. Friday's, but the decor is thoroughly Caribbean, thanks to psychedelic tropical colors, underwater sea themes, and jaunty maritime decorative touches. A bar dispenses everything from conventional mai tais to embarrassingly oversized 48-ounce "sparklers"—with a combination of rum, amaretto, vodka, and fruit punch that is about all most serious drinkers can handle. Menu items include burgers, barbecued or fried chicken, ribs with Caribbean barbecue sauce, meal-size salads, and pizzas topped with everything from lobster to jerk chicken.

Paradise Island Shopping Plaza, at Paradise Island and Casino drives. (©) **242/363-3152.** www.anthonysgrillparadiseisland.com. Main courses $8–$15 lunch; $14–$32 dinner. AE, DISC, MC, V. Daily 7:30am–11pm.

Atlas Bar & Grill AMERICAN   The blare of its dozen or so TVs competes with the jangling of slot machines. This is the sports bar with the most elaborate array of screens on Paradise Island. It's set up in two separate ovals, each of which rings, at different perimeters, an oval-shaped bar. Decor includes lots of statues depicting Atlas and his many macho struggles. What should you get here?

Consider a burger with beer, a burger with scotch, or a burger with a soda.

Atlantis Casino, Casino Dr. ✆ **242/363-3000.** www.atlantis.com. Reservations not necessary. Main courses $10–$36. AE, DC, MC, V. Daily 11am–4pm; Thurs–Sun 4pm–3am, though days and hours (especially at dinner) may vary.

BEACHES & OUTDOOR PURSUITS

Visitors interested in more than lazing on the beach have only to ask hotel staff to make the necessary arrangements. Guests at Atlantis, for example, have access to a surprising number of diversions without so much as leaving the hotel property: They can splash in private pools; play tennis, ping-pong, and shuffleboard; ride the waves; snorkel; or rent WaveRunners, jet skis, banana boats, and catamarans from contractors located in kiosks.

Hitting the Beach

On Paradise Island, **Cabbage Beach ★★** (also known as **West Beach**) is the real showcase. Its broad white sands stretch for at least 3km (1¾ miles) and are bordered by casuarinas, palms, and sea grapes. It's likely to be crowded in winter, but you can find more elbow room by walking to the beach's northwestern stretch. You can reach Paradise Island from downtown Nassau by walking over the bridge, taking a taxi, or boarding a ferryboat at Prince George Wharf. Cabbage Beach does not have public restrooms, but if you patronize one of the handful of bars and restaurants nearby, you can use its facilities. Note that during the construction of Atlantis's soon-to-come waterfront timeshare property, access to some sections of this beach might be off-limits.

Our other favorite beach in this area is the white-sand **Paradise Beach ★★**, which is used mainly by guests of the Cove Atlantis and the Reef Atlantis hotels, as it lies at the island's far western tip. If you're not a resident, access is difficult. If you're staying at a hotel in Nassau and want to come to Paradise Island for a day at the beach, it's better to go to Cabbage Beach. However, sunsets viewed from the sands of Paradise Beach look particularly beautiful.

Fishing

Anglers can fish close to shore for grouper, dolphinfish, red snapper, crabs, even lobster. Farther out, in first-class fishing boats fitted with outriggers and fighting chairs, they troll for billfish or giant marlin.

The best way to pursue this pastime is to go to your hotel's activities desk, where the staff can set you up with a local charter operator for a half or full day of fishing. Also see "Beaches & Outdoor Pursuits" in chapter 3.

Golf

Ocean Club Golf Course ★★, Paradise Island Drive (*© 242/363-2510*; www.oneandonlyresorts.com), at the island's east end, is an 18-hole championship golf course designed by Tom Weiskopf that overlooks both the Atlantic Ocean and Nassau Harbour. Attracting every caliber of golfer, the par-72 course is known for its hole 17, which plays entirely along the scenic Snorkelers Cove. Greens fees, including use of a golf cart, are $120 to $300 for 18 holes of play, without reductions for guests at any individual hotels. Rental clubs and shoes are available.

Golfers seeking more variety will find one other course on New Providence Island, the **Cable Beach Golf Club** (p. 73).

Snorkeling & Scuba Diving

Bahama Divers, Nassau Yacht Haven Marina, on East Bay Street (*© 800/398-3483* or 242/393-5644; www.bahamadivers.com), is the area's best all-around center for watersports, specializing in scuba diving and snorkeling. A two-tank morning dive goes for $109, a single-tank afternoon dive costs $70, and a half-day snorkeling trip is $50. Dive packages are also offered.

For more scuba sites in the area, see "Snorkeling & Scuba Diving" under "Beaches & Outdoor Pursuits" in chapter 3.

Tennis

No other hotel in The Bahamas pays as much attention to tennis as the **One&Only Ocean Club,** Ocean Club Drive (*© 242/363-2501*; www.oneandonlyresorts.com), which has six Har-Tru courts, four lit for night play. Guests here can practically roll out of bed and onto the courts, which are often filled with first-class competitors, although beginners and intermediate players are welcome. One&Only Ocean Club guests have free access to the courts; they can also play with the resident pro for $75 per hour. Nonguests are not admitted.

Other hotels with courts include **Atlantis,** Casino Drive (*© 242/363-3000*; www.atlantis.com), with six hard-surface and clay courts. Atlantis guests (nonguests are not admitted) pay $20 per hour for access to the courts; they can play with the resident pro for an additional $70 per hour. Ball rentals go for $10 per hour, tennis racquets for another $10 per hour.

SEEING THE SIGHTS

Most of the big hotels here maintain activity-packed calendars, especially for that occasional windy, rainy day that comes in winter. Similar to life aboard a large cruise ship, the resorts offer diversions (some of them age-specific) that include water volleyball games, bingo, fish-feeding demonstrations, and movie screenings. And that doesn't include the disco parties for teens and preteens that tend to be scheduled for late afternoons or early evenings. To an increasing degree, hotels such as Atlantis have configured themselves as destinations in their own right.

Atlantis Paradise Island ★★ Regardless of where you're staying—even if it's at New Providence Island's most remote hotel—you'll want to visit this lavish theme park, hotel, restaurant complex, casino, and entertainment center. It is, hands-down, Paradise Island's biggest attraction. You could spend all day here—and all night, too—wandering the resort's shopping arcades, sampling the eateries' international cuisine, or gambling at roulette wheels, slot machines, poker games, and blackjack tables. And once you're here, don't even think about leaving without a walk along the marina or a visit to the Dig, a theme-driven marine attraction that celebrates the eerie, tragic legend of the lost continent of

Atlantis. During the day you can wear casual clothes, but at night you should dress up a bit, especially to try one of the better restaurants.

The most crowded time to visit is between 9am and 5pm on days when cruise ships are berthed in the nearby harbor—usually every Tuesday, Friday, and Saturday. The casino is at its most packed between 8 and 11pm any night of the week. There is no cover to enter: You pay just for what you eat, drink, and gamble away (and that could be considerable). Ironically, it's illegal for Bahamian citizens or residents to gamble. That restriction, however, most definitely does not apply to visitors from other countries. Except for the price of the liquor, entertainment within the bars—which usually includes live salsa, Goombay, and calypso music provided by local bands—is free.

Casino Dr. (C) **242/363-3000.** Free admission. Daily 24 hr.

The Cloister ★ Located in the Versailles Gardens of the One&Only Ocean Club, this 12th-century cloister built by Augustinian monks in southwestern France was reassembled here stone by stone. Huntington Hartford, the A&P heir, purchased the cloister from the estate of William Randolph Hearst. Regrettably, after the newspaper czar originally bought the cloister, it was hastily dismantled in France for shipment to The Bahamas. However, the parts had not been numbered—they all arrived unlabeled on Paradise Island. The reassembly of the complicated monument baffled most, and defied conventional methods of construction, until artist and sculptor Jean Castre-Manne set about doing it piece by piece. It took him 2 years, and what you see today presumably bears some similarity to the original. The gardens, which extend over the rise to Nassau Harbour, are filled with tropical flowers and classical statues. Though the monument retains a timeless beauty, recently erected buildings have encroached on either side, marring Hartford's original vision.

One&Only Ocean Club, Ocean Club Dr. (C) **242/363-2501.** www.oneandonly resorts.com. Free admission. Daily 24 hr.

 A Special Place of Beauty

Paradise Island's loveliest spot is Ocean Club's **Versailles Gardens,** far removed from the glitz and faux glamour of Atlantis. Within its seven terraces, the sites of many a wedding, are statues of some of Huntington Hartford's favorite people, including Mephistopheles, Franklin D. Roosevelt, and Doctor Livingstone. The gardens are open anytime, day or night, and admission is free.

SHOPPING

Many of Nassau's major stores also have outlets on Paradise Island. For serious shopping, however, cross over the Paradise Island Bridge into downtown Nassau (see chapter 3).

The **Shops at Atlantis** (© 242/363-3000; www.atlantis.com) is the largest concentration of shopping and boutiques on Paradise Island, rivaling anything else in The Bahamas in terms of size, selection, and style. The boutiques are subdivided into two different sections: The well-appointed **Crystal Court Shops** corridor meanders between the Royal Towers and the Coral Towers, encompassing 3,252 sq. m (35,004 sq. ft.) of prime high-traffic retail space. The waterfront **Marina Village Shops** are newer. Another handful of emporiums is scattered randomly throughout other parts of the resort. It's all about flagrantly conspicuous consumption that's sometimes fueled by the gaming frenzy in the nearby casino.

The resort contains two branches of **Colombian Emeralds** (one in the Marina Village, another in Atlantis's Beach Tower), where the colored gemstones far outnumber the relatively limited selection of diamonds. Other boutiques include **Lalique,** the French purveyor of fine crystal and accessories for men and women; **Versace,** which has not only clothing but also a charming home division; **Façonnable,** a sporty French label; **Bulgari,** producer of some of the world's most enviable jewels, as well as watches, gifts, and perfumes; and **Gucci** and **Ferragamo,** in case you forgot your best dancing shoes. For bathing suits, **Cole's of Nassau** sells swimwear by Gottex, Pucci, and Fernando Sanchez. Finally, pioneer watchseller **John Bull,** known for its Bay Street store in Nassau, has an interesting assortment of timepieces, jewelry, and designer accessories.

If you've had your fill of upscale gems and fashion, stop by one of our favorite shops, **Doongalik Studios,** Marina Village (© 242/394-1886). At press time, it's still the complex's only art gallery. Owned and operated by Jackson Burnside, the architect and art connoisseur who designed Marina Village, it's a bastion of authentic Bahamian culture within the glittering row of shops otherwise devoted to luxury goods. Come here for insight into who is creating contemporary art in The Bahamas. Oil paintings by locally famous artists (including John Cox, John Paul, Jessica Colebrooke, and Eddie Minnis) range from $800 to $2,500. Prints—sometimes of works by the same artists—are priced between $15 and $100. Sculptures can be especially interesting, with some crafted from gnarled driftwood.

PARADISE ISLAND AFTER DARK

Paradise Island has the country's best nightlife, and most of it centers on Atlantis.

Atlantis Paradise Island ★★★   There's no other spot in The Bahamas, with the possible exception of the Crystal Palace complex on Cable Beach, with such a wide variety of after-dark attractions, and absolutely nothing that approaches its inspired brand of razzle-dazzle. Even if you stay in Nassau or Cable Beach, you'll want to drop by this artfully decorated, self-contained temple to decadence, even if gambling isn't your passion. Love it or hate it, this place is simply a jaw-dropper.

The **Atlantis Casino** is the most lavishly planned, most obviously themed venue of its kind this side of Vegas. Its managers claim that it's the only casino in the world built above a body of water. Designed in homage to the lost continent of Atlantis, it appears to have risen directly from the waters of the lagoon. The gaming area is centered on buildings representing a Temple of the Sun and a Temple of the Moon, with a painted replica of the zodiac chart overhead. Rising from key locations are four of the most elaborate sculptures in the world. Massive and complex, they were crafted by teams of artisans spearheaded by Dale Chihuly, the American-born master whose glass-blowing skills are heralded globally. Other than the decor, the casino's gaming tables, open daily from 10am to 4am, are the main attraction in this enormous place, and about a thousand whirring and clanging slot machines operate 24 hours a day.

Recent additions include a lineup of poker tables and the **Pegasus Race & Sports Book,** with an illuminated and computerized display that lists the odds for many of the world's upcoming sporting events. Thanks to instantaneous communications with a centralized betting facility in Las Vegas, the staff here will make odds on a staggering number of sports events. This facility also contains a miniamphitheater with a battery of TV screens displaying the sporting and/or racing events for which money is changing hands.

Upstairs from the casino is **Aura,** a totally upscale nightclub experience that manages to attract a few local hipsters as well as Atlantis guests. Come anytime during casino hours for a drink. The club gets going around 10pm nightly, with a cover of $50 for females and $100 for males, unless they're guests of Atlantis, in which case they enter without charge. (Note that the cover for nonguests is usually waived for women if they're hip or beautiful enough.) Drinks inside carry big-city price tags, usually hovering around $17 for a scotch and soda.

Also in Atlantis, **Joker's Wild** is the only real comedy club in The Bahamas, with a talented company of funny people who work hard to make you laugh. Showtimes are Tuesday through Sunday at 9:30pm. There's a per-person cover of $15 for everyone. At least two comedians appear on any given night, and most of them hail from either the U.S. or the U.K. Midway btw. Beach and Coral towers, on Casino Dr. *Ⓒ* **242/363-3000.** www.atlantis.com.

The Bar Scene

Bimini Road   At many bars in this sprawling resort, the bartenders seem to ignore you. Not here—they're a lively bunch, slinging drinks like the sour-apple Gussie Mae in a setting imbued with a Junkanoo theme. The place is especially popular with yachties, who tie up at the nearby marina. A costumed dance troupe performs 4 nights a week (times vary), and live bands pump out island music. The restaurant (p. 107) serves food daily from around noon to 11pm. Both bars here (one on the terrace, the other indoors) are open daily until 1:30am. Marina Village at Atlantis, Casino Dr. *Ⓒ* **242/363-3000.** www.atlantis.com.

Dune Bar   This luxe dining room (p. 105) is also the setting for the island's most sophisticated lounge; it's becoming increasingly popular as a plush meeting spot for singles. The action centers around a translucent white marble bar illuminated from behind. The terrace here can be undeniably romantic. One&Only Ocean Club, Ocean Club Dr. *Ⓒ* **242/363-2501.** www.oneandonlyresorts.com. Call for hours, which vary.

Plato's Lounge   This is Atlantis's most popular bar, a sensual spot where you can escape the din of the slot machines and relax in an upscale environment that's flanked with replicas of Greek texts that might have been hand-lettered by Plato himself when he wrote about the lost continent of Atlantis. A pianist sets the mood during cocktail hour, and you'll get the sense that you're right in the heart of everything. In the sunlit hours, the site doubles as a cafe, serving pastries and snacks from 6am until 4pm. Open until 1am nightly. Royal Towers at Atlantis, Casino Dr. *Ⓒ* **242/363-3000.** www.atlantis.com.

GRAND BAHAMA (FREEPORT/ LUCAYA)

5

Fabulous beaches, unspoiled beauty, and warm waters continue to make Grand Bahama Island, just 50 miles east of Florida, a year-round destination. Of its two main urban centers, Freeport is a stimulating mix of restaurants, shops, and nightlife, while Lucaya, called the "Garden City," pleases with its restaurants, fine beaches, and marketplace shops. The rest of the island is filled with long stretches of beach, broken by inlets and fishing villages. Away from the beach, Rand Nature Centre—the island's national park—invites peaceful strolls along paths of casuarina, palmetto, and pine trees.

THINGS TO DO Grand Bahama has enough shoreline space for everyone, and you'll find plenty of spots in the sand to sun at **Xanadu Beach** and **Lucaya Beach.** If you want to get away from it all, **Fortune Beach** is a gem of secluded white sand. Get in the water to commune with dolphins on a **dolphin dive** at the Underwater Explorer Society. For a more fragrant and surprising experience, immerse yourself in the invigorating scent of pine trees as you wander through **Lucayan National Park,** with its underwater caves, forest trails, and quiet beach.

SHOPPING The brightly-painted huts at **Port Lucaya Marketplace,** along the waterfront, are filled with handicrafts and souvenirs. At Freeport's **International Bazaar,** you can fill your shopping bag full of duty-free cameras, perfumes, and clothing. A **straw market** next door to the International Bazaar contains

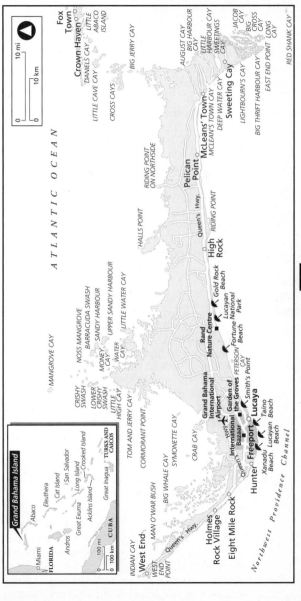

5

GRAND BAHAMA | Introduction

items with that special Bahamian touch—brightly hued baskets, hats, handbags, placemats, and an endless array of T-shirts.

NIGHTLIFE & ENTERTAINMENT   Lively restaurants and bars keep things hopping at **Port Lucaya,** while DJs keep the dance floors rocking in the clubs around the International Bazaar in **Freeport.** Spin the slot machines at the **Isle of Capri** casino at **Our Lucaya Beach Resort.** For the island's best live music, check out what's playing at **Count Basie Square** in the Port Lucaya Marketplace.

RESTAURANTS & DINING   Bahamian cuisine dominates the dining rooms in Grand Bahama, but you can also expect everything from steak and kidney pie (from the days of British colonial rule) in the backstreets of **Freeport** to creative Italian and Pacific Rim fare at the resort restaurants. Along **Taíno Beach** and at **Lucaya,** beach shacks serve up sumptuous specialties such as conch, grouper, Bahamian lobster, and **conch salad,** the Bahamian favorite. A traditional dish to try is **meat souse** (boiled mutton), accompanied with fried plantain, macaroni pie, or peas 'n' rice.

ORIENTATION

Arriving

A number of airlines fly to Freeport's **Grand Bahama International Airport** (FPO; ☏ **242/352-6020**) from the continental United States. **American Airlines** (☏ **800/433-7300;** www. aa.com) and **Bahamasair** (☏ **800/222-4262** or 242/377-3218; www.bahamasair.com) both offer daily flights from Miami. **Continental Connection** (☏ **800/231-0856;** www.continental.com) flies to Freeport from Miami and West Palm Beach once daily, and from Fort Lauderdale five times daily. **Delta Connection** (☏ **800/221-1212;** www.delta.com) has daily service from Atlanta. **US Airways** (☏ **800/428-4322;** www.usairways.com) operates flights to Freeport from Charlotte, NC, and Philadelphia.

Many visitors arrive in Nassau and then hop on one of the five daily Bahamasair flights to Freeport. These 30-minute hops run $155 to $420 round-trip.

No buses run from the airport to the major hotel zones, but many hotels provide airport transfers, especially if you've bought a package deal. If yours does not, no problem; **taxis** meet arriving flights and can take you from the airport to hotels in Freeport or Lucaya for about $15 to $39. The ride shouldn't take more than about 10 minutes.

Discovery Cruise Line (℡ **800/259-1579** or 242/351-1339; www.discoverycruiseline.com) offers daily passage between Fort Lauderdale and Grand Bahama. Frankly, the vessels making this 89km (55-mile) jaunt aren't the newest or glitziest, but they fit the bill with the requisite pool deck and bar, along with a casino, show lounge, and dining facilities. The trip from Florida takes about 5 hours, and you'll disembark very well fed. Fares are $55 to $180 per person.

Visitor Information

Information is available at the **Grand Bahama Tourism Board,** in the Fidelity Financial Centre, West Mall Drive at Poinciana Drive (℡ **242/350-8600;** www.bahamas.com). It's open Monday to Friday 9am to 5pm. That organization maintains three smaller information booths, each open daily from 9am to 5pm. They're located at **Grand Bahama International Airport** (℡ **242/352-2052**), at **Port Lucaya Marketplace** (℡ **242/373-8988**), and at the cruise-ship docks adjacent to **Lucayan Harbour** (℡ **242/350-8600**).

Island Layout

Other than the perhaps unexpected novelty of driving on the left, getting around Freeport/Lucaya is fairly easy due to the flat terrain. Although Freeport and Lucaya are frequently mentioned in the same breath, newcomers should note that Freeport is a landlocked collection of hotels and shops rising from the island's center, while the better-maintained and more appealing Lucaya, about 4km (2½ miles) away, is a bustling waterfront section of hotels, shops, and restaurants clustered next to a saltwater pond on the island's southern shore.

Freeport lies midway between Grand Bahama's northern and southern shores. Bisected by some of the island's largest roads, it was originally conceived as the site of the biggest hotels. Until a few years ago, the **International Bazaar** here was one of the country's most visited. Now in a lackluster state of disrepair, it's merely a theme-oriented mall that has seen better days. Immediately adjacent is the local **straw market,** where you can buy inexpensive souvenirs and Bahamian handicrafts.

To reach **Port Lucaya** from Freeport, head east from the International Bazaar along East Sunrise Highway, and then turn south at the intersection with Seahorse Road. The intersection—actually an oversize roundabout—is marked with a prominent stone marker that says PORT LUCAYA. Less than a mile from that roundabout, you'll be in the heart of the Lucaya complex. Know in advance that the shops and restaurants on the marina side of Seahorse Road are identified as being within the **"Port Lucaya"** subdivision. Conversely, the Radisson hotels, their restaurants, and their shops, all of which are clustered on the landward side of Seahorse Road, are identified as **"Our Lucaya."**

Port Lucaya's architectural centerpiece is **Count Basie Square,** named for the great entertainer who used to have a home on the island. A short walk east or west of the square will take you to most of the hotels, rising above the narrow strip of sand that separates the sea from a saltwater pond.

Life on Grand Bahama Island doesn't get more glamorous after you leave the Lucaya area. To the west of Freeport and Lucaya, the West Sunrise Highway passes grim industrial complexes that include the Bahamas Oil Refining Company. Once you pass the built-up waterfront sprawl of Freeport's western end, you can take Queen's Highway northwest all the way to **West End,** some 45km (28 miles) from Freeport's center. Along the way you pass the not-very-picturesque wharves of **Freeport Harbour,** where cruise ships dock. Just to the east lies **Hawksbill Creek,** a nondescript village that's home to some of the local port workers.

Much less explored is Grand Bahama's isolated **East End.** Its most distant tip lies about 72km (45 miles) from the center of Freeport and is reached via the Grand Bahama Highway. Despite its name, the route is bumpy and potholed in places and, along extensive stretches of its central area, is either blocked by piles of sand, rock, and fallen trees or is under construction. For access to the East End's most distant reaches from Freeport or Lucaya, allow about 2 hours of driving time. You'll first pass the **Rand Nature Centre,** about 5km (3 miles) east of Freeport. About 11km (6¾ miles) on is **Lucayan National Park,** and 8km (5 miles) farther lies the hamlet of **Free Town;** east of that is **High Rock,** known for its Emmanuel Baptist Church. The road now becomes considerably rougher until it ends in **McLean's Town,** which celebrates Columbus Day with an annual conch-cracking contest. From here, you can take a water taxi across Runners Creek to the exclusive **Deep Water Cay Club,** which caters to serious anglers.

Note: In Freeport/Lucaya, but especially on the rest of Grand Bahama Island, you will almost never find a street number on a hotel or a store. Sometimes in the more remote places, including sparsely populated areas on Lucaya's outskirts, you won't even find street signs. In lieu of numbers, locate places by their relation to hotels, beaches, or landmarks.

GETTING AROUND
By Taxi

The government sets the taxi rates, and the cabs are metered (or should be). Metered rates are $3 for the first .3km (¼ mile) and 40¢ for each additional 1.6km (1 mile). Extra passengers over the age of 2 pay $3 each. If there's no meter, agree on a price with the driver in advance. Typical taxi rates from the cruise dock are as follows: Xanadu Beach Hotel, $23; Port Lucaya Marketplace, $28; Flamingo Beach Resort, $27; and Viva Fortuna Beach, $34. Rates from the airport are as follows: Port Lucaya or Our Lucaya, $23; Viva Fortuna, $25; Royal Oasis, $22; and Xanadu $18.

You can call for a taxi, though most cabs wait at the big hotels or the cruise dock to pick up passengers. One major dispatcher is **Freeport Taxi Company,** Logwood Road (© **242/352-6666**), open 24 hours. Another is **Grand Bahama Taxi Union,** at Grand Bahama International Airport, Old Airport Road (© **242/352-7101**), also open 24 hours.

By Rental Car

If you plan to confine your exploration to the center of Freeport, with its International Bazaar, and Lucaya, with its beaches, you can rely on public transportation. However, if you'd like to explore the rest of the island (perhaps to find a more secluded beach), a rental car is the way to go. Terrain here is universally flat, a fact that's appreciated by drivers trying to conserve gasoline. Try **Avis** (© **800/331-1212** or 242/332-7666; www.avis.com) or **Hertz** (© **800/654-3131** or 242/352-9250; www.hertz.com), which both maintain offices in small bungalows near Grand Bahama International Airport. From inside the terminal, an employee of either company will contact a colleague, who will direct you to the curb outside the baggage pickup point. Then someone will arrive in a company car or van to drive you to the car pickup location.

One of the best companies is **Dollar Rent-a-Car,** Old Airport Road (© **800/800-3665** or 242/352-9325; www.dollar.com), which rents everything from a new Kia Sportage to a VW Jetta. Rates start at $60 per day for a car with a manual transmission, or $75 for an automatic. Mileage is unlimited, but the collision damage waiver (CDW) costs another $17 per day ($350 deductible). Remember to drive on the left, as British rules apply.

By Bus

Public bus service runs from the International Bazaar and downtown Freeport to Lucaya. The typical fare is $1.50 for adults, 50¢ for children. Check with the Grand Bahama Tourism Board

(p. 119) for bus schedules; there is no number to call for information.

By Scooter

A scooter is a fun way to get around, as most of Grand Bahama is flat with well-paved roads. Scooters can be rented at most hotels or, for cruise-ship passengers, in the Freeport Harbour area. You can also find dozens of stands along the roads in Freeport and Lucaya, as well as in major parking lots, charging from $40 to $65 per day. Helmets are required and provided by the outfitter.

On Foot

You can explore the center of Freeport or Lucaya on foot, but if you want to venture into the East End or West End, you'll need to rent a car, hire a taxi, or try Grand Bahama's erratic public transportation.

[FastFACTS] GRAND BAHAMA

ATMs Most banks here have ATMs that accept Visa, MasterCard, American Express, and any other bank or credit card on the Cirrus, Honor, Novus, and PLUS networks. Americans need not bother exchanging their money into Bahamian dollars because the currencies are on par, and U.S. dollars are readily accepted everywhere.

Doctors For the fastest and best service, head to **Rand Memorial Hospital** (see "Hospitals," below).

Emergencies Call ☎ **911,** or dial **0** for the operator.

Eyeglass Repair The biggest specialist in eyeglasses and contact lenses is the **Optique Shoppe,** 7 Regent Centre, downtown Freeport (☎ **242/352-9073**).

Hospitals If you need medical care, go to the government-operated, 90-bed **Rand Memorial Hospital,** East Atlantic Drive (☎ **242/352-6735,** or 352-2689 for ambulance; www.phabahamas.org).

Laundry & Dry Cleaning Try **Jiffy Cleaners Number 3,** West Mall at Pioneer's Way (☎ **242/352-7079**), open Monday 8am to 1pm, Tuesday to Saturday 8am to 6pm.

Newspapers & Magazines The *Freeport News* is a morning paper published Monday to Saturday, except holidays. Nassau's two dailies, the *Tribune* and the *Nassau Guardian,* are also available here, as are some New York and Miami papers, especially the *Miami Herald,* usually on the date of publication. American newsmagazines, such as *Time* and *Newsweek,* are flown in on the day of publication.

Pharmacies For prescriptions and other pharmaceutical needs, go to Mini Mall, 1 West Mall, Explorer's Way, where you'll find

L. M. R. Drugs (📞 **242/352-7327**), next door to Burger King. Hours are Monday through Saturday from 8am to 8pm and Sunday from 8am to 3pm.

Police Dial 📞 **911.**

Post Office The main post office (📞 **242/352-9371**) is on Explorer's Way, in Freeport.

Safety Avoid walking or jogging along lonely roads. There are no particular danger zones, but stay alert: Grand Bahama is no stranger to drugs and crime.

Taxes There is no sales tax on any purchase made within The Bahamas, though there is a 12% hotel tax. Visitors leaving The Bahamas pay a $20 departure tax, a tariff that's automatically included in the price of any airline or cruise-ship ticket.

Weather Grand Bahama Island, in the north of The Bahamas, has winter temperatures varying from around 61° to 75°F (16°–24°C) daily. Summer variations range from 79°F to the high 80s (26°C to the low 30s Celsius). In Freeport/Lucaya, phone 📞 **915** for weather information.

WHERE TO STAY

Most accommodations are in the Freeport area, near the International Bazaar, or in the Lucaya area, which is closer to the beach. *Remember:* In most cases, a resort levy of 8% and a 15% service charge will be added to your final bill. Be prepared, and ask if it's already included in the price you're quoted.

Freeport
EXPENSIVE

Island Seas Resort   A three-story timeshare property that rents units to nonmembers, this peach-colored resort opens onto a secluded beach midway between downtown Freeport and Port Lucaya. The location is convenient to both the Port Lucaya Marketplace and the Lucaya and Reef golf courses. The resort offers its own water fun with a pool, hot tub, and waterfall—plus a tiki-hut restaurant and bar. Because the condos are individually owned, each has unique furnishings and decor. All of the one- and two-bedroom units contain a full kitchen and balcony. Although technically they're not associated with the hotel, many watersports outfitters are located right on the beach.

William's Town, Freeport, Grand Bahama, The Bahamas. 📞 **800/801-6884** or 242/373-1271. Fax 242/373-1275. www.islandseas.com. 197 units. Year-round $179–$299 1-bedroom unit; $219–$359 2-bedroom unit. AE, DISC, MC, V. **Amenities:** Restaurant; bar; bikes; exercise room; Internet (free in lobby); outdoor pool; tennis court (lit for night play). *In room:* A/C, TV/DVD, kitchen.

Hotels & Restaurants in Freeport/Lucaya

Hotels ■
Castaway Resort & Suites **3**
Dundee Bay Villas **7**
Flamingo Bay Hotel & Marina **17**
Island Palm Resort **2**
Island Seas Resort **9**
Ocean Reef Yacht Club & Resort **11**
Old Bahama Bay by Ginn sur Mer **18**
Paradise Cove Beach Resort **19**
Pelican Bay at Lucaya **13**
Radisson at Our Lucaya Beach & Golf Resort **14**
Royal Islander Hotel **4**
Royal Palm Resort & Suites **1**
Taíno Beach Resort **15**
Viva Wyndam Fortuna Beach **20**
Xanadu Beach Resort and Marina **8**

Grand Bahama International Airport
Grand Bahamian Hwy.

Settlers Way

FREEPORT

Santa Maria Ave.
Pioneers Way
Cadwallader Dr.
Explorers Way
Nansen Ave.
West Atlantic Drive
West Mall Drive
East Mall Drive
Frobisher Drive
Pioneers Way East

Bahamia Princess Ruby Golf Course

Adventurers Way

SUNRISE PARK

West Sunrise Hwy.

International Bazaar

Princess Casino

Poinciana St.

Coral Rd.

Ranfurly Circus

Tamarind St.

Gambier St.

Hydroflora Gardens

East Sunrise Hwy.

Pinetree Stables

Santa Maria Ave.

Bahamia Princess Emerald Golf Course

E. Beach Dr.

CARAVEL BEACH

Pinta Ave.
The Mall South
Drumfish St.
Glover St.

Beachway Dr.
Tahiti St.

ROYAL BAHAMIA ESTATES

Lunar Blvd.

BAHAMAS TERRACE

WILLIAM'S TOWN

Bahama Re

Xanadu Beach
JOHN JACK PT.

Port-of-Call St.

MADIOCA PT.

East Palm Beach

Silver Pt. Dr.

Northwest Providence Channel

SILVER PT.

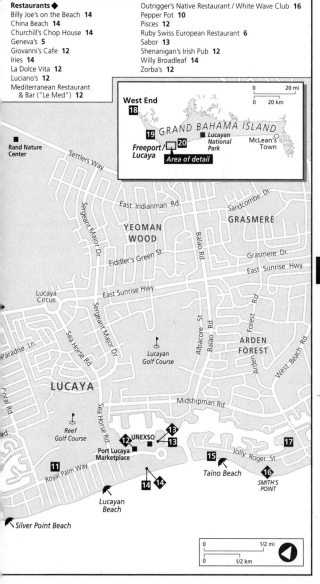

Restaurants ◆
Billy Joe's on the Beach **14**
China Beach **14**
Churchill's Chop House **14**
Geneva's **5**
Giovanni's Cafe **12**
Iries **14**
La Dolce Vita **12**
Luciano's **12**
Mediterranean Restaurant
& Bar ("Le Med") **12**

Outrigger's Native Restaurant / White Wave Club **16**
Pepper Pot **10**
Pisces **12**
Ruby Swiss European Restaurant **6**
Sabor **13**
Shenanigan's Irish Pub **12**
Willy Broadleaf **14**
Zorba's **12**

West End **18**

GRAND BAHAMA ISLAND

Freeport / Lucaya **19** **20**
Area of detail

Lucayan National Park

McLean's Town

0   20 mi
0   20 km

Rand Nature Center

Settlers Way

East Indianman Rd.

Sandcombe Dr.

YEOMAN WOOD

GRASMERE

Fiddler's Green St.

Baillou Rd.

Grasmere Dr.

East Sunrise Hwy.

Sergeant Major Dr.

Lucaya Circus

East Sunrise Hwy.

Albacore St.

Balao Rd.

Forest Rd.

ARDEN FOREST

Arden Rd.

West Beach Rd.

Paradise Ln.

Sea Horse Rd.

LUCAYA

Lucayan Golf Course

Midshipman Rd.

Royal Rd.

Reef Golf Course

Sea Horse Rd.

12 UNEXSO **13**
Port Lucaya Marketplace **13**

17

15

Jolly Roger St.

11

Royal Palm Way

14 **14**

Lucayan Beach

Taíno Beach

16
SMITH'S POINT

Silver Point Beach

0   1/2 mi
0   1/2 km

MODERATE

Castaways Resort & Suites ☺ Castaways is a modest and unassuming hotel that's almost immediately adjacent to the International Bazaar in downtown Freeport. A mix of vacationers and business travelers come here for the clean, well-maintained motel-style accommodations and the moderate prices. Pink-walled, green-shuttered rooms surround a quartet of landscaped courtyards, creating shelter from the traffic outside. It's not on the water, but a free shuttle will take you to nearby William's Town Beach. The four-story hotel is surrounded by gardens and has an indoor-outdoor garden lobby with a gift shop and kiosks selling island tours and watersports opportunities. The Flamingo Restaurant serves Bahamian and American fare daily from 7:30am to 10pm; it also has one of the island's best breakfasts. The pool area has a wide terrace and adjoining playground, plus a bar serving sandwiches and cool drinks.

E. Mall Dr., Freeport, Grand Bahama, The Bahamas. ℂ **866/410-9676** or 242/352-6682. Fax 242/352-5087. www.castaways-resort.com. 118 units. Winter $125–$155 double, $185–$195 suite; off-season $105–$135 double, $150–$160 suite. Children 12 and under stay free in parent's room. AE, MC, V. **Amenities:** Restaurant; 2 bars; babysitting; outdoor pool. *In room:* A/C, TV, DVD and VCR in some, hair dryer, Wi-Fi (free).

Royal Palm Resort & Suites ☺ Don't confuse this hotel with some of its competitors, whose names and amenities are roughly equivalent. The staff here mentioned to us that taxis often arrive with passengers booked at other properties with similar names, such as the Royal Islander, the Island Palm, and the more expensive Island Seas. This particular choice is a well-maintained, two-story pink motel that's the closest lodging to the airport. Though inland from the beach, it provides an oasis of resort-style living, with its wings wrapping around a pool. Rooms are outfitted in tropical motel style: tile floors, simple furniture, and floral upholsteries. Each sleeps up to four people, making this an economical choice for families. Although it's usually a bit more expensive than either the Royal Islander or the Island Palm, its repeat clientele—about 50% of whom are here for business reasons—don't seem to mind.

E. Mall Dr. at Settlers Way, Freeport, Grand Bahama, The Bahamas. ℂ **888/790-5264** or 242/352-3462. Fax 242/352-5759. 48 units. $60–$150 double. AE, DC, MC, V. **Amenities:** Restaurant; pool bar; children's playground; Internet (free in cafe); outdoor pool; tennis court (lit for night play). *In room:* A/C, TV, hair dryer, Wi-Fi (free).

INEXPENSIVE

Dundee Bay Villas 🏷 These well-furnished and affordable accommodations open onto ocean or canal views, with a good beach only 100 yards away. The place has a sort of down-home feeling, providing that home for you means Florida. All of the studios and the one-, two-, and three-bedroom units are comfortably decorated in a sort of tropical motif and come with fully equipped kitchens. To save money, many guests cook some of their own meals here. The two- and three-bedroom units are sought out by families. The larger ones with a loft can sleep eight comfortably and include a step-up jetted tub in the master bathroom.

15 Dundee Bay Dr., Freeport, Grand Bahama, The Bahamas. ☏ **866/771-7778** or 242/352-8038. Fax 416/247-4561. www.dundeebayvillas.com. 10 units. Year-round $79–$100 studio; $99–$129 1-bedroom unit; $139–$179 2-bedroom unit; $169–$219 3-bedroom unit. AE, DISC, MC, V. **Amenities:** Outdoor pool; Wi-Fi (free in lobby). *In room:* A/C, TV, kitchen.

Island Palm Resort 🏷 Set within the commercial heart of Freeport, this simple three-story motel comprises four buildings separated by parking lots and greenery. An easy walk to virtually everything in town and 2km (1¼ miles) from the International Bazaar, it offers good value in no-frills, eminently serviceable rooms with well-kept bathrooms. Complimentary shuttle service ferries guests to nearby William's Town Beach (also called Island Seas Beach), where you can jet-ski and snorkel at its sibling property, the Island Seas.

E. Mall Dr., Freeport, Grand Bahama, The Bahamas. ☏ **800/790-5264** or 242/352-6648. Fax 242/352-6640. www.islandpalm.com. 143 units. Winter $139–$169 double; off-season $99–$149 double. Extra person $15. AE, DISC, MC, V. **Amenities:** Bar; outdoor pool; Wi-Fi (free in lobby). *In room:* A/C, TV.

Royal Islander Hotel 😊 This hotel was built during an unfortunate Disney-style period in Freeport's expansion during the early 1980s. Its improbable-looking pyramidal roofs, inspired by a trio of Mayan pyramids, were rendered somewhat less obvious in 2004 when they were covered with dark-gray metal. Hospitable rooms are arranged around a verdant courtyard that seems far removed from the busy traffic and sterile-looking landscape outside. Rooms on the street level have white-tile floors, while those upstairs have wall-to-wall carpeting. Bathrooms are on the small side. Throughout, the motif is Floridian tropical, with some pizzazz and rates that tend to be lower than the Castaways Resort across the street. Lots of families check in here, so it's a safe environment for those with kids, who will enjoy the on-site playground. They can also take advantage of the free hourly shuttles to the more opulent Xanadu (p. 131), under the same ownership, without paying that resort's higher prices. There's a snack bar and a small restaurant on the premises, but otherwise you'll have to wander a short distance, perhaps to the International Bazaar across the street, to find dining and diversions.

E. Mall Dr., Freeport, Grand Bahama, The Bahamas. © **242/351-6000.** Fax 242/351-3546. http://royalislanderhotel.com. 100 units. Year-round $82-$102 double. Children 14 and under stay free in parent's room. AE, MC, V. **Amenities:** Restaurant; snack bar; bar; children's playground; outdoor pool. *In room:* A/C, TV, Wi-Fi ($10).

Lucaya

EXPENSIVE

Pelican Bay at Lucaya ★★   Here's a hotel with more architectural charm than any other small property on Grand Bahama. Built on a peninsula jutting into a labyrinth of inland waterways, it evokes a Dutch seaside village with rows of whimsically trimmed town houses, each painted a different color. Its location couldn't be better: It's immediately adjacent to Port Lucaya Marketplace, where restaurants and entertainment spots abound. Lucayan Beach, one of the best stretches of white sand on the island, is a 5-minute walk away. The equally appealing Taíno Beach lies immediately to the east, on the opposite side of a saltwater channel with hourly ferryboat service. UNEXSO, which provides some of the best dive facilities in The Bahamas, is next door. If that's not enough, the extensive amenities of Our Lucaya Resort, a very short walk away, are also available for use. Accommodations—especially suites—are about as stylish as you'll find on Grand Bahama, rivaled only by the Radisson compound at Our Lucaya. Each has a veranda or balcony, usually with water views; floors of buffed, tinted concrete; and rustic art objects and handicrafts from all over the world.

Seahorse Rd., Port Lucaya, Grand Bahama, The Bahamas. © **800/852-3702** in the U.S., or 242/373-9550. Fax 242/373-9551. www.pelicanbayhotel.com. 183 units. Winter $185 double, $215-$235 suite; off-season $165 double, $195-$215 suite. Rates include breakfast. AE, MC, V. **Amenities:** Restaurant (Sabor, p. 138); bar; babysitting; Jacuzzi; 3 outdoor pools. *In room:* A/C, TV, fridge, hair dryer, minibar (in suites), Wi-Fi ($13).

Radisson at Our Lucaya Beach & Golf Resort ★★★ ☺

This massive resort is one of the country's largest—and without a doubt it's the finest, most appealing, and best-accessorized property on Grand Bahama Island. The resort is set beside Lucayan Beach, one of the top white strands in The Bahamas. Although the area had been losing tourist business to Paradise Island, it got a big boost with the opening of this sprawling metropolis.

The first of the resort's three subdivisions is the **Radisson at Our Lucaya Resort.** With a vague South Beach Art Deco design, it's laid out in a massive open-sided, stone-trimmed hexagon. About half of the rooms face the beach and the pool; the other half look toward the gardens. The 513-room resort is contemporary but relaxed, with a young vibe that draws many families. Bedrooms are whimsical and fun, with maple-veneered furniture and loud fabric designs, all put together with artful simplicity.

Two newer, more upscale subdivisions are located immediately next door. The smaller and somewhat more private of the two buildings is **Radisson Pointe,** a 322-unit low-rise condo and timeshare complex that focuses on an adult clientele. Its larger counterpart is the 536-unit **Breakers Cay.** This grand 10-story, white-sided tower has edges that bend in a postmodern S-curve beside the beach. There's also the **Lanai Suites** in a small two-story compound flanking the sea, with 23 sprawling two-bedroom suites that blend colonial Caribbean style with 21st-century amenities.

The complex's various subsections stretch along a narrow beach strip, allowing guests to drop in to any of the bars, restaurants, and gardens that flank its edges. A resort this big contains an impressive array of dining options, each with a different theme and ambience. The most intriguing are reviewed under "Where to Eat," below. Each of the subdivisions also has an unconventional pool: The Sheraton's seems to flow around a replica of a 19th-century sugar mill and ancient Roman aqueduct, while the Radisson's is separated from the powder-white sands of Lucayan Beach by a trio of lap pools, each 15m (49 ft.) long and 1.2m (4 ft.) deep, with edges replicating the hotel's sinuous "S" shape. The pools culminate in a watery crescent whose infinity edge seems to merge directly into the Atlantic. The swim-up bar and hot tubs add more watery appeal.

Recent years have seen the addition of a spa, a convention center, and an upscale shopping mall. Kids 2 to 12 can be entertained during daylight hours at the country's best-run children's venue, **Camp Lucaya.** There's an increasing emphasis on golf here, thanks to the opening of the spectacular **Reef Golf Course** (p. 144). Tennis players will enjoy the **Ace Tennis Center,** which features replicas of the world's best-known court surfaces—like the red clay of the French Open, the manicured grass of Wimbledon, the Rebound Ace of the Australian Open, and the DecoTurf of the U.S. Open.

Royal Palm Way, Our Lucaya, Grand Bahama, The Bahamas. 📞 **866/870-7148** in the U.S., or 242/373-1333. Fax 242/327-5968. www.ourlucaya.com. 1,218 units. Year-round $249–$430 double; $519–$849 suite. $30 extra per day for 3rd and 4th occupants. Lanai 2-bedroom suites year-round $1,400–$1,700 per night for up to 6 occupants. AE, DC, DISC, MC, V. **Amenities:** 11 restaurants; 10 bars; babysitting; concierge; children's programs and camp; 2 18-hole golf courses; health club and spa; room service; 4 tennis courts (lit for night play); watersports equipment/rentals; Wi-Fi (free in lobby). *In room:* A/C, TV, hair dryer, Internet (free), minibar.

ESPECIALLY FOR kids

Radisson at Our Lucaya Beach & Golf Resort

(p. 128)   Camp Lucaya is the best-run, most amenities-packed kids' camp in The Bahamas, a full-service child-minding facility for infants to 12-year-olds. The camp is open only to children of guests at the Radisson at Our Lucaya and is open daily year-round from 9am to 5pm. It includes a supervised children's pool and classes on Bahamian culture (politics, arts, ecosystems, and crafts). A day's involvement might include learning native dances, creating island-inspired art, coconut bowling, or exploring a garden reserved just for kids. The **Marine Explorer's Club,** co-sponsored by the **Underwater Explorer Society (UNEXSO),** offers ocean and marine experiences to youngsters, including an opportunity to go nose-to-nose with dolphins. For children 2 and under, the staff imposes a 2-hour time limit for babysitting services. Children 3 to 12, however, can remain within the camp premises all day without charge, though parents are advised to check on them periodically.

Viva Wyndham Fortuna Beach (p. 133)   This all-inclusive
beachfront hotel, a 10-minute drive east of Port Lucaya (making it the island's most easterly resort), maintains its **Kid's Club** exclusively for children ages 2 to 11. It provides sports, games, and lessons throughout the day, under the supervision of trained staff members who know when to get parents involved and when to let them slip away for pursuits of their own.

MODERATE

Ocean Reef Yacht Club & Resort ★   Opening onto a marina and the water, this tropically furnished resort lies half a mile from a good beach and a 10-minute drive from Port Lucaya. It caters mainly to yachties but welcomes all vacationers to its individually owned one-, two-, and three-bedroom town houses and suites, which are rented out when the owners are away. Rental units come in various shapes and sizes, the least expensive being the narrow but comfortable efficiencies. Some units have bathrooms with Jacuzzis. Three meals a day are served at the outdoor Groupers Bar & Grill, where the namesake grouper and Bahamian lobster are specialties.

Royal Palm Way, Port Lucaya, Grand Bahama, The Bahamas. ℂ **242/373-4661.** Fax 242/373-8261. www.oryc.com. 60 units. Winter $130–$160 double, $170–$230 2-bedroom apt for 4; off-season $130–$140 double, $165–$175 2-bedroom apt for 4. MC, V. **Amenities:** Restaurant; bar; bikes; 2 outdoor pools; dive shop. *In room:* A/C, TV, kitchen or kitchenette, Wi-Fi ($5).

Taíno Beach

MODERATE

Taíno Beach Resort ★ ☺ This hotel lies across a saltwater canal from the grounds of the Radisson at Our Lucaya. It's also adjacent to Taíno Beach, the sister shore of the better-known Lucayan Beach. Enveloped by semitropical gardens, but not as posh as the Radisson, it dates back to 1995, when construction began on what evolved into a three-phase development. All units are in coral-painted concrete buildings and range from efficiencies, studios, and one-bedroom suites up to elaborate villas and penthouses. The rooms are spacious, well furnished, and nicely maintained. The quality, size, and amenities of your accommodations depend on how much you want to pay. Penthouses (on the fourth floor) are multi-level studios with their own deck and private pool. The hotel's ferry service ($2.50 per person each way, free for children 2 and under) makes frequent trips across the canal to a dock associated with Our Lucaya. From there, the restaurants, shops, and bars of the Port Lucaya Marketplace are within a 10-minute walk.

Jolly Roger Dr., Taíno Beach, Lucaya, Grand Bahama, The Bahamas. ℂ **888/311-7945** or 242/373-4682. Fax 242/373-4421. www.tainobeach.com. 157 units. Year-round $150 efficiency, $200 studio (shower only), $250 penthouse. Children 12 and under stay free in parent's room. AE, MC, V. **Amenities:** Restaurant; bar; babysitting; outdoor pool; tennis court; watersports equipment/rentals. *In room:* A/C, TV, hair dryer, Wi-Fi (free).

INEXPENSIVE

Flamingo Bay Hotel & Marina This hotel is set back from the water, about a 5-minute walk from a highly appealing length of white sand. Built of painted concrete, with three stories, it offers midsize, unpretentious, and uncomplicated bedrooms that are furnished in a Caribbean motif. Each has a well-maintained bathroom and such extras as a microwave and toaster. From a nearby 20-slip marina, frequent ferry service ($2.50 per person each way, free for children 2 and under) takes guests across a narrow saltwater canal to a pier operated by Our Lucaya, which is a short walk from Port Lucaya Marketplace.

Jolly Roger Dr., Taíno Beach, Lucaya, Grand Bahama, The Bahamas. ℂ **800/824-6623** or 242/373-5640. Fax 242/373-4421. www.tainobeach.com. 58 units. Year-round $90–$150 double. Children 12 and under stay free in parent's room. AE, DISC, MC, V. **Amenities:** W-Fi (free in lobby). *In room:* A/C, TV, hair dryer, kitchenette.

Xanadu Beach

MODERATE

Xanadu Beach Resort & Marina ★ Permeated with one of the most quirky and idiosyncratic histories of any lodging in The Bahamas, this hotel is radically different from the way it was back when it housed the reclusive billionaire Howard Hughes. Today, Xanadu soars above a scrub-dotted landscape that's crisscrossed with canals, mysteriously upscale villas, and reminders of the hurricane damage of the past several years. This hotel continues to strive admirably to provide comfort and good service to its guests, despite negative fortunes and a visitor scene that has shifted increasingly away from Freeport and toward Port Lucaya. The place benefited in 2005 from a big influx of cash that reconfigured the lobby area into a Spanish Baroque fantasy. Guest rooms are comfortable, and the nearby beach is alluring. Is the ghost of Howard Hughes still lurking in the penthouse? Perhaps.

Freeport, Grand Bahama, The Bahamas. ℰ **888/790-5264** or 242/352-6783 or 242/351-6777. Fax 242/352-5799. 186 units, plus 3 1-bedroom waterfront villas. Year-round $129 double; $225–$300 suite; $375 villa for up to 4 occupants. AE, DC, MC, V. **Amenities:** Babysitting; exercise room; outdoor pool; 2 tennis courts (lit for night play); watersports equipment/rentals; Wi-Fi (free in lobby). *In room:* A/C, TV, kitchen (in some).

Elsewhere on Grand Bahama
EXPENSIVE
Old Bahama Bay by Ginn sur Mer ★★ One of the most dramatic real-estate developments in The Bahamas lies at this outpost on the island's extreme western tip. Built on a site that in the early 1980s was the setting for the unsuccessful Jack Tar Village, the project centers around a cluster of upscale hotel units, a state-of-the-art 72-slip marina, and a palm-flanked beach. Accommodations are situated in nine two-story beach houses, each with four to six units. The spacious and breezy living quarters are outfitted in a colonial Caribbean style with a tropical country-club feel. Two on-site restaurants serve well-prepared Bahamian and international dishes.

The Ginn sur Mer resort encompasses much more than just hotel units. Its owners envision it as an entire village-in-the-making, relentlessly upscale and dotted with celebrity references. There's even an airplane landing strip less than a half-kilometer ($\frac{1}{3}$-mile) away. Future plans will expand the marina and improve the beachfront. Building sites, many sold already, range from $400,000 to $1 million each.

Bayshore Rd., West End, Grand Bahama, The Bahamas. ℰ **888/800-8959** in the U.S., or 242/350-6500. Fax 242/350-6565. www.oldbahamabay.com. 73 units. Winter $245–$520 suite, from $1,150 2-bedroom suite; off-season $245–$395 suite, $790–$1,510 2-bedroom suite. Breakfast and dinner $115 per person extra per day. AE, MC, V. **Amenities:** 2 restaurants; 2 bars; babysitting; exercise room; outdoor pool; room service; watersports equipment/rentals. *In room:* A/C, TV/DVD, CD player, CD library, hair dryer, kitchenette, Wi-Fi (free).

Viva Wyndham Fortuna Beach ★ ☺ Some visitors to this easternmost resort on the island argue that the beachfront here is even better than the more extensively developed strands at Port Lucaya. (The pool, however, packs a lot less drama than those at the Radisson at Our Lucaya.) Established in 1993, this all-inclusive resort lies 9.5km (6 miles) east of the International Bazaar along the island's southern coast, amid a landscape of casuarinas and scrubland. The sprawling 10-hectare (25-acre) compound of remote and breezy beachfront property is loaded with sports activities that are included in your room rate (as are all meals and drinks). Stylish, comfortably furnished bedrooms lie in a colorful group of two-story outbuildings. Most rooms have a private balcony, and about three-quarters have ocean views; the others overlook the surrounding scrublands.

In addition to an ongoing series of all-you-can-eat buffet feasts, you'll find Italian and Asian restaurants with a la carte dining. Know in advance that if you stay here, you'll be far from Port Lucaya (though a shuttle bus brings guests to the International Bazaar in downtown Freeport twice each day). For clients who appreciate the all-inclusive format, it's a worthwhile choice. Note, however, that singles pay 40% more than the per-person double-occupancy rate.

1 Doubloon Rd. (at Churchill Dr.), Freeport, Grand Bahama, The Bahamas. ℭ **877/999-3223** or 242/373-4000. Fax 242/373-5555. www.wyndham.com. 276 units. Winter $254–$294 double; off-season $204–$294 double. Extra person $80. Rates are all-inclusive. AE, DC, MC, V. **Amenities:** 3 restaurants; 3 bars; babysitting; kids' club; exercise room; Jacuzzi; outdoor pool; watersports equipment/rentals; Wi-Fi ($15 in lobby). *In room:* A/C, TV, fridge, hair dryer.

MODERATE

Paradise Cove Beach Resort ★ 🎁 Destroyed by the hurricane of 2005, this small resort has bounced back and is better than ever. It lies near the secluded beach of Paradise Cove just a 15-minute drive from Freeport's International Airport. Snorkelers along with seekers of tranquillity will like the resort's remote location. Each cottage comes with a full kitchen and a large screened-in porch, and is built on stilts rising above the beach, where you can not only swim and snorkel, but go kayaking. Guests gather at the Red Bar for tropical drinks, a limited menu, conch burgers, and one of the island's best piña coladas.

Deadman's Reef, Grand Bahama, The Bahamas. ℭ **242/349-2677.** www.dead mansreef.com. 2 cottages. Year-round $175 1-bedroom; $225 2-bedrooms. AE, MC, V. **Amenities:** Bar; watersports equipment/rentals. *In room:* TV, kitchen.

WHERE TO EAT

Foodies will find that the cuisine on Grand Bahama doesn't match the more refined fare served at dozens of places on New Providence (Nassau/Paradise Island). However, a few places here do specialize in fine dining; the others get by with rather standard food. The good news is that the dining scene is more affordable here.

Freeport

EXPENSIVE

Ruby Swiss European Restaurant ★★ CONTINENTAL The dishes you may remember from that European vacation are served here, without losing too much flavor in crossing the Atlantic. We're talking Wiener schnitzel, veal cutlets, and that retro favorite of the '50s, lobster Thermidor. Some of the best and freshest seafood is also featured here, along with affordably priced vintages. Ruby Swiss is also a great place for a snack after midnight, when you might be in the mood for a burger or Southern fried chicken. Live dinner music is sometimes featured.

Atlantic Way, off W. Sunrise Hwy. ✆ **242/352-8507.** Reservations recommended. Main courses $12–$48. AE, DISC, MC, V. Mon–Fri 11am–2am; Sat 6pm–4am.

INEXPENSIVE

Geneva's BAHAMIAN/SEAFOOD To eat where the locals eat, head for this unpretentious spot, where food is made the old-fashioned way. This restaurant is one of the best places to sample conch, which has nourished Bahamians for centuries. The Monroe family will prepare it for you stewed, cracked, or fried, or as part of a savory conch chowder that makes an excellent starter. Grouper also looms large, prepared in every imaginable way. The bartender will get you in a good mood with a rum-laced Bahama Mama.

Kipling Lane and E. Mall Dr., at W. Sunrise Hwy. ✆ **242/352-5085.** Lunch sandwiches and platters $10–$12; dinner main courses $12–$28. DISC, MC, V. Daily 7am–11pm.

Pepper Pot BAHAMIAN The Pepper Pot might be the only place on Grand Bahama that focuses exclusively on Bahamian-style takeout. It's popular all day, but it's especially mobbed on weekends after midnight, when clubbers descend to squelch their after-disco munchies. (It's the only 24-hr. eatery we know of on the island.) Don't expect glamour, as it's in a cramped, ordinary-looking building within a shopping center a 5-minute drive east of the International Bazaar. Order takeout portions of the island's best guava duff (a Bahamian dessert that resembles a jelly roll), as well as pork chops, fish dishes (usually deep-fried), chicken souse (an acquired taste), sandwiches, and an array of daily specials.

E. Sunrise Hwy. and Coral Rd. ✆ **242/373-7655.** Breakfast items $3–$8; main courses $9–$18; vegetarian plates $7–$9. No credit cards. Daily 24 hr.

Our Lucaya Resort & Taíno Beach
EXPENSIVE

Churchill's Chop House ★★ AMERICAN One of the island's most elegant and formal restaurants is imbued with a sense of the faded grandeur of the British Empire. Surpassed only by Luciano's (p. 137), in our opinion, Churchill's lures diners from other parts of the island to a room that opens onto the lobby of the Radisson at Our Lucaya. The venue includes a British colonial–style bar with dark-wood flooring and trim, potted plants, a grand piano, and views over the sea. The island's best chophouse, it features succulent steaks flown over from the mainland and locally caught seafood. Regrettably, it's open less frequently than we'd like, sometimes operating only on weekends during low and shoulder seasons.

Radisson at Our Lucaya Resort, Royal Palm Way. ✆ **242/373-1333.** www.our lucaya.com. Reservations required. Main courses $16–$42. AE, DC, DISC, MC, V. Usually Mon–Sat 6–10pm, though off-season hours may vary based on resort occupancy.

Iries ★ CARIBBEAN This is one of the newer restaurants at Our Lucaya, where a team of food and beverage experts threw tons of money and research into developing an appropriate blend of Caribbean tradition and modern marketing methods. The result looks like the dining room of a colonial Jamaican manor house. Decor is replete with replicas of pineapples (the region's traditional symbol of hospitality), Rastafarian paintings, and elaborately carved mahogany furniture similar to what might have graced the home of a 19th-century Caribbean planter. It's permeated by a sense of spaciousness and old-fashioned dignity and restraint. Menu items include cracked conch with spicy sauce and sweet potato wedges, grilled sirloin steak with cumin and thyme, blackened grouper with fire-roasted peppers and pineapple sauce, and tamarind-glazed hen. On your way in, check out the Bahamian Junkanoo costume on display—it's one of the most elaborate, outrageous, and costly examples of its kind.

Radisson at Our Lucaya Resort, Royal Palm Way. ✆ **242/373-1333.** www.our lucaya.com. Reservations recommended. Main courses $16–$34. AE, MC, V. Sat–Wed 6–10pm, though hours may vary based on resort occupancy.

MODERATE

China Beach ★ ASIAN FUSION   Within its own stone-and-stucco building on the seafront grounds of Our Lucaya, this restaurant proffers a culinary passport to the Pacific Rim. Exotic delights include the spicy cuisines of Vietnam, Thailand, Korea, Indonesia, and Malaysia. The menu changes monthly, but some dishes appear with regularity. Our favorites are a savory Hong Kong roast duckling and a zesty Thai chicken. The beef marinated in soy sauce is served with fresh spring onion, while the grouper filet appears with ginger and scallions. Other specialties include a seafood teppanyaki and stir-fried conch. The decor is particularly imaginative, with scarlet parasols doubling as chandeliers, and architecture that seems to float above one of the resort's serpentine swimming pools.

Radisson at Our Lucaya Resort, Royal Palm Way. ℭ **242/373-1333.** www.our lucaya.com. Reservations recommended. Main courses $15–$30. AE, DC, DISC, MC, V. Tues–Sat 6–10pm, though hours may vary based on resort occupancy.

Willy Broadleaf ★ INTERNATIONAL   Set on the ground level of the Radisson at Our Lucaya, facing one of its S-shaped swimming pools, this imaginatively decorated restaurant is centered on one of the most lavish buffet breakfasts we've ever seen in The Bahamas. The decor fits the cuisine, with various sections evoking a Mexican courtyard, a marketplace in old Cairo, the dining hall of an Indian maharajah (including tables that are cordoned off with yards of translucent fabric), and an African village. Food stations serve cold and hot breakfast foods—try the omelets, pancakes, and French toast, the best version of which is laced with coconut.

Radisson at Our Lucaya Resort, Royal Palm Way. ℭ **242/373-1333.** www.our lucaya.com. Reservations not necessary. Breakfast buffet $15 for cold foods, $20 for both hot and cold foods; dinner buffet $38. AE, DC, DISC, MC, V. Daily 6:30–11am and 6–11pm.

INEXPENSIVE

Billy Joe's on the Beach BAHAMIAN   In an act of generosity, the developers of the Radisson have preserved a Bahamian tradition, allowing the famous Billy Joe to keep his stand on the beach after they bought the property. As in days gone by, patrons can still go barefoot on the white sand while sampling the chef's fixins. "Fresh, sexy conch" is his reason for living, and Billy Joe sells it on the spot. His conch salad is hailed as the island's best; he'll also grill or "crack" the conch for you. On occasion, he'll offer sautéed Bahamian lobster. Fish and chips are on the menu, too, and if you tire of the fresh snapper or grouper (highly unlikely), he's also known for making the best cheeseburger on the island.

Lucayan Beach. ℭ **242/373-1300,** ext. 5803. Reservations not needed. Main courses $11–$15. No credit cards. Daily 10am–10pm (closing times can vary).

Port Lucaya

EXPENSIVE

Luciano's ★ FRENCH/CONTINENTAL   With its tables usually occupied by local government officials and dealmakers, Luciano's is the grande dame of the area's restaurants. It's the only place in Port Lucaya offering caviar, foie gras, and oysters Rockefeller, all served with a flourish by a formally dressed waitstaff, who, fortunately, have a definite sense of charm and humor. Inside, you'll find a bar and elegantly set tables; additional seating on a breezy upstairs veranda overlooks the marina. For a good opener, opt for the lightly smoked salmon, seafood crepe, or snails in garlic butter. Fresh fish and shellfish are delicately prepared, allowing natural flavor to shine through without heavy sauces. Steak Diane is one of Luciano's classics, along with a delectable veal medallion sautéed with shrimp and chunks of lobster.

Port Lucaya Marketplace. ✆ **242/373-9100.** www.thebahamasguide.com/lucianos. Reservations required in winter. Main courses $26–$48. AE, MC, V. Daily 5:30–9:45pm (last order).

MODERATE

Giovanni's Cafe ★ ITALIAN/SEAFOOD   Tucked into one of the pedestrian thoroughfares of Port Lucaya Marketplace, this cream-colored clapboard house contains a charming 38-seat Italian trattoria. The chefs serve Italian-influenced preparations of local seafood, highlighted by seafood pasta and a lobster special. Giovanni stamps each dish with his Italian verve and flavor, whether it be Bahamian conch, local seafood, or scampi. Choices showing off his precision and rock-solid technique include sirloin steak with fresh mushrooms, shrimp scampi, and extremely good spaghetti carbonara.

Port Lucaya Marketplace. ✆ **242/373-9107.** Reservations recommended. Main courses $14–$37. AE, MC, V. Mon–Sat 4–10pm; Sun 5–10pm.

Mediterranean Restaurant & Bar ("Le Med") ★ 🏷 FRENCH/GREEK/BAHAMIAN   This is a simpler and more cost-effective version of **Luciano's** (above), which is under the same management. The decor consists of sand-colored floor tiles, refrigerator cases loaded with pastries and salads, and bare tables that look like they belong in a coffee shop. Don't let this simplicity fool you: The place serves well-flavored, surprisingly sophisticated food that has attracted its share of celebrities. It's crowded in the morning, when omelets (including a feta-and-spinach Greek version), eggs and bacon, and Bahamian stewed fish and steamed conch are crowd-pleasers. Lunch and dinner feature assorted Greek- and Turkish-style mezes and Iberian-influenced tapas that include marinated octopus and grilled calamari. Crepes come in both sweet and savory varieties. Other tempters include a seafood combo piled high with lobster, shrimp, conch, fish, and mussels; *shashlik* (marinated kabobs redolent with herbs); and braised lamb shank cooked in red wine.

Port Lucaya Marketplace. © **242/374-2804.** Breakfast items $5–$13; crepes $8–$10; main courses $12–$26. AE, DC, MC, V. Daily 8am–10pm.

Pisces ★ SEAFOOD/PIZZA/INTERNATIONAL This ranks high among our favorites in the Port Lucaya Marketplace—and we're seconded by the locals and sailors who pack it every weekend. The place is outfitted with a quirky mixture of nautical accessories and dark-varnished wood, with a prominent bar where more gossip is exchanged the later it gets. Tabletops contain laminated seashells, fake gold coins, and sand. The charming all-Bahamian staff serves more than 20 different varieties of pizzas, including a version with conch, lobster, shrimp, and chicken, as well as one with Alfredo sauce. Dinners are more elaborate, with a choice of curries of all kinds, fish, shellfish, and several pastas.

Port Lucaya Marketplace. © **242/373-5192.** www.the-bahamas-restaurants. com/pisces. Reservations recommended. Pizzas $12–$30; main courses $9–$37. AE, DISC, MC, V. Mon–Sat 5pm–2am.

Sabor SEAFOOD Located in the garden of the Pelican Bay hotel, this restaurant opens onto a panoramic sweep over the yachts in Port Lucaya Marina. Diners peruse the menu as exotic lounge music fills the night air. This has become a favorite watering hole of local yachties, who sample such appetizers as herb-laden escargots baked in garlic butter, steamed curry mussels, or perhaps the salad of pear, blue cheese, and greens mixed with a sweet nut vinaigrette. If you're here for lunch, Sabor has the best burger menu in town, including one flavored with Cajun spices. Sunday brunch from noon to 2pm is an event here, featuring three varieties of eggs Benedict.

Pelican Bay at Lucaya, Seahorse Rd., Port Lucaya. © **242/373-5588.** www. sabor-bahamas.com. Reservations recommended for dinner. Burgers $12–$14; main courses $16–$29. MC, V. Daily 11:30am–10pm.

Shenanigan's Irish Pub IRISH/INTERNATIONAL Dark and beer-stained from the thousands of pints of Guinness, Harp, and Killian's that have been served and spilled here, this pub and restaurant is the premier Irish—or Bostonian-Irish—hangout on Grand Bahama. Many visitors come just to drink, sometimes for hours at a time, soaking up the suds and perhaps remembering to eventually order some food. They still serve steak-and-kidney pie, burgers, and surf and turf, but newer items include French-style rack of lamb for two, seafood Newburg, and chicken Connemara drenched in whiskey sauce.

Port Lucaya Marketplace. © **242/373-4734.** www.irishpubbahamas.com. Main courses $11–$51. AE, DISC, MC, V. Mon–Thurs 5pm–midnight; Fri–Sat 5pm–2am (last food order at 9:45pm).

INEXPENSIVE

Outrigger's Native Restaurant/White Wave Club BAHAMIAN
Cement-sided and simple with a large deck extending out toward the sea, this restaurant was here long before the Port Lucaya Marketplace, which lies 4 blocks away. It's the domain of Gretchen Wilson, whose kitchens produce a rotating series of lip-smacking dishes such as lobster tails, minced lobster, steamed or cracked conch, pork chops, chicken, fish, and shrimp, usually served with peas 'n' rice and macaroni. Every Wednesday from 5pm to 2am, **Outrigger's Famous Wednesday Night Fish Fry** draws as many as 1,000 diners who line up for platters of fried or steamed fish ($10–$16). A DJ and dancers provide entertainment. Almost as well attended are the Tuesday and Thursday **Bonfire Nights,** when all-you-can-eat barbecue dinners go for $30 per person. You can order drinks at the restaurant, but you might consider stepping into the nearby ramshackle bar called the **White Wave Club,** which serves only drinks. *Note:* If you make reservations for a Bonfire Night through your hotel, you may pay an extra $20.

Smith's Point. © **242/373-4811.** Reservations not required. Main courses $10–$16. No credit cards. Sat–Thurs noon–8pm.

Zorba's ◢ BAHAMIAN/GREEK
Zorba's provides some of the best food value at Port Lucaya Marketplace. A narrow veranda overlooks a relatively uninteresting pedestrian alleyway outside, and the blue-and-white Formica-clad interior might remind you of a diner. A TV blasts a Greek-language news broadcast. Big photos of Alan Bates and Anthony Quinn (playing Zorba, get it?) dancing on a beach add a touch of nostalgia for *ouzo* and *retsina.* The cuisine is a quirky mixture of Greek and Bahamian, and if you don't remember exactly what *taramosalata* is, the good-looking Bahamian staff will rattle off the ingredients like Peloponnesian pros. First thing in the morning, you'll see locals standing in line for the Bahamian breakfasts, which include chicken souse, corned beef and grits, and an array of pancakes, waffles, and omelets. Lunch could be a fat gyro, burger, or souvlaki. Dinner can begin with a Greek salad and then move on to moussaka, grilled chicken on a bed of spinach, or any of several pasta dishes. End with baklava, those honey and nut-studded pastries, for a sweet finish.

Port Lucaya Marketplace. © **242/373-6137.** http://zorbasbahamas.com. Main courses lunch $4–$15; dinner $12–$29. AE, DISC, MC, V. Daily 7am–10:30pm.

The East End

Bishop's Beach Club & Bar BAHAMIAN   If you're heading to the East End to visit Lucayan National Park (p. 148), you might want to make this your luncheon stopover. After you've explored the park, you can drive east for about 6 miles to High Rock. (Just continue east along Queens Highway, the major boulevard.) Locals, expats, fishermen, and visitors alike patronize this very authentic eatery, which serves local recipes based on time-tested favorites. Cracked conch is the chef's specialty and it's a savory choice, though often a bit rubbery. If you're not a conch aficionado, there are other choices, such as savory barbecued ribs and broiled Bahamian lobster. Peas 'n' rice accompany most dishes. If you're arriving in the East End in the morning, consider a breakfast here—nothing special, just ham (or bacon) and eggs. If you're using a credit card, a $30 minimum is required.

High Rock, Queens Hwy. (©) **242/353-5485.** Reservations not needed. Breakfast from $6; main courses $6–$15. MC, V. Daily 9am–6pm.

The West End

Pier One AMERICAN/BAHAMIAN/SEAFOOD   This is a favorite restaurant of visitors because it's close to the cruise-ship dock, and it's also an ideal place to sample some fresh Bahamian seafood. Guests from all over the world choose between picnic tables set out on the veranda, or else they dine inside in a large room decorated with nautical paraphernalia. The owner presents shark feedings at 7, 8, and 9pm. The house specialty is actually baby shark, which is most often served smoked. You can also order it sautéed with garlic; or else stuffed with cheese and fresh crab. A fresh fish of the day, perhaps grouper or snapper, is also featured. For the non-seafood eater, there are juicy steaks and poultry dishes such as chicken curry.

Freeport Harbour. (©) **242/352-6674.** Reservations not needed. Main courses $17–$23. AE, MC, V. Mon–Sat 11am–10pm; Sun 4–10pm.

BEACHES & OUTDOOR PURSUITS

Hitting the Beach

Grand Bahama Island has enough beaches for everyone. The best ones open onto Northwest Providence Channel at Freeport and sweep eastward for some 97km (60 miles) to encompass Xanadu Beach, Lucaya Beach, Taíno Beach, and others, eventually ending at such remote eastern outposts as Rocky Creek and McLean's

A Secluded Beach Hideaway

More and more visitors are discovering the secluded beach of **Paradise Cove,** at Deadman's Reef (② 242/349-2677), just a 15-minute drive from Freeport's Grand Bahama International Airport. This has become an all-around recreation center with snorkeling, swimming, ocean kayaking, fishing, beach bonfires, and much more. The on-site Red Bar is the social center, renting underwater cameras and other items needed for the beach, as well as quenching your thirst with Bahama Mamas and serving food such as conch burgers or lobster with pasta salad.

Town. Once you leave the Freeport/Lucaya area, you can virtually have your pick of white sandy beaches all the way. When you get past the resorts, you'll see a series of secluded beaches used mainly by locals. If you like people, a lot of organized watersports, and easy access to hotel bars and rest rooms, stick to Xanadu, Taíno, and Lucayan beaches.

Xanadu Beach ★★ is one of our favorites, immediately south of Freeport and the site of the famed Xanadu Beach Resort. The 1.6km-long (1-mile) beach may be crowded in winter, but that's because of those gorgeous soft white sands, which open onto tranquil waters. The beach is set against a backdrop of coconut palms and Australian pines. You can hook up here with an assortment of watersports, including snorkeling, boating, jet-skiing, and parasailing.

Immediately east of Xanadu is little **Silver Point Beach,** site of a timeshare complex whose guests ride the waves on water bikes and play volleyball. You'll see horseback riders from Pinetree Stables (p. 145) galloping along the sands here.

Despite the allure of other beaches on Grand Bahama, most visitors go to **Lucayan Beach,** right off Royal Palm Way and immediately east of Silver Point Beach. This is one of the best strands in The Bahamas, with long stretches of white sand. In the vicinity of the Radisson hotels, you'll also encounter a worthy scattering of beach bars. At any of the resorts along this beach, you can hook up with an array of watersports or get a frosty drink from a hotel bar. It's definitely not for those seeking seclusion, but it is a fun beach-party scene.

Immediately to the east of Lucayan Beach, and separated from it by a saltwater canal, **Taíno Beach** is a family favorite and a good place for watersports. This, too, is a fine wide beach of white sands, opening onto usually tranquil waters.

5

GRAND BAHAMA

Beaches & Outdoor Pursuits

Another choice, not too far east, is **Gold Rock Beach,** a favorite picnic spot for weekending locals; you'll usually have it to yourself on weekdays. A 19km (12-mile) drive from Lucaya, it's at the doorstep of **Lucayan National Park** (p. 148), a 16-hectare (40-acre) park filled with some of the island's longest, widest, and most fabulous secluded beaches.

Biking

A guided bike trip is an ideal way to see parts of Grand Bahama that most visitors miss. You'll start at **Barbary Beach** and pedal a mountain bike along the southern coast parallel to the sands. After stopping for a snack, lunch, and a dip, you'll finally reach **Lucayan National Park,** some 19km (12 miles) away. You can explore the cave in which the natives, centuries before the coming of Columbus, buried their dead. Crabs here occasionally come up through holes in the ground carrying bits of bowls once used by the Lucayans. **Grand Bahama Nature Tours,** also known as Kayak Nature Tours (© **866/440-4542** or 242/373-2485; www.grandbahama naturetours.com), runs these bike trips and transports you home to your hotel by van so you don't exhaust yourself in the heat while cycling back. Other tour options give you more time kayaking or snorkeling. All excursions last 5 to 6 hours and cost $79 for adults, $40 for children 11 and under. Rates include all equipment, sustenance, and round-trip transportation from your hotel.

Boat Cruises

Ocean Wonder, Port Lucaya Dock (© **242/373-5880;** www. bahamasvacationguide.com/reeftours), run by Reef Tours, is a gargantuan 18m (59-ft.) Defender glass-bottom boat. Any tour agent can arrange for you to board this vessel. You'll get a panoramic view of the beautiful underwater life off the coast of Grand

Bahama. Cruises depart from Port Lucaya behind the straw market on the bay side at 9:30am, 11:15am, 1:15pm, and 3:15pm, except Friday, when only the earlier two tours are offered. The excursion lasts 1½ hours and costs $30 for adults and $18 for children 6 to 12. During high season in midwinter, make reservations a day or two in advance, as the boat does fill up quickly.

Superior Watersports, Freeport (© **242/373-7863**; www.superiorwatersports.com), offers trips on its *Bahama Mama,* a two-deck, 22m (72-ft.) catamaran. The **Robinson Crusoe Beach Party** is offered four times a week and costs $59 for adults and $39 for children 11 and under. Schedules vary with the season, from 11am to 4pm October through March, but from noon to 5pm April through September. There's also a shorter sunset **Booze Cruise** that goes for $39; it's offered Tuesday, Thursday, and Saturday evenings and lasts 2 hours.

For an underwater cruise, try the *Seaworld Explorer,* the company's quasi-submarine. The sub itself does not descend; instead, you walk down into the hull and watch the sea life glide by. It departs daily at 9:30am, 11:30am, and 1:30pm. The 2-hour ride costs $45 for adults and $25 for children 2 to 12.

The Dolphin Experience

A pod of bottle-nosed dolphins is involved in a unique dolphin-human familiarization program at the **Dolphin Experience,** located at Underwater Explorer Society (UNEXSO), next to Port Lucaya, opposite the entrance to the Radisson at Our Lucaya (© **800/992-DIVE** [3483] or 242/373-1244; www.unexso.com). This close-encounter program allows participants to observe these intelligent, friendly animals and hear a talk by a member of the animal-care staff. This is the world's largest dolphin facility, so conditions aren't cramped. In addition, the dolphins can swim out to sea, passing through an underwater gate that prevents their natural predators from entering the lagoon; the dolphins later return of their own free will to their protected marine habitat.

After a 25-minute ferryboat ride from Port Lucaya, you'll step onto a shallow wading platform to interact with the dolphins. At press time, the dolphin colony had 17 members. This educational, fun adventure for all ages costs $75 for adults and $50 for kids 4 to 7; children 3 and younger participate free. If you like to document your life's unusual experiences, bring your camera.

For certified divers, UNEXSO offers a dolphin dive, wherein a school of dolphins swims out from its marine habitat in Sanctuary Bay for a closely supervised diver-to-dolphin encounter. The cost is $199. If business warrants, the dolphin dive is offered daily.

Swimming with dolphins has its supporters as well as its highly vocal critics. For insight into the various points of view surrounding this issue, visit the Whale and Dolphin Conservation Society's website at www.wdcs.org. For more information about responsible travel in general, check out www.ecotourism.org.

Fishing

In the waters off Grand Bahama, you can fish for barracuda, snapper, grouper, yellowtail, wahoo, and kingfish, along with other denizens of the deep.

Reef Tours, Port Lucaya Dock (© **242/373-5880** or 373-5891; www.bahamasvacationguide.com/reeftours), offers one of the least expensive ways to go deep-sea fishing around Grand Bahama. Adults pay $130 if they fish, $60 if they go along only to watch. Four to six people can charter the entire 13m (43-ft.) craft for $750 per half-day or $1,350 per whole day. The 9.6m (31-ft.) boat can be chartered for $480 per half-day or $850 per full day. Departures for the 4-hour half-day excursions are daily at 8:30am and 1pm, while the 8-hour full-day excursions leave daily at 8:30am. Bait, tackle, and ice are included in the cost.

Golf

Since two of the island's older courses, the Ruby and the Emerald, closed after the hurricane damage of the early millennium, Grand Bahama is not as rich in golf courses as it used to be. But golf on the island recently experienced a resurgence, thanks to the improvements to the courses described below. They're open to the public year-round; their pro shops can rent you clubs.

Fortune Hills Golf & Country Club, Richmond Park, Lucaya (© **242/373-2222**), was originally intended to be an 18-hole course, but the back 9 were never completed. You can replay the front 9 for 18 holes and a total of 6,324m (6,916 yd.) from the blue tees. Par is 72. Greens fees are $50 for 9 holes, $64 for 18; carts are included. Club rental costs $20 for 18 holes, $16 for 9 holes.

The island's best kept and most manicured course is **Lucayan Golf Course,** Lucayan Beach, at Our Lucaya (© **242/373-1333**). Made over after 2004's Hurricane Jeanne, this beautiful course is a traditional golf layout with rows of pine trees separating the fairways. Greens are fast, with a couple of par 5s more than 457m (500 yd.) long, totaling 6,240m (6,824 yd.) from the blue tees and 5,933m (6,488 yd.) from the whites. Par is 72.

Its sibling golf course, with an entirely separate clubhouse and staff, is the slightly older **Reef Golf Course ★★**, Royal Palm Way, at Our Lucaya (© **242/373-1333**). Designed by Robert

Trent Jones, Jr., who called it "a bit like a Scottish course but a lot warmer," the course boasts 6,328m (6,920 yd.) of links-style playing grounds. It features a wide-open layout without rows of trees to separate its fairways and lots of water traps—you'll find water on 13 of the 18 holes and various types of long grass swaying in the trade winds. Play requires patience and precise shot-making to avoid the numerous lakes.

At either the Lucayan or Reef courses, guests at the Radisson hotels, with which the courses are associated, pay between $75 and $120, depending on the time of day, for 18 holes. The 9-hole special goes for $55. Nonguests are charged between $85 and $130 for 18 holes, $65 for 9 holes. Rates include use of an electric-powered golf cart.

Horseback Riding

Pinetree Stables, North Beachway Drive, Freeport (© **242/373-3600** or 305/433-4809; www.pinetree-stables.com), has the country's best and—with a boarded inventory of more than 50 horses—biggest riding stables, superior to rivals on New Providence Island (Nassau). Pinetree offers trail rides to the beach Tuesday through Sunday year-round at 9 and 11:30am. The cost is $85 per person for a 2-hour trail ride. Children 8 and under are not allowed. The weight limit for riders is 91kg (200 lb.).

Sea Kayaking

To explore the waters off the island's north shore, call **Grand Bahama Nature Tours** (© **866/440-4542** or 242/373-2485; www.grandbahamanaturetours.com) and go on kayak excursions through the mangroves, where you can see wildlife as you paddle along. The cost is $79 for adults and $40 for children 11 and under, with lunch included. Double kayaks are used on these jaunts, and children must be at least 3 years old. For the same price, you can take a 30-minute kayak trip to an offshore island, with 1½ hours of snorkeling included along with lunch. Call ahead to book reservations for either of these tours. A van will pick you up at your hotel between 9 and 10am and deliver you back at the end of the tour, usually sometime between 3 and 4pm. A popular variation on this tour, which operates during the same hours and at the same prices, includes more time devoted to snorkeling above a series of shallow offshore reefs and slightly less time allocated to kayaking.

Snorkeling & Scuba Diving

Though there's fine snorkeling along the shore, you should book a snorkeling cruise aboard one of the catamarans to see the most stunning reefs. **Reef Tours** (© 242/373-5880; www.bahamas vacationguide.com/reeftours) offers highly recommended snorkeling tours. Lasting just under 2 hours each, they depart from Port Lucaya thrice daily (10am, 12:30pm, and 2:30pm). Tours are priced at $35 for adults and $18 for children 6 to 12, with all equipment included. Another option is a 3-hour sail-and-snorkel-tour that departs daily at 9:30am and 1:30pm; it's priced at $45 for adults and $25 for children 6 to 12.

Serious divers are attracted to Grand Bahama sites like the **Wall,** the **Caves** (one of the most interesting of which is **Ben's Cavern**), **Treasure Reef,** and the most evocative of all, **Theo's Wreck ★★**, a freighter that was deliberately sunk off Freeport to attract marine life. Today it teems with everything from horse-eyed jacks to moray eels. Other top locales include **Spit City, Ben Blue Hole, Pygmy Caves, Gold Rock, Silver Point Reef,** and the **Rose Garden.**

One of the premier dive outfitters in the Caribbean, **Underwater Explorer Society (UNEXSO) ★★★** (© 800/992-DIVE [3483] or 242/373-1244; www.unexso.com) offers seven dive trips daily, including reef trips, shark dives, wreck dives, and night dives. Divers can even meet dolphins in the open ocean here—a rare experience offered by very few facilities in the world (see "The Dolphin Experience," p. 143).

UNEXSO also has a popular 3-hour learn-to-dive course, the **Mini-B Pool and Reef Adventure,** offered daily. Over the outfitter's 30-year history, more than 50,000 people have successfully completed either this course or its similar predecessors. For $109, students learn the basics in UNEXSO's training pools and dive the beautiful shallow reef with an instructor.

Tennis

The island's best tennis facilities are part of the **Ace Tennis Center,** at Our Lucaya (© **242/350-5294**), where four tennis courts feature different playing surfaces. They include a grass court ($100 per hour) that resembles that of Wimbledon, a clay surface ($50 per hour) like that of the French Open, a Rebound Ace rubber surface that's equivalent to the norm at the Australian Open ($35 per hour), and a hard DecoTurf ($25 per hour) that's similar to the surface at the U.S. Open. Advance reservations are necessary, and there is no discount of any kind for resort guests. A resident pro offers individual 1-hour tennis lessons for $90 per person, or $130 for a couple.

Watersports in General

Ocean Motion Watersports Ltd., Sea Horse Lane, Lucayan Beach (© **242/374-2425**; www.oceanmotionbahamas.com), is one of the island's largest watersports companies. It offers a wide variety of activities daily from 9am to 5pm, weather permitting, including snorkeling, parasailing, Hobie Cats, banana boating, water-skiing, jet skis, windsurfing, and other activities. **Parasailing,** for example, costs $70 per person for 5 to 7 minutes in the air. **Snorkeling trips** cost $35 for adults, $18 for kids 11 and under, for 1½ hours. **Water-skiing** goes for $40 per 3.2km (2-mile) pull, $60 for a 30-minute lesson. **Hobie Cats** are $50 for the 4.2m (14 ft.), $75 for the 4.8m (16 ft.), $30 for a lesson. **Windsurfing** costs $30 per hour, $100 for a 2-hour lesson. **Kayaking** costs $20 for a single kayak, $25 for a double. The **water trampoline** is $20 for a full day, $10 for a half-day. **Banana boating** goes for $15 per person for a 3.2km (2-mile) ride along a white-sand beach. Call for reservations, especially for windsurfing.

    Lucaya Watersports, Taíno Beach (© **242/373-6375**), also offers options for fun in the surf, including **WaveRunners,** which cost $70 per 30 minutes; **double kayaks,** which are $20 per hour for two passengers; and **paddle boats,** which hold four people and go for $20 per hour. The **sunset cruise**—a 2-hour sailboat ride offered every Wednesday between 5 and 7pm—is especially popular and costs $45 per person.

SEEING THE SIGHTS

Several informative tours of Grand Bahama Island are available. One reliable company is **H. Forbes Charter Services Ltd.,** West Sunrise Highway, Freeport (© **242/352-9311;** www.forbes charter.com). From its headquarters in the International Bazaar, this company operates half- and full-day bus tours. The most popular option is the half-day Super Combination Tour, priced at $35 per adult and $25 per child age 5 to 12. It includes drive-through tours of residential areas and the island's commercial center, stops at the island's deep-water harbor, shopping, and a visit to a wholesale liquor store. Departures are Monday through Saturday at 9am and 1pm; the tour lasts 3½ hours. Full-day tours, conducted whenever business warrants, last from 9am to 3:30pm. In addition to everything included in the half-day tours, they bring participants in a bus or van, with guided commentary, all the way to the Caves, near Grand Bahama Island's easternmost tip, for $40 per adult, $30 per child.

See also the "Beaches & Outdoor Pursuits" section for details on UNEXSO's **Dolphin Experience** (p. 143), as well as the "Shopping" section, below, for descriptions of the International Bazaar and the Port Lucaya Marketplace.

Garden of the Groves ★★★ ☺ This 5-hectare (12-acre) botanical garden, filled with waterfalls, ponds, and fountains, is a place of enchantment. Destroyed by the hurricanes of 2004 and 2005, it has been rebuilt by the Grand Bahama Port Authority. Today it is filled with some 10,000 species of plants, including orchids. The park is also a birdwatcher's paradise. In addition to the flora and fauna, there is a petting zoo that's home to pot-belly pigs and pygmy goats. Other features include a children's playground and an arts and crafts village. Nature trails cut through the grounds, where you can see a hanging garden, a bougainvillea walk, a banana plantation, and even a tilapia pond. Guides are available to take you on tours, and food and drink are sold at an on-site cafe.

Midshipman Rd. and Magellan Dr., 11km (7 miles) east of International Bazaar. ℂ **242/374-7778.** http://thegardenofthegroves.com. Admission $15 adults, $10 children 4-12. Daily 9am–5pm.

Lucayan National Park This 16-hectare (40-acre) park is filled with mangrove, pine, and palm trees. It also contains one of the island's loveliest, most secluded beaches—a long, wide, dune-covered stretch reached by following a wooden pathway that winds through the trees. Bring snorkeling gear with which to glimpse the colorful creatures living beneath the turquoise waters of the offshore coral reef. As you wander through the park, you'll cross Gold Rock Creek, fed by a spring from what is said to be the world's largest underground freshwater cavern system. There are 36,000 entrances to the caves, some only a few feet deep. You can explore two of the caves because they became exposed when a portion of ground collapsed. The pools in them (accessible via spiral wooden steps) are composed of 2m (6½ ft.) of fresh water atop a heavier layer of saltwater.

The freshwater springs once lured native Lucayans, those Arawak-connected tribes who lived on the island and depended on fishing for their livelihood. They would come inland to get fresh water for their habitats on the beach. Lucayan bones and artifacts, such as pottery, have been found in the caves, as well as on the beaches.

Settlers Way, eastern end of E. Sunrise Hwy. *(C)* **242/352-5438.** Admission $3; tickets available only at the Rand Nature Centre (see below). Daily 9am–5pm. Drive east along Midshipman Rd., passing Sharp Rock Point and Gold Rock.

Rand Nature Centre This 40-hectare (99-acre) pineland sanctuary, located 3km (1¾ miles) east of Freeport's center, is the regional headquarters of The Bahamas National Trust, a nonprofit conservation organization. Nature trails highlight native flora, including bush medicine plants, and provide ample opportunities for seeing the wild birds that abound here. As you stroll, keep your eyes peeled for the lush blooms of tropical orchids or the brilliant flash of green and red feathers in the trees. You can join a bird-watching tour on the first Saturday of every month at 8am. Other highlights include native animal displays, an education center, and a gift shop selling nature books and souvenirs.

E. Settlers Way. *(C)* **242/352-5438.** Admission $5 adults, $3 children 5–12. Mon-Fri 9am–5pm.

SHOPPING

Shopping hours in Freeport/Lucaya are generally Monday through Saturday from 9am to 6pm. However, in the International Bazaar, hours vary widely, with shops usually closing a bit earlier in the day.

Port Lucaya Marketplace

Port Lucaya and its Marketplace took precedence over the International Bazaar (described below) in the mid-1990s, when it became clear that the future of merchandising on Grand Bahama had shifted. Today, Port Lucaya Marketplace on Seahorse Road rocks and rolls with a spankingly well-maintained facility set within a shopping, dining, and marina complex on 2.4 hectares (6 acres) of low-lying seafront land. Regular free entertainment, such as steel-drum bands and strolling musicians, as well as recorded music that plays throughout the evening hours, adds to a festival atmosphere.

The complex emulates the 19th-century clapboard-sided construction style of the Old Bahamas, all within a short walk of the island's most desirable hotel accommodations, including the Radisson at Our Lucaya. The development arose on the site of a former Bahamian straw market. Today, in addition to dozens of restaurants and upscale shops, it incorporates rows of brightly painted huts from which local merchants sell handicrafts and souvenirs.

The waterfront location is a distinct advantage. Lots of the business that fuels this place derives from the expensive yachts and motor craft that tie up at the marina here. Most of those watercraft are owned by Floridians. You might get the sense that many of them have just arrived from the U.S. mainland, disgorging their passengers out onto the docks here.

Below are the most recommended shops at Port Lucaya Marketplace:

Animale Trendy fashionistas would define this as a hot boutique featuring clingy, sophisticated tropical looks. Come here for long cotton dresses that make the female form look more provocative than usual, accompanied by the kind of accessories—oversized straw hats, chunky necklaces, animal-print scarves—that emphasize the feline, the *animale,* and perhaps, the seductress. ℭ **242/374-2066.**

Bandolera The staff can be rather haughty here, but despite its drawbacks, the store carries a collection of chic women's clothing that's many cuts above the T-shirts and tank tops that are the norm for many of its competitors. ℭ **242/373-7691.**

Colombian Emeralds This branch of the world's foremost emerald jeweler offers a wide array of precious gemstone jewelry and one of the island's best watch collections. Careful shoppers can get significant savings over U.S. prices. The outlet offers certified appraisals and free 90-day insurance. ℭ **242/373-8400.**

Flovin Gallery II This branch of the gallery located in the International Bazaar sells a collection of oil paintings by Bahamian and international artists, along with lithographs and posters. In its limited field, it's the best in the business. Also for sale here are a number of gift items, such as handmade Bahamian dolls, decorated corals, and Christmas ornaments. ℭ **242/373-8388.**

UNEXSO Dive Shop The nation's premier dive shop sells everything related to the water—swimsuits, wet suits, underwater cameras, video equipment, shades, hats, souvenirs, and state-of-the-art dive equipment. ℭ **800/992-3483** or 242/373-1244.

International Bazaar

The older and less glamorous of Grand Bahama Island's two main shopping venues, the International Bazaar has steadily declined since the collapse of the mega-resort Crowne Plaza, immediately next door. Originally conceived as a warren of alleyways loaded with upscale, tax-free boutiques, and still plugging away valiantly

Shopping

GRAND BAHAMA

at its location at East Mall Drive and East Sunrise Highway, it encompasses 4 hectares (10 acres) in the heart of Freeport.

It's currently a pale shadow of what it was during its peak in the mid-1980s, when it boasted 130 purveyors of luxury goods, when the Marketplace at Port Lucaya was still a dream, and when bus-loads of cruise-ship passengers would be unloaded in front of its gates at regular intervals. With many shops permanently closed and cracks in its masonry, its aggressively touted role as an "international" venue seems a bit theme-driven and tired. Even worse for the retailers here, its rising competitor, the Port Lucaya Market-place, is looking better every day.

Buses at the entrance of the complex aren't numbered, but those marked INTERNATIONAL BAZAAR will take you right to the entrance at Torii Gate on West Sunrise Highway. The fare is $1. Visitors walk through this much-photographed gate, a Japanese symbol of welcome, into a miniature World's Fair setting (think of it as a kitschy and somewhat run-down version of Epcot). The bazaar blends architecture and cultures from some 25 countries, each re-created with cobblestones, narrow alleys, and a layout that evokes a somewhat dusty casbah in North Africa.

In the approximately 34 shops that remain in business today, you might find something that is both unique and a bargain. You'll see African handicrafts, Chinese jade, British china, Swiss watches, Irish linens, and Colombian emeralds. Many of the enterprises represented here also maintain branches within the Port Lucaya Marketplace. Various sections evoke the architecture of the Ginza in Tokyo, with merchandise—electronic goods, art objects, luxury products—from Asia. Other subdivisions suggest the Left Bank of Paris, various regions of India and Africa, Latin America, and Spain.

Some merchants claim their prices are 40% lower than compa-rable costs in the U.S., but don't count on that. If you're contem-plating a big purchase, it's best to compare prices before you leave home. Most merchants can ship your purchases back home at relatively reasonable rates.

A **straw market** next door to the International Bazaar contains items with that special Bahamian touch—colorful baskets, hats, handbags, placemats, and an endless array of T-shirts, some of which make worthwhile gifts. Be aware that some items sold here are actually made in Asia, and expect goodly amounts of the tacky and tasteless.

Below are the best shops that remain in the bazaar:

Flovin Gallery   This gallery sells original Bahamian and inter-national art, frames, lithographs, posters, decorated coral, and

Bahamian-made Christmas ornaments. It also offers handmade Bahamian dolls, coral jewelry, and other gift items. Another branch is at the Port Lucaya Marketplace. © **242/352-7564.**

Perfume Factory Fragrance of The Bahamas   This is the country's top fragrance producer. The shop is housed in a re-creation of an 1800s mansion, in which visitors are invited to hear a 5-minute commentary and see the mixing of fragrant oils. There's even a "mixology" department where you can create your own fragrance from a selection of oils. The Perfume Factory's well-known products include Island Promises, Goombay, Paradise, and Pink Pearl (with conch pearls in the bottle). The shop also sells Guanahani, created to commemorate the 500th anniversary of Columbus's first landfall, and Sand, the leading Bahamian-made men's fragrance. © **242/352-9391.**

Unusual Centre   Where else can you get an array of items made of walrus skin or peacock feathers? There's another branch at the Port Lucaya Marketplace. © **242/373-7333.**

GRAND BAHAMA AFTER DARK

Many resorts stage entertainment at night, and these shows are open to the general public.

The Club & Bar Scene

Located in the center of Port Lucaya Marketplace, **Count Basie Square** contains a vine-covered bandstand where the island's best live music is performed several nights a week, usually beginning around 7:30 or 8pm. And it's free! The square honors the "Count," who used to have a grand home on Grand Bahama. Steel bands, small Junkanoo groups, even gospel singers from a local church are likely to be heard here, their voices or music wafting across the marina and the nearby boardwalk and wharves. Sip a beer or a tropical rum concoction while tapping your feet.

Club Amnesia   This is one of the most popular discos and pickup joints on Grand Bahama, a local spot that seems a world away from the somewhat sanitized version of nightlife at the island's tourist hotels. Positioned across the street from the Castaways Resort, it features an interior outfitted with big mirrors, strobe lights, and psychedelic Junkanoo colors. Recorded music grooves and grinds, and live bands are often imported either from the mainland of Florida or from nearby Caribbean islands. Crowds

Bahamian Theater

Instead of one of those Las Vegas–style leggy-showgirl revues, call the 450-seat **Regency Theater,** West Sunrise Highway (ⓒ 242/352-5533; www.regencytheatregbi.com), and ask what performance is scheduled. This is the home of two nonprofit companies, the Freeport Players' Guild and the Grand Bahama Players. The season runs from September to June, and you're likely to see reprises of such Broadway and London blockbusters as *Mamma Mia!,* as well as contemporary works by Bahamian and Caribbean playwrights. Some very intriguing shows are likely to be staged every year by both groups, which are equally talented. Tickets cost $10 to $40.

range in age from 18 to 35, and the cover charge, depending on who's playing that night, is from $10 to $24 per person (concerts cost up to $50 per ticket). Open nights vary with the season, but it's a good bet that the place is operating Thursday through Saturday from 8:30pm until around 2am. E. Mall Dr. ⓒ **242/351-2582.**

Margaritavilla Sand Bar Arguably the hottest bar on the island is this lively "jump-up" place opening onto an isolated stretch of Mather Town Beach, about a 15-minute drive southeast of Lucaya. It's really a one-room sand-floor shack, but a lot of fun. Before this bar opened, this part of Grand Bahama used to be relatively sleepy. No more. A weekly bonfire cookout is staged Tuesday night from 6:30 to 9:30pm, with fish or steak on the grill along with a DJ. Main courses cost $10 to $16 if you'd like to stick around to eat. The place rocks on Wednesday night with younger Bahamians; Sunday is for an older crowd that prefers singalongs. The bar opens at 11am. As for closing times, the owner, Jinx Knowles, says it "might be 7 at night if it's quiet or 7 in the morning if it's jumpin'." Millionaire's Row, Mather Town Beach. ⓒ **242/373-4525.**

Prop Club Also an informal restaurant, this sports bar and dance club flourishes as a singles venue that rocks at high intensity, fueled by high-octane cocktails. A lot happens here, including occasional bouts of karaoke, cultural showcasing of emerging Bahamian and Caribbean bands, and both Junkanoo and retro-disco revival nights, depending on the season. You can also expect a "get down with the DJ" night on Sundays and game nights on slow Mondays. The DJ arrives at 10pm every night. Radisson at Our Lucaya Resort, Royal Palm Way. ⓒ **242/373-1333.**

Grand Bahama After Dark

A SIDE TRIP TO WEST END

If you crave a refreshing escape from the plush hotels of Freeport/Lucaya, head to West End, 45km (28 miles) from Freeport. At this old fishing village, and along the scrub-flanked coastal road that leads to it, you'll get glimpses of how things used to be before tour groups began descending on Grand Bahama Island.

To reach West End, head north along Queen's Highway, going through Eight Mile Rock, to the northernmost point of the island.

A lot of the old village buildings had become seriously dilapidated even before the destructive hurricanes of 2004 and 2005, but those that remain hint at long-ago legends and charm. From about 1920 to 1933, when Prohibition rather unsuccessfully held America in its grip, the docks buzzed with activity day and night. West End was (and is) so close to the U.S. mainland that rum-running became a lucrative business, with booze flowing out of West End by day and into Florida by night. No surprise, then, that Al Capone was supposedly a frequent visitor here.

Villages along the way to West End have colorful names like **Hawksbill Creek.** For a glimpse of local life, try to visit the **fish market** along the harbor. You'll pass some thriving harbor areas, too, but the vessels you'll see will be oil tankers, not rumrunners. Don't expect too many historic buildings en route.

Eight Mile Rock is a hamlet of mostly ramshackle houses that stretches along both sides of the road. At **West End,** you come to an abrupt stop. By far the most compelling developments here are associated with **Old Bahama Bay** (p. 132), a good spot for a meal, a drink, and a look at what might one day become one of the most important real-estate developments in The Bahamas.

FAST FACTS: THE BAHAMAS

African-American Travelers Soul of America (www.soulofamerica.com) is a comprehensive website, with travel tips, event and family-reunion postings, and sections on historically black beach resorts.

Agencies and organizations that provide resources for black travelers include **Rodgers Travel** (☎ 888/823-1775; www.rodgerstravel.com) and the **African American Association of Innkeepers International** (☎ 877/422-5777; www.africanamericaninns.com). For more information, check out the following collections and guides: *Go Girl: The Black Woman's Book of Travel & Adventure* (Eighth Mountain Press), a compilation of travel essays by writers including Jill Nelson and Audre Lorde; *The African-American Travel Guide,* by Wayne Robinson (Hunter Publishing; www.hunterpublishing.com); *Steppin' Out,* by Carla Labat (Avalon); and *Pathfinders Travel* (☎ 215/438-2140; www.pathfinderstravel.com), which includes articles on destinations from Rio de Janeiro to Ghana, as well as information on upcoming ski, diving, golf, and tennis trips.

American Express Representing American Express in The Bahamas is **Destinations,** 303 Shirley St. (btw. Charlotte and Parliament sts.), Nassau (☎ 242/322-2931; www.destinations.com.bs). Hours are Monday through Friday from 9am to 5pm. The travel department is also open Saturday from 9am to 1pm. If you present a personal check and an Amex card, you can buy traveler's checks here.

ATMs See "Money & Costs," p. 21.

Area Code The country code for The Bahamas is **242.**

Business Hours In Nassau, Cable Beach, and Free-port/Lucaya, commercial banking hours are Monday through Thursday from 9:30am to 3pm, Friday from 9:30am to 5pm. Most government offices are open Monday through Friday from 9am to 5pm, and most shops are open Monday through Saturday from 9am to 5pm.

Car Rental See "Getting Around," p. 20.

Cellphones The three letters that define much of the world's wireless capabilities are GSM (Global System for Mobiles), a big, seamless network that makes for easy cross-border cellphone use in countries worldwide. In general, reception is good. In the U.S., T-Mobile, AT&T Wireless, and Cingular use this quasi-universal system; in Canada, Microcell and some Rogers customers use GSM; and all Europeans and most Australians use GSM.

For many, **renting** a phone is a good idea. While you can rent a phone from any number of overseas sites, including kiosks at airports and at car-rental agencies, we suggest renting the phone before you leave home. North Americans can rent one before leaving home from **InTouch USA** (✆ **800/872-7626** or 703/222-7161; www.intouchglobal. com) or **Roadpost** (✆ **888/290-1616** or 905/272-5665; www.road post.com). InTouch will also, for free, advise you on whether your existing phone will work overseas.

Buying a phone can be economically attractive, as many nations have cheap prepaid phone systems. Once you arrive at your destination, stop by a local cellphone shop and get the cheapest package; you'll probably pay less than $100 for a phone and a starter calling card. Local calls may be as cheap as 10¢ per minute, and in many countries incoming calls are free.

Wilderness adventurers might consider renting a **satellite phone ("satphone")**. It's different from a cellphone in that it connects to satellites and works where there's no cellular signal or ground-based tower. You can rent satellite phones from **Roadpost** (see above). **InTouch USA** (see above) offers a wider range of satphones but at higher rates. Per-minute call charges can be even cheaper than roaming charges with a regular cellphone, but the phone itself is more expensive. Satphones are outrageously expensive to buy, so don't even think about it.

Crime When going to Nassau (New Providence), Cable Beach, Paradise Island, or Freeport/Lucaya, exercise the same caution you would if visiting Miami. Whatever you do, if people peddling drugs approach you, steer clear of them.

Crime is increasing, and visitors should use caution and good judgment when visiting The Bahamas. While most criminal incidents take place in a part of Nassau not usually frequented by tourists (the "Over-the-Hill" area south of downtown), crime and violence have moved into more upscale tourist and residential areas.

Women, especially, should take caution if walking alone on the streets of Nassau after dark, particularly if those streets appear to be deserted.

In the past few years, the U.S. Embassy has received several reports of sexual assaults, including some against teenage girls. Most assaults have been perpetrated against intoxicated young women, some of whom were reportedly drugged. To minimize the potential for sexual assault, the embassy recommends that young women stay in groups, consume alcohol in moderation, and not accept rides or drinks from strangers.

Pickpockets (often foreigners) work the crowded casino floors of both Paradise Beach and Cable Beach. See that your wallet, money, and valuables are well secured.

Travelers should avoid walking alone after dark or in isolated areas, and avoid placing themselves in situations in which they are alone with strangers. Be cautious on deserted areas of beaches at all hours. Don't leave valuables such as cameras and purses lying unattended on the beach while you go for a swim.

If you're driving a rental car, always make sure your car door is locked, and never leave possessions in view.

Hotel guests should always lock their doors and should never leave valuables unattended, especially on beaches. Visitors should store passport/identity documents, airline tickets, credit cards, and extra cash in hotel safes. Avoid wearing expensive jewelry, particularly Rolex watches, which criminals have specifically targeted. Use only clearly marked taxis and make a note of the license plate number for your records.

The loss or theft of a passport overseas should be reported to the local police and the nearest embassy or consulate. A lost or stolen birth certificate and/or driver's license generally cannot be replaced outside the United States. U.S. citizens may refer to the Department of State's pamphlets, *A Safe Trip Abroad* and *Tips for Travelers to the Caribbean,* for ways to promote a trouble-free journey. The pamphlets are available by mail from the Superintendent of Documents, U.S. Government Printing Office, Washington, DC 20402; via the Internet at **www.gpoaccess.gov**; or via the Bureau of Consular Affairs' home page at **www.travel.state.gov**.

Customs Bahamian Customs allows you to bring in 200 cigarettes, or 50 cigars, or 1 pound (.45 kg) of tobacco, plus 1 quart (1L) of spirits (hard liquor). You can also bring in items classified as "personal effects" and all the money you wish.

Visitors leaving Nassau or Freeport/Lucaya for most U.S. destinations clear U.S. Customs & Border Protection before departing The Bahamas. Charter companies can make special arrangements with the Nassau or Freeport flight services and U.S. Customs & Border Protection for pre-clearance. No further formalities are required upon arrival in the United States once the pre-clearance has taken place in Nassau or Freeport.

Collect receipts for all purchases you make in The Bahamas. *Note:* If a merchant suggests giving you a false receipt, misstating the value of the goods, beware—the merchant might be an informer to U.S. Customs. You must also declare all gifts received while abroad.

If you purchased an item during an earlier trip abroad, carry proof that you have already paid Customs duty on the item at the time of your previous reentry. To be extra careful, compile a list of expensive carry-on items and ask a U.S. Customs agent to stamp your list at the airport before your departure.

For information on what you're allowed to bring home, contact one of the following agencies:

o **U.S. Citizens: U.S. Customs & Border Protection (CBP),** 1300 Pennsylvania Ave., NW, Washington, DC 20229 (© **877/287-8667;** www.cbp.gov).

o **Canadian Citizens: Canada Border Services Agency,** Ottawa, Ontario, K1A 0L8 (© **800/461-9999** in Canada, or 204/983-3500; www.cbsa-asfc.gc.ca).

o **U.K. Citizens: HM Customs & Excise,** Crownhill Court, Tailyour Road, Plymouth, PL6 5BZ (© **0845/010-9000;** from outside the U.K., 020/8929-0152; www.hmce.gov.uk).

o **Australian Citizens: Australian Customs Service,** Customs House, 5 Constitution Ave., Canberra City, ACT 2601 (© **1300/363-263;** from outside Australia, 612/6275-6666; www.customs.gov.au).

o **New Zealand Citizens: New Zealand Customs,** The Customhouse, 17–21 Whitmore St., Box 2218, Wellington, 6140 (© **04/473-6099** or 0800/428-786; www.customs.govt.nz).

Disabled Travelers A disability should not stop anyone from traveling to The Bahamas. Because these islands are relatively flat, it is fairly easy to get around, even for persons with disabilities.

Many travel agencies offer customized tours and itineraries for travelers with disabilities. Among them are **Flying Wheels Travel** (© **877/451-5006** or 507/451-5005; www.flyingwheelstravel.com), **Access-Able Travel Source;** www.access-able.com), and **Accessible Journeys** (© **800/846-4537** or 610/521-0339; www.disabilitytravel.com.

Organizations that offer assistance to travelers with disabilities include **MossRehab** (© **800/225-5667;** www.mossresourcenet.org), the **American Foundation for the Blind** (AFB; © **800/232-5463** or 212/502-7600; www.afb.org), and **SATH** (Society for Accessible Travel & Hospitality; © **212/447-7284;** www.sath.org). **AirAmbulanceCard.com** (© **877/424-7633**) is partnered with SATH and allows you to preselect top hospitals in case of an emergency.

Also check out the quarterly magazine *Emerging Horizons* (www.emerginghorizons.com) and *Open World* magazine, published by SATH.

British travelers can contact the Royal Association for Disability and Rehabilitation (RADAR), Unit 12, City Forum, 250 City Rd., London, EC1V 8AF (© **020/7250-3222;** www.radar.org.uk).

For more on organizations that offer resources to travelers with disabilities, go to www.frommers.com.

You can call the **Bahamas Association for the Physically Disabled** (BAPD; © **242/322-2393;** www.bahamas.com) for information about accessible hotels in The Bahamas. This agency will also send a van to the airport to transfer you to your hotel for a fee and can provide ramps.

Drinking Laws Alcohol is sold in liquor stores and various convenience stores; it's readily available at all hours, though not for sale on Sundays. The legal drinking age in The Bahamas is 18.

Driving Rules See "Getting Around," p. 20.

Drug Laws Importing, possessing, or dealing unlawful drugs, including marijuana, is a serious offense in The Bahamas, with heavy penalties. Customs officers may at their discretion conduct body searches for drugs or other contraband goods.

Electricity Like Canada and the U.S., The Bahamas normally uses 110–120 volts AC (60 cycles), compared to 220–240 volts AC (50 cycles) in most of Europe, Australia, and New Zealand. American appliances are fully compatible; British or European appliances will need both adapters and downward converters that change 220–240 volts to 110–120 volts.

Embassies & Consulates The embassy of the **United States** is at 42 Queen St., P.O. Box N-8197, Nassau (☏ **242/322-1181;** http://nassau.usembassy.gov).

The consulate of **Canada** is at Shirley Street Plaza, P.O. Box SS-6371, Nassau (☏ **242/393-2123;** cdncon@batelnet.bs).

There is no British High Commission in The Bahamas. U.K. travelers should contact the **British High Commission** in Jamaica, at 28 Trafalgar Rd., Kingston (☏ **876/510-0700;** http://ukinjamaica.fco.gov.uk).

Entry Requirements To enter The Bahamas, citizens of Britain and Canada coming in as visitors *must* bring a passport to demonstrate proof of citizenship. Under new Homeland Security regulations that started December 31, 2005, U.S. travelers were required to have a valid passport to re-enter the United States by January 1, 2008.

Onward or return tickets must be shown to immigration officials in The Bahamas. Citizens of other countries, including Australia, Ireland, and New Zealand, should carry a valid passport.

For information about how to get a passport, see "Passports," below. The websites listed provide downloadable passport applications as well as the current fees for processing passport applications. For an up-to-date, country-by-country listing of passport requirements around the world, go to the "Foreign Entry Requirement" Web page of the U.S. State Department at **http://travel.state.gov**.

Family Travel The Bahamas is one of the top family-vacation destinations in North America. The smallest toddlers can spend blissful hours on sandy beaches and in the shallow seawater, or in swimming pools constructed with them in mind. There's no end to the fascinating pursuits offered for older children, ranging from boat rides to shell collecting, to horseback riding, hiking, or even dancing. Some children are old enough to learn to snorkel and to explore an underwater wonderland. Some resorts will even teach kids to swim or windsurf.

Most families with kids head for New Providence (Nassau), Paradise Island, or Grand Bahama Island (Freeport). Look for our "Kids" icon, indicating attractions, restaurants, or hotels and resorts that are especially family-friendly.

See "The Best Family Vacations," in chapter 1, for additional recommendations.

Every country's regulations differ, but in general, children traveling abroad should have plenty of documentation on hand, particularly if they're traveling with someone other than their own parents (in which case a notarized form letter from a parent is often required).

For details on entry requirements for children traveling abroad, go to the U.S. State Department website (http://travel.state.gov).

Recommended family travel websites include **TravelwithYourKids. com, Family Travel Forum** (www.familytravelforum.com), **Family Travel Network** (www.familytravelnetwork.com), and **Family Travel Files** (www.thefamilytravelfiles.com).

Gasoline (Petrol) Gasoline is plentiful on New Providence Island (Nassau/Cable Beach) and Grand Bahama Island (Freeport/Lucaya), but be prepared to pay almost twice the price you would in the United States. Watch out for Sunday closings.

For more information on holidays, see "The Bahamas Calendar of Events," p. 16.

Health We list **hospital** and **emergency numbers** in each chapter under "Fast Facts."

The major health risk here is not tropical disease, as it is in some Caribbean islands, but rather the bad luck of ingesting a bad piece of shellfish or exotic fruit (or too many rum punches). If your body is not accustomed to these foods or they haven't been cleaned properly, you may suffer diarrhea. If you tend to have digestive problems, drink bottled water and avoid ice, unpasteurized milk, and uncooked food such as fresh salads. However, fresh food served in hotels is usually safe to eat.

The Bahamas has excellent medical facilities. Physicians and surgeons in private practice are readily available in Nassau, Cable Beach, and Freeport/Lucaya. If intensive or urgent care is required, patients are brought by the Emergency Flight Service to **Princess Margaret Hospital** (© **242/322-2861;** www.phabahamas.org) on Shirley Street, Nassau. Some of the big resort hotels have in-house physicians or can quickly secure one for you.

There is also a government-operated hospital, **Grand Bahamas Health Services** (© **242/352-6735**), on East Atlantic Drive, Freeport, and several government-operated clinics on Grand Bahama Island. Nassau and Freeport/Lucaya also have private hospitals.

Dentists are plentiful in Nassau, somewhat less so on Grand Bahama. Where dentists aren't readily available, hotel staff should know where to send you for emergencies.

Contact the **International Association for Medical Assistance to Travellers (IAMAT;** ✆ **716/754-4883,** or 416/652-0137 in Canada; **www.iamat.org)** for tips on travel and health concerns in the countries you're visiting, and for lists of local English-speaking doctors. The United States **Centers for Disease Control and Prevention** (✆ **800/232-4636;** www.cdc.gov) provides up-to-date information on health hazards by region or country and offers tips on food safety. The website **www.tripprep.com**, sponsored by a consortium of travel medicine practitioners, may also offer helpful advice on traveling abroad. You can find listings of reliable clinics overseas at the **International Society of Travel Medicine** (www.istm.org).

Getting too much sun can be a real issue in The Bahamas. You must, of course, take the usual precautions you would anywhere against sunburn and sunstroke. Your time in the sun should be wisely limited for the first few days until you become accustomed to the more intense rays of the Bahamian sun. Also bring and use strong UVA/UVB sunblock products.

In most cases, your existing health plan will provide the coverage you need. But double-check; you may want to buy **travel medical insurance** instead (see the section on insurance). Bring your insurance ID card with you wherever you travel.

We list **hospitals** and **emergency numbers** under "Fast Facts" in each chapter.

If you suffer from a chronic illness, consult your doctor before your departure. Pack **prescription medications** in your carry-on luggage, and carry them in their original containers, with pharmacy labels—otherwise, they won't make it through airport security. Carry the generic name of prescription medicines, in case a local pharmacist doesn't know the brand name.

For travel abroad, you may have to pay medical costs upfront and be reimbursed later. See "Medical Insurance," under "Insurance."

Hospitals On New Providence Island (Nassau/Cable Beach), patients are treated at the government-operated **Princess Margaret Hospital,** on Shirley Street, Nassau (✆ **242/322-2861;** www.phabahamas.org).

On Grand Bahama Island, patients are seen at the government-operated **Rand Memorial Hospital,** on East Atlantic Drive, Freeport (✆ **242/352-6735;** www.phabahamas.org), and at several government-operated clinics.

Many resorts also have either in-house physicians or on-site medical clinics. If intensive or urgent care is required, patients are brought to Nassau by the Emergency Flight Service.

Insurance For travel overseas, most U.S. health plans (including Medicare and Medicaid) do not provide coverage, and the ones that do often require you to pay for services upfront and reimburse you only after you return home.

As a safety net, you may want to buy travel medical insurance, particularly if you're heading to a remote or high-risk area where emergency evacuation might be necessary. If you require additional medical insurance, try **MEDEX Assistance** (© 800/537-2029 or 410/453-6300; www.medexassist.com) or **Travel Assistance International** (© 800/821-2828; www.travelassistance.com; for general information on services, call the company's **Worldwide Assistance Services** at © 800/777-8710; www.worldwideassistance.com).

Canadians should check with their provincial health plan offices or call **Health Canada** (© 866/225-0709; www.hc-sc.gc.ca) to find out the extent of their coverage and what documentation and receipts they must take home in case they are treated overseas.

Travelers from the U.K. should carry their **European Health Insurance Card (EHIC),** which replaced the E111 form as proof of entitlement to free or reduced-cost medical treatment abroad. Call © **0845/605-0707,** or 44/191-212-7500 outside the U.K., or go to www.ehic.org.uk for information. Note that the EHIC only covers "necessary medical treatment."

Travel Insurance The cost of travel insurance varies widely depending on the destination, cost, and length of your trip; your age and health; and the type of trip you're taking. Expect to pay between 5% and 8% of the total cost of your vacation. You can get estimates from various providers through **Insuremytrip.com** (© **800/487-4722**). Enter your trip's cost and dates, your age, and other information to get prices from more than a dozen companies.

U.K. citizens and their families who make more than one trip abroad per year may find that an annual travel insurance policy works out cheaper. Check **www.moneysupermarket.com** (© **0845/345-5708**), which compares prices across a wide range of providers for single- and multi-trip policies.

Most big travel agents offer their own insurance and will probably try to sell you their package when you book a holiday. Think before you sign. **Britain's Consumers' Association** recommends that you insist on seeing the policy and reading the fine print before buying. The **Association of British Insurers** (© **020/7600-3333;** www.abi.org.uk) gives advice by phone and publishes *Holiday Insurance,* a free guide to policy provisions and prices. You might also shop around for better deals: Try **Columbus Direct** (© **0870/033-9988;** www.columbusdirect.net).

Trip-Cancellation Insurance Trip-cancellation insurance will help you retrieve your money if you have to back out of a trip or depart early, or if your travel supplier goes bankrupt. Trip cancellation traditionally covers such events as sickness, natural disasters, and State Department advisories. The latest news in trip-cancellation insurance is the availability of expanded hurricane coverage and the "any-reason" cancellation coverage—which costs more but covers cancellations made for any reason. You won't get back 100% of your prepaid trip cost, but you'll be refunded a substantial portion. **TravelSafe** (© 888/885-7233; www.travelsafe.com) offers both types of coverage. **Expedia** also offers any-reason cancellation coverage for its air-hotel packages. For other options, contact one of the following recommended insurers: **Access America** (© 800/284-8300; www.accessamerica.com), **AIG Travel Guard** (© 800/228-9792; www.travelguard.com), **Travelex Insurance Services** (© 888/457-4602; www.travelex-insurance.com), and **Travel Insured International** (© 800/243-3174; www.travelinsured.com).

Internet & Wi-Fi Internet cafes are not common on the islands, but in Nassau you can try **Cybercafe,** in the Mall at Marathon (© 242/394-6254).

If you're traveling with your own computer, Web access via **Wi-Fi** hot spots is increasingly common at hotels. But if this issue is especially important to you, see our hotel reviews throughout this book and check with specific accommodations before booking.

More and more hotels, cafes, and retailers are signing on as Wi-Fi (wireless fidelity) "hot spots." Mac owners have their own networking technology: Apple AirPort. **T-Mobile Hotspot** (© 877/822-SPOT [7768]; hotspot.t-mobile.com or www.t-mobile.co.uk) serves up wireless connections at coffee shops nationwide. **Boingo** (www.boingo.com) and **Wayport** (www.wayport.com) have set up networks in airports and high-class hotel lobbies. iPass providers (see below) also give you access to a few hundred wireless hotel lobby setups.

For wired access, most business-class hotels offer dataports for laptop modems. In addition, major Internet service providers (ISPs) have **local access numbers** around the world, allowing you to go online by placing a local call. The **iPass** network also has dial-up numbers around the world. You'll have to sign up with an iPass provider, who will then tell you how to set up your computer for your destination(s). For a list of iPass providers, go to www.ipass.com and click on "Individuals Buy Now." One solid provider is **i2Roam** (© 866/811-6209 or 920/233-5863; www.i2roam.com).

Wherever you go, bring a **connection kit** of the right power and phone adapters, a spare phone cord, and a spare Ethernet network cable—or find out whether your hotel supplies them to guests.

To find **cybercafes,** check www.cybercaptive.com and www.cybercafe.com.

Aside from formal cybercafes, most **public libraries** have Internet access. Avoid **hotel business centers** unless you're willing to pay exorbitant rates.

Most major airports now have **Internet kiosks** scattered throughout their gates. These give you basic Web access for a per-minute fee that's usually higher than cybercafe prices.

Language In The Bahamas, locals speak English, but sometimes with a marked accent that provides the clue to their ancestry—African, Irish, or Scottish, for example.

LGBT Travelers In addition to the destination-specific resources listed below, please visit Frommers.com for other specialized travel resources.

Generally speaking, The Bahamas isn't a gay-friendly destination. Think twice before choosing to vacation here. Although many gay people visit or live here, the country has very strict anti-homosexuality laws. Same-sex relations, even when between consenting adults, are subject to criminal sanctions carrying prison terms. If you would like to make visiting gay beaches, bars, or clubs part of your vacation, consider South Miami Beach, Key West, or Puerto Rico instead.

Of course, the big resorts welcome one and all, even if forced to do so. For many years, the all-inclusive Sandals Royal Bahamian on Cable Beach refused to accept same-sex couples and booked only heterosexual guests. However, rights groups in Canada and Great Britain lobbied successfully, and the Sandals people found they could no longer advertise their resorts, and their discriminatory policies, in those countries. As a result, Sandals capitulated and ended its previous ban. However, gay and lesbian couples looking for a carefree holiday should seriously consider whether they want to spend their hard-earned dollars in a resort like Sandals that did not end its ban against gay and lesbian travelers until forced to do so by more liberal governments.

Single gays and gay couples should travel here with great discretion. If you're intent on visiting, the **International Gay & Lesbian Travel Association** (IGLTA; ✆ 800/GAYTRAVEL; www.iglta.org) is the trade association for the gay and lesbian travel industry, and offers an online directory of gay- and lesbian-friendly travel businesses; go to their website and click on "Members."

Many agencies offer tours and travel itineraries specifically for gay and lesbian travelers. Among them are **Now, Voyager** (✆ 800/255-6951; www.nowvoyager.com) and **Olivia Cruises & Resorts** (✆ 800/631-6277; www.olivia.com).

Gay.com Travel (✆ 415/834-6500; www.gay.com or www.planetout.com) is an excellent online successor to the popular *Out & About* print magazine. It provides regularly updated information about gay-owned, gay-oriented, and gay-friendly lodging, dining, sightseeing, nightlife, and shopping establishments in every important destination worldwide.

The following travel guides are available at many bookstores, or you can order them from any online bookseller: *Spartacus International Gay Guide* (Bruno Gmünder Verlag; www.spartacus.de) and *Odysseus: The International Gay Travel Planner* (Odysseus Enterprises Ltd.); and the *Damron* guides (http://damron.com), with separate annual books for gay men and lesbians. For more gay and lesbian travel resources, go to www.frommers.com.

Lost & Found Be sure to notify all of your credit card companies the minute you discover your wallet has been lost or stolen. Also file a report at the nearest police precinct: Your credit card company or insurer may require a police report or record of the loss. Most credit card companies have an emergency toll-free number to call; they may be able to wire you a cash advance immediately or deliver an emergency credit card in a day or two. **American Express** cardholders and traveler's check holders should call ⓒ **800/221-7282. MasterCard** holders should call ⓒ **800/307-7309.** The emergency contact for **Visa** is **800/847-2911.** For other credit cards, call the toll-free number directory at ⓒ **800/555-1212.**

If you need emergency cash over the weekend, when all banks and American Express offices are closed, you can have money wired to you via **Western Union** (ⓒ **800/325-6000;** www.westernunion.com).

Mail You'll need Bahamian (not U.S.) postage stamps to send postcards and letters from The Bahamas. Most of the kiosks selling postcards also sell the stamps you'll need to mail them, so you probably won't need to visit the post office.

Sending a postcard or an airmail letter (up to ½ oz. in weight) from The Bahamas to anywhere outside its borders (including the U.S., Canada, and the U.K.) costs 65¢, with another charge for each additional half-ounce of weight.

Medical Requirements Unless you're coming from an area suffering from an epidemic, inoculations or vaccinations are not required for entry into The Bahamas.

Mobile Phones See "Cellphones," above.

Newspapers & Magazines Three newspapers are circulated in Nassau and Freeport: the *Nassau Guardian,* the *Tribune,* and the *Freeport News.* In Nassau, you can find such papers as the *New York Times,* the *Wall Street Journal, USA Today,* the *Miami Herald,* London's *Times,* and the *Daily Telegraph* at newsstands in your hotel and elsewhere around town.

Packing For helpful information on packing for your trip, download our convenient Travel Tools. Go to www.frommers.com/tips/packing_tips and click on "Smart Traveler" for either domestic or international flights.

Passports See www.frommers.com/planning for information on how to obtain a passport.

o **For Residents of Australia:** Contact the Australian Passport Information Service at ⓒ **131-232,** or visit www.passports.gov.au.
o **For Residents of Canada:** Contact the central **Passport Office,** Department of Foreign Affairs and International Trade, Ottawa, ON K1A 0G3 (ⓒ **800/567-6868;** www.ppt.gc.ca).
o **For Residents of Ireland:** Contact the **Passport Office,** Setanta Centre, Molesworth Street, Dublin 2 (ⓒ **01/671-1633;** www.foreignaffairs.gov.ie).

o **For Residents of New Zealand:** Contact the **Passports Office,** Department of Internal Affairs, 47 Boulcott St., Wellington, 6011 (© **0800/225-050** in New Zealand or 04/474-8100; www.passports.govt.nz).

o **For Residents of the United Kingdom:** Visit your nearest passport office, major post office, or travel agency, or contact the **Identity and Passport Service (IPS),** 89 Eccleston Sq., London, SW1V 1PN (© **0300/222-0000;** www.ips.gov.uk).

o **For Residents of the United States:** To find your regional passport office, check the **U.S. State Department** website (http://travel.state.gov/passport) or call the **National Passport Information Center** (© **877/487-2778**) for automated information.

Senior Travel In The Bahamas, the standard adult rate usually applies to everyone 21 years of age and over. The careful, frugal travel shopper, however, might find some deals if arrangements are made before you go.

Members of **AARP,** 601 E St. NW, Washington, DC 20049 (© **888/687-2277;** www.aarp.org), get discounts on hotels, airfares, and car rentals. AARP offers members a range of benefits, including *AARP The Magazine* and a monthly newsletter. Anyone over 50 can join.

Many reliable agencies and organizations target the 50-plus market. **Road Scholar** (© **800/454-5768;** www.roadscholar.org), formerly Exploritas/Elderhostel, arranges study programs for those aged 55 and over.

Recommended publications offering travel resources and discounts for seniors include the quarterly magazine *Travel 50 & Beyond* (www.travel50andbeyond.com); *Travel Unlimited: Uncommon Adventures for the Mature Traveler* (Avalon); *101 Tips for Mature Travelers,* available from Grand Circle Travel (© **800/959-0405** or 617/350-7500; www.gct.com); and *Unbelievably Good Deals and Great Adventures That You Absolutely Can't Get Unless You're Over 50* (McGraw-Hill), by Joan Rattner Heilman. For more information and resources about travel for seniors, go to www.frommers.com.

Single Travelers Single tourists often find the dating scene better in The Bahamas during the winter when there are more visitors, especially unattached ones.

On package vacations, single travelers are often hit with a "single supplement" to the base price. To avoid it, you can agree to room with other single travelers or find a compatible roommate before you go, from one of the many roommate-locator agencies.

TravelChums (www.travelchums.com) is an Internet-only travel-companion matching service with elements of an online-personals-type site, hosted by the respected New York–based Shaw Guides travel service. Many reputable tour companies offer singles-only trips.

For more information, check out Eleanor Berman's guide *Traveling Solo: Advice and Ideas for More Than 250 Great Vacations* (Globe Pequot), with advice on traveling alone, either solo or as part of a group tour. For more information on traveling single, go to www.frommers.com.

Police Dial ℂ **919.**

Smoking The government is on a drive to crack down on smoking in public places. Health officials are now in the process of drafting legislation that will ensure that nonsmokers are not subjected to secondhand smoke.

Taxes A 6% to 12% tax is imposed on hotel bills; otherwise, there is no sales tax on any purchase made within The Bahamas. Visitors leaving The Bahamas pay a $20 departure tax, a tariff that's automatically included in the price of any airline or cruise-ship ticket.

Telephones Though some of the Out Islands are still difficult to reach by telephone, direct long-distance dialing is available between North America and Nassau (New Providence Island), Grand Bahama Island, the Abacos, Andros, the Berry Islands, Bimini, Eleuthera, Harbour Island, Spanish Wells, the Exumas, and Stella Maris on Long Island.

To call The Bahamas:

1. Dial the international access code: 011 from the U.S.; 00 from the U.K., Ireland, or New Zealand; or 0011 from Australia.
2. Dial the country code: 242.
3. Dial the seven-digit local number.

To make international calls from The Bahamas: First dial 00 and then the country code (U.S. or Canada 1, U.K. 44, Ireland 353, Australia 61, New Zealand 64). Next, dial the area code and local number. For example, if you wanted to call the British Embassy in Washington, D.C., you would dial 00-1-202-588-7800.

o **For local calls within The Bahamas:** Simply dial the seven-digit number. To call from one island to another within The Bahamas, dial 1-242 and then the seven-digit number.

o **For directory assistance:** Dial ℂ **916** if you're looking for a number inside The Bahamas, **0** for numbers to all other countries.

o **For operator assistance:** To reach an international or domestic operator within The Bahamas, dial ℂ **0.**

o **Toll-free numbers:** Numbers beginning with 881 within The Bahamas are toll-free. However, calling a normally toll-free number within the U.S. (that is, one beginning with 800, 866, 887, or 888) usually involves a charge if made from The Bahamas. In fact, it usually costs the same as an overseas call unless the merchant has made arrangements with local telephone authorities. *Note:* Major airlines generally maintain toll-free 800, 866, 887, or 888 provisions for calls made to them within The

Bahamas. If you dial what you think is a toll-free phone number and it ends up costing the long-distance rate, an automated recording will inform you of this fact. In some cases, the recording will suggest a local toll-free alternative—usually one beginning with 881.

To reach the major international services of **AT&T,** dial ✆ **800/ CALL-ATT** (225-5288), or head for any phone with AT&T or USA Direct marked on the side of the booth. Picking up the handset will connect you with an AT&T operator. These phones are often positioned beside cruise-ship docks for disembarking passengers. **MCI** can be reached at ✆ **800/888-8000.**

Note that the old coin-operated phones are still prevalent in The Bahamas and do still swallow coins. Those old phones, however, are gradually being replaced by phones that use calling cards (debit cards) that come in denominations of $5, $10, $20, and $50. They can be bought from any office of **BATELCO** (Bahamas Telephone Co.). BATELCO's main branch is on Kennedy Drive, Nassau (✆ **242/302-7102;** www2.btcbahamas.com), although a popular local branch lies in the heart of Nassau, on East Street off Bay Street.

Useful Phone Numbers Sources of information include:

o **U.S. Department of State Travel Advisory:** ✆ 202/647-5225; www.travel.state.gov (24 hr.)
o **U.S. Passport Agency:** ✆ 202/647-0518.
o **U.S. Centers for Disease Control International Traveler's Hotline:** ✆ 800/232-4636; www.cdc.gov.

Time Eastern Standard Time (EST) is used throughout The Bahamas, and daylight saving time is observed in the summer.

Tipping Many establishments in The Bahamas add a service charge, but it's customary to leave something extra if service has been especially fine. If you're not sure whether service has been included in your bill, don't be shy—ask.

Bellhops and **porters,** at least in the expensive hotels, expect a tip of $1 to $2 per bag. It's also customary to tip the **chamber staff** at least US$2 per day—more if she or he has performed special services such as getting a shirt or blouse laundered. Most service personnel, including **taxi drivers, waiters,** and the like, expect 15%, or 20% for waiters in deluxe restaurants.

Visas The Commonwealth of The Bahamas does not require visas. On entry to The Bahamas, you'll be given an immigration card to complete and sign. The card has a carbon copy that you must keep until departure, at which time it must be turned in. You'll also have to pay a departure tax before you can exit the country.

Toilets Public toilets are few and far between, except in hotel lobbies, bars, restaurants, museums, department stores, bus stations, and service stations. Large hotels and fast-food restaurants are often the best bet for clean facilities. Restaurants in resorts or heavily visited areas may reserve their toilets for patrons.

Visitor Information One of the best information sources to contact before you leave home is your nearest Bahamas Tourist Office. Start off by visiting the country's official tourism website at www.bahamas.com or calling ☏ **800/BAHAMAS** (224-2627) or 242/302-2000.

You can also stop by any of the following branch offices:

- **Chicago:** 8600 W. Bryn Mawr Ave., Ste. 820, Chicago, IL 60631 (☏ **312/693-1500**)
- **Dallas:** 3102 Oak Lawn Ave., Ste. 700, Dallas, TX 75219 (☏ **214/550-2280**)
- **Fort Lauderdale:** 1100 Lee Wagener Blvd., Ste. 204, Fort Lauderdale, FL 33315 (☏ **954/359-8099**)
- **London:** 10 Chesterfield St., London W1J 5JL (☏ **020/7355-0800**)
- **Los Angeles:** 3450 Wilshire Blvd., Ste. 208, Los Angeles, CA 90010 (☏ **213/385-0033**)
- **Miami:** 1 Turnberry Place, 19495 Biscayne Blvd., Ste. 80, Aventura, FL 33180 (☏ **305/932-0051**)
- **Montreal:** 1130 Sherbrooke St. W., Ste. 750, Montreal, Quebec H3A 2MB (☏ **800/667-3777**)
- **New York:** 150 E. 52nd St., 28th floor, New York, NY 10022 (☏ **212/758-2777**)
- **Toronto:** 121 Bloor St. E., Ste. 1101, Toronto, Ontario M4W 3M5 (☏ **416/968-2999**)

You may want to contact the **U.S. State Department** for background bulletins, which supply up-to-date information on crime, health concerns, import restrictions, and other travel matters. Call ☏ **888/407-4747** or visit www.travel.state.gov.

A travel agent can also be a great source of information. Make sure yours is a member of the **American Society of Travel Agents (ASTA).** If you get poor service from an ASTA agent, you can write to the ASTA Consumer Affairs Department, 1101 King St., Alexandria, VA 22314 (☏ **800/440-ASTA** [2782] or 703/739-2782; www.asta.org).

Useful Bahamas websites include:

- **The Bahamas Ministry of Tourism** (www.bahamas.com), the country's official tourism site.
- **Bahamas Tourist Guide** (www.geographia.com/bahamas), for general information and listings.
- **Bahamas Vacation Guide** (www.bahamasvacationguide.com), for general information and various service listings.
- **Nassau/Paradise Island Promotion Board** (www.nassauparadiseisland.com), the official tourism site for these areas.

Women Travelers Should a woman travel alone to The Bahamas? Opinions and reports vary. Women traveling alone in The Bahamas rarely encounter aggressive, potentially dangerous behavior from males and are usually treated with respect. However, some Bahamian men may assume that a woman traveling alone is doing so in order to find a male partner. To avoid such unwanted attention, dress a bit conservatively and don't go wandering the streets of Nassau unescorted at night. It's always advisable to wear a cover-up over your swimsuit when leaving the beach and heading into town.

Women Welcome Women World Wide (5W; 📞 01494/465441; www.womenwelcomewomen.org.uk) works to foster international friendships by enabling women of different countries to visit one another (men can come along on the trips; they just can't join the club). It's a big, active organization, with more than 3,500 members from all walks of life in some 70 countries.

Also check out the award-winning website **Journeywoman** (www. journeywoman.com), a "real life" women's travel-information network where you can sign up for a free e-mail newsletter and get advice on everything from etiquette to safety; or the travel guide *Safety and Security for Women Who Travel,* by Sheila Swan and Peter Laufer (Travelers' Tales, Inc.), offering common-sense tips on safe travel. For general travel resources for women, go to www. frommers.com.

Water Technically, tap water is drinkable throughout The Bahamas. Still, we almost always opt for bottled. Resorts tend to filter and chlorinate tap water more aggressively than other establishments; elsewhere, bottled water is available at stores and supermarkets, and tastes better than that from a tap.

Index

See also Accommodations and Restaurant indexes, below.

General Index

A

B